Corporate DNA

Corporate DNA

Using Organizational Memory to
Improve Poor Decision-Making

ARNOLD KRANSDORFF

GOWER

Published by
Gower Publishing Limited
Gower House
Croft Road
Aldershot
Hants GU11 3HR
England

Gower Publishing Company
Suite 420
101 Cherry Street
Burlington VT 05401–4405
USA

Arnold Kransdorff has asserted his right under the Copyright, Designs and Patents Act 1988 to be identified as the author of this work.

British Library Cataloguing in Publication Data
Kransdorff, Arnold
    Corporate DNA: using organizational memory to improve poor
    decision-making
    1. Knowledge management 2. Organizational behaviour 3. Decision
    making 4. Corporate culture
    I. Title
    658.4'038

    ISBN 0 566 08681 6

Library of Congress Cataloging-in-Publication Data
Kransdorff, Arnold.
        Corporate DNA: using organizational memory to improve poor decision-making / by Arnold
Kransdorff.
        p. cm.
    Includes index.
    ISBN 0-566-08681-6
    1. Corporate culture. 2. Decision making. 3. Industrial productivity 4. Organizational effectiveness.
5. Knowledge management. I. Title.

HD58.7.K697 2005
658.4'03--dc22

                                                                                            2005024155

Typeset in 9 point Stone Serif by IML Typographers, Birkenhead, Merseyside
Printed and bound in Great Britain by TJ International Ltd, Padstow, Cornwall.

Contents

List of Figures and Tables   *xi*
List of Abbreviations   *xiii*
Preface and Acknowledgements   *xv*

Introduction: The Boiler is Running out of Steam   **1**
   When profit margins crumple   2
   Using comparative values   4
   Drucker's productivity challenge   4
   Where the blame lies   5
   Knowledge dispossession: the unnoticed revolution   6
   The three ways of acquiring knowledge   7
   The many types of learning   7
   Decision-making techniques   8
   Where new productivity can come from   9
   The three ages of organizational memory   10
   The critical importance of organizational memory   11
   The arguments for better management of OM   12
   Explaining experience-based management (EBM)   12

1 When Experience-Rich Falls Short of Experience-Poor   **15**
   The phenomenon of corporate amnesia   16
   The two experiential learning approaches   17
   The peanuts and flight syndrome   18
   Fair trade   18
   Contemporary non-learning   19
   The Big Black Hole   20
   The quality of management skills   20
   Where organizations fall down   23
   The inheritors   23
   Paying lip service to genuine learning   24
   Untrained managers   25
   Some understandings about management   27
   The need to teach decision-making   27

2 How More Equals Less   **31**
   Bureaucratic ineffectiveness   32
   Higher cost, lower value   33
   Two steps forward, one step back   33

A possible answer – to unlearn or purge beliefs   34
The reason for Germany's and Japan's slippage   35
Excuses, excuses in the UK   35
Where real 'wealth' resides   37
'You've just got to wait'   38
The UK's lack of clever systems   38
No one is perfect   39
The effects of rapid job turnover   41
The domino effect   41
The cost of lost know-how   43
Western philosophical differences with the East   44
An explanation for non-reflection   45
No inheritance   45
The history of experiential learning   46
The reason for decision-making's neglect   47
Instinct is not enough   48

3   The Gaping Holes in Business Education   53
Failures in start-ups and acquisitions   54
The lip service treatment of corporate and business history   55
Two other disregarded subjects   56
'There is no relation between business education and success' 57
The shortcomings of business education   58
'Dangerous' MBAs   59
The history of business instruction in the UK   61
The unprepared professionals   63
'World-class UK management researchers are as rare as world-class UK managers' 64
The importance of reflectiveness   65
The dearth of experiential learning   65
A story of failure   66
Grudge, friction and neglect   68
Needed – another look at business education   69

4   Productivity – The New Corporate Imperative   75
How productivity is calculated   75
Productivity down the years   77
The enormous potential still in hand   77
The history of productivity   78
The arrival of hire'n'fire   79
Job churn 'above recognized danger levels'   79
Redundancy and the inability to grow   80
Rewarding failure – and its justification   80
World ranking in staff turnover   81
The US: an exception to the rule   81
The other agents of OM dispersal   83
Short and selective memory recall   83
Defensive reasoning   84

Denial in politics 85
Hostile defensiveness 86
The culture of deception 87
The confusion surrounding knowledge management and the learning organization 88
What are data, information and knowledge? 90
The educational neglect of experiential learning 92

5 **Where Failure is not Delayed Success** 95
Management by rote 96
The cost of bad decision-making 96
Prevention – less costly than cure 98
A country-by-country survey: the US 98
The UK 100
New Zealand 104
South Africa 107
Israel 109

6 **Going for 20:20 Vision** 115
Unconscious learning 115
Incidental learning 115
Planned learning 116
Proactive learning 116
Defensive learning 116
Action learning 117
Prospective learning 117
Case studies: company-specific experiential learning 118
The improvement principle 118
Selective learning 118
Postmortems 119
The tacit input 119
Remember hard copy? 120
Socializing: the other knowledge-sharing medium 121
Why modern systems are not working well 122
Addressing the innate problems 123

7 **Cutting the Workload** 127
The Knowledge Chart 128
The Project Map 128
The Employee Transit Audit 129
The Knowledge Retrieval Plan 130

8 **Talk Talk** 133
From cave drawings to DVDs 133
The history of oral debriefing 135
Oral debriefing in the US military 135
Oral debriefing in industry 136
Embarking on an oral debriefing programme 139

Knowledge is mine. Why should i share it?   139
The four types of debriefing   140
Dealing with false memory   142
Capturing the evidence   142
The introduction letter   142
Serious research   143
The debrief – and follow-up questions   143
Transcripts and editing   144
Ethics and legal issues   144
Confidentiality   145
Defamation and freedom of information   146
Copyright differences   146
To pay or not to pay?   147
Telephone interviews   147
Summary   148

9   **From Hagiography to a Powerful Management Tool**   **149**
Externally funded corporate histories   149
Independent corporate histories   149
Unauthorized corporate histories   151
Independent corporate histories with company cooperation   151
PR: the main motivation   153
The sponsored corporate history   154
Some corporate history disasters   156
A successful example   159
The history of corporate history   161
The acknowledged limitations of corporate history   162
How to improve corporate histories   163
Formulate a code of conduct   163
Change departments   164
Develop a new mindset   165
Construct an arm's-length approach   166
Wider applications   167
Why corporate and business history?   168
History is knowledge   169

10   **Lighting the Lamp**   **171**
The make-up of survival   172
Chains and weak links   172
Experiential learning explained   173
Kolb's unique contribution   174
The origins of modern experiential learning   174
Lewin's group dynamics   175
Upending Pavlov   175
Life experiences = learning = knowledge   176
EBM's contribution   178
Kolb's Experiential Learning Theory (ELT)   178

EBM's learning stages: reflection   179
The Lessons Audit   180
Reprocessing   180
Evaluation   181

Epilogue: The Future of the Past   **185**
How one point can make the difference   186
Working smarter is the answer   187
Where is business going?   188
Demand is the key   189
Catch 22   190
Restructuring learning within the corporate setting   191
Messages for the learning organization   194
Decision-making made easier   195
Business and academia: intelligent cooperation   196
Two addendums   197

Appendix 1: GDP Per Person Employed 1950–2003   **201**
Appendix 2: The World Competitiveness Scoreboard 2004   **203**
Appendix 3: OECD Productivity Scoreboard 2003   **205**
Appendix 4: Productivity as a Percentage of US Productivity   **207**

Index   *209*

List of Figures and Tables

Figures

I.1   OECD countries: productivity per capita   2

I.2   Productivity growth not sustained   3

1.1   Business executive perceptions of the quality of their own management   21

2.1   The working profile of British companies post-Second World War   41

2.2   Annual job turnover by industry, late 1990s   41

6.1   The continuous six-stage EBM learning spiral   124

8.1   Example copyright release form   145

Tables

1.1   The cost of wasted productivity   22

2.1   Jobs: the OECD discontinuity league   43

2.2   Annual jobs turnover, by industry, 1990s   43

List of Abbreviations

ABH	Association of Business Historians
AHP	analytic hierarchy process
ASSI	Associazione di Storia e Studi sull'Impresa
BHU	Business History Unit (at the SE)
BRICK	Brazil, Russia, India, China, Korea
CBI	Confederation of British Industry
CEO	chief executive officer
CEML	Council for Excellence in Management and Leadership
CHOC	Centre for the History of Chemistry
CILT	Centre for Information on Language Teaching
CIPD	Chartered Institute of Personnel and Development
CMI	Chartered Management Institute
DEC	Digital Computer Corporation
DFES	Department for Education and Science
DTI	Department of Trade and Industry
EBHA	European Business History Association
EBM	experienced-based management
ECB	European Central Bank
ELT	Experiential Learning Theory
ENA	Ecole Nationale de l'Administration
EoT	end of tour (military)
ESRC	Economic and Social Research Council
GDP	gross domestic product
GUG	Gesellschaft für Unternehmensgeschichte
HEFCE	Higher Education Funding Council for England
IDS	Incomes Data Service
IIP	Investors in People
IMCA	International Management Centers Association
IMPM	International Masters in Practising Management
IoD	Institute of Directors
IS	information systems
IT	information technology
ITT	International Telephone and Telegraph Corporation
KM	knowledge management
LSC	Learning and Skills Council
LSE	London School of Economics
MBA	Masters in Business Administration
MGI	McKinsey Global Institute

MIS	management information systems
NAFIS	National Automated Fingerprint Identification System
Nasa	National American Space Agency
NEHA	Nederlands Economisch-Historisch Archief
OECD	Organization for Economic Cooperation and Development
Ofsted	Office for Standards in Education
OL	organizational learning
OLAF	Office Européen de Lutte Anti-Fraude (European Anti-Fraud Office)
OM	organizational memory
ONS	Office for National Statistics
PPP	purchasing power parity
QAHCS	Quality in Australia Health Care Study
RAE	Research Assessment Exercise
RAMBA	Real-Alternative MBA
ROCE	return on capital employed
RSA	Royal Society of Arts
SADC	South African Development Community
SNZ	Standards New Zealand
SRA	Strategic Rail Authority
SSRC	Social Science Research Council
TUC	Trades Union Congress
TPA	Taxpayers' Alliance
TQM	total quality management
UoAs	units of assessment
WHO	World Health Organization

Preface and Acknowledgements

People write books because publishers think they have something interesting or important to say. In the process there is usually a long list of people to whom appreciation is due because the author's ideas are rarely one person's exclusive output.

Take chemistry. Many people think that the great motivators in this field just pop up irregularly in the scientific community. Not so. In the world of Nobel prize winners, for example, Stern 'begat' Rabi and Rabi 'begat' Chamberlain. In turn, Lawrence's work, without which there wouldn't have been Seaborg's strivings, would not have been possible without Compton. There is a genealogy among them. So is it with books. It's a Darwinian thing. Just like the learning I'm advocating.

My thank-you list is also long although, perversely, I will be acknowledging people and institutions that have resisted the central concept of this book.

But government organizations, many trade and professional bodies, countless private companies and a whole raft of British business schools have – through their noticeable disregard for experiential learning – played an important role in the genesis of my interest in the concept in general and experience-based management (EBM) in particular. I should add that my experience also bears out a wider geographical resistance.

Apart from those relatively few organizations that already employ formal experiential learning, however effective, I have reasoned that anyone who cannot find fault with its universal conception and then, in almost the very same breath, decline to consider its use or even assess its validity as an educational tool is displaying a perplexing inconsistency. If resistance then continues after attention is drawn to a pattern of repeated mistakes, reinvented wheels, other unlearned lessons and low productivity – all of which have already burned an expensive hole in an unpatched pocket and will continue to drain resources if no darning is done – the phenomenon becomes even more puzzling. Intellectually challenging as these contradictions are, they have stubbornly dominated my attention for two decades with the nineteenth-century US philosopher and author Henry Thoreau's advice ringing in my ears: '… he who travels with another must wait till that other is ready'.[1] As a result, I've come to realize that, however lofty the intellect, non-learners can travel only short distances in long intervals and also that frustration from others' indifference can be a great personal motivator as well as being educational in its own right.

That organizations and academia are *potentially* interested in experiential learning is not in doubt. The benefits – a better bottom line – are as desirable as the theory is iron-clad. Even babies do it – quite instinctively when they learn to walk, for example. But it appears to become more difficult with age. And managers' ability to put experiential learning into practice – ironically what corporate supervision and decision-making is all about – seems to be especially difficult.

Given that 'experience' is the focal point of this book, my own encounters are helpful in confirming this phenomenon, if only for the excuses used to sidestep its use and the pretext they provide me to continue refining my arguments and improving the methodology.

In the case of the UK's Department of Trade and Industry (DTI), which many want to abolish because of its perceived inadequacy, this government unit has voiced a well-publicized concern over the UK's acknowledged low productivity and the uncertain quality of management education – problems that have dominated government's attention for more than two decades. The disquiet that British business schools are not as good as equivalent educational establishments in the US and elsewhere is also mirrored – albeit less audibly – over at the Department of Education and Skills. Even the Treasury and the now independent Bank of England has flagged up their concern over the nation's low productivity, so any fresh approach that might help to rectify the problems should, one would imagine, at least be explored. While launching the 2003 government-sponsored report by the Council for Excellence in Management and Leadership, Patricia Hewitt MP, the then Trade and Industry Secretary, said publicly that, although there were concerns about the quality and supply of managers, the DTI could help to make a difference by taking a lead role in stimulating demand for better management skills from employers and in encouraging them to deploy skilled people more effectively. By improving management and leadership skills and by establishing stronger links between employers' investment in skills and improvements in their productivity, 'we can significantly improve the competitiveness of many individual firms,' she said. By this, I thought she was encouraging the DTI to be proactive.

In an effort to pilot experiential learning in a practical environment, an enthusiastic senior official in the DTI, who agreed that many lessons of past endeavours had not been learned, spent nine months in 2002/3 trying to interest his department in such a project. The plan was to first ratify the methodology internally before proposing its wider application. In turning down the opportunity, the department's head eventually decided that his staff were 'too busy' to participate, a response that ignored the reality that increased efficiency would reduce the workload of individuals. In fact, the learning project's required specification included a small number of decision-makers putting aside 20 minutes every two weeks and to attend two one-day workshops over a period of six months – the first to apply the lessons of the first three months to the second period and the second to apply the lessons of the whole project to future projects. Whilst confirming the underlying need for genuine experiential learning, the senior official, whose efforts went far beyond his call of duty, is hopeful that his boss will return to the issue when people start to answer the question, 'How are we going to make things different this time?' It was just a few months later that Brian Leeming, the DTI's best-practice champion for the East of England, commenting on some DTI research[2] into how individuals learn to be better managers and increase productivity, said:

While learning from mistakes can be a useful experience, this can be a lengthy process and create wastage of both time and resources. We want to encourage businesses to see what works at other organizations and urge managers to try and learn from examples of management best practice to increase productivity and avoid making unnecessary mistakes.

His words spoke volumes. Even though the research indicated clearly that the majority of managers said that they learned best from their own mistakes, Leeming (like most of industry and commerce) was more fixated on the corporate equivalent of horticultural hybridization – better known as benchmarking – believing that the grafting of someone else's successes will necessarily improve things. Of course, sometimes this is the case, but what is invariably forgotten is that the root stock first has to be of a quality that is receptive to splicing. This applies not only to worker skills but to manager's ability to adapt their decision-making to their employer's special circumstances. Whatever changes are made – whether internally or externally initiated – they still have to be managed from inside the organization. So why just depend on the things outside one's front door?

The follow-through to approaches made to many other British universities and business schools, where learning is supposed to thrive, has been almost as fruitless.

My first inkling that experiential learning was of interest to academia came through an approach to one of the cash-strapped offshoots of the University of London, my motivation being that it might be more successful to initiate a new idea in collaboration with a relevant and respected academic institution that needed funds. The idea I put to them included a proposal to jointly offer industry a dedicated service to help it capture its departing 'memory' so that future incumbents might benefit. The timing looked right as the country was in the midst of the early 1990s downsizing boom. A pilot project was successfully completed with the Rothschild bank, but negotiations foundered when the institution decided that it wanted to embark on the project without me.

The second clue that experiential learning was of interest came through an approach to the Open University's business school, the UK's largest institution of business teaching. My proposal to them was that we jointly undertake a project to record the memories and experiences of as many as possible of the UK's dwindling band of senior post-Second World War managers in much the same way as Allen Nevins, a Professor of American History at Columbia University, organized the interview, in the early 1950s, of more than 400 people in order to compile a history of the Ford Motor Company. Nevins had already introduced oral history as a tool for serious scholarship through the Columbia University Oral History Collection, which he set up in the late 1940s to preserve the reminiscences of former slaves and so-called 'unlettered rural folk'. Since then, other universities, including Harvard, Princeton and the University of California at Berkeley, have also developed extensive collections of oral history. In the business area, the only comparable project in the UK is a project called 'City Lives' in which the British Library National Sound Archive interviewed about 100 top men and women from financial institutions who lived through the changes since the Second World War.

One idea put to the Open University was that the UK material would be eventually used to compile a history of British management, of which there was none so far produced. Some unused funds for a pilot project were arranged by a senior academic but were subsequently diverted to another, unrelated, project being undertaken by the same individual while he was on sabbatical.

Another of my memories is of a top administrator in one the UK's top university business schools giving me an original and entirely unconvincing explanation for inaction. Having politely voiced a sympathetic view to the idea of introducing more rigorous experiential learning into the curriculum through corporate history, she pointed to the rows of bound copies of the business school's charter in her office and said that any modification to teaching approaches would require changes to the university's articles of association. The process of change, she said, was just too cumbersome, although she would run the idea past several of her colleagues. It was a familiar managerial ruse to proclaim disinterest.

Elsewhere, a not untypical reaction by the higher educational establishment came from Henley Management Centre, one of the top independent providers of executive and postgraduate management training, which approached me following the publication of my first book on experiential learning. Alas, it took others a further 18 months to try to arrange a requested teach-in for the faculty (based on the suggestion that 'it may yield some pay-off for the college'), by which time my regular polite enquiries as to 'progress' had begun to generate irritable responses. It was an experience that sadly confirmed both an inability to follow up management initiatives and a singular lack of curiosity undeserving of an academic establishment. At closure I constructively suggested that there were relevant experiential learning lessons to be gained from our discourse but, not unexpectedly, this was met by a deafening silence. Lip service to the concept has been evident at most other of Britain's older educational institutions with the notable exception of the University of Nottingham Business School, which has appointed me a Visiting Fellow. My thanks are due to Professor John Wilson, who has tried boldly and unsuccessfully on several occasions to arouse the interest of his fellow academics.

Professor Wilson's close association with The Association of Business Historians (ABH), the logical academic conduit through which experiential learning could be promoted to education and industry, has also proved unrewarding. As a representative body, it has all but given up the ghost at championing their chosen genre in the UK, with its long-time leading light, Reading University's Professor Geoffrey Jones, leaving the field of battle for Harvard Business School. An even earlier champion of the concept, Leslie Hannah, the UK's first Professor of Business History, has also left British shores for the University of Tokyo. Alongside these defections, the Business History Unit of the London School of Economics, which was set up in the late 1970s by a campaigning sector of industry to inject the concept of experiential learning into the curriculum, has all but faded into obscurity. After decades of trying, the main activity in business history has moved across to the more recently formed and more active European Business History Association (EBHA).

Curiously, it has been the UK's new universities, the old polytechnics, which have shown more interest – but, again, with little management follow-through. One of the London-based institutions approached me after seeing something I wrote for one of the UK's national newspapers. Like the independent provider of executive and postgraduate management training, it took the university a long time – two years – to try to arrange (also unsuccessfully) its requested meetings with its own faculty to even discuss the idea. Thanks, too, to one of the near-London universities, which also saw the potential, but was unable to find a role through its Competitiveness Centre because the appointed heads of the Centre kept leaving.

Elsewhere in the institutional hierarchy, I remember contacting Stuart Bishell, an ex-chief executive of Understanding Industry, a UK foundation dedicated to increasing links between business and education, with the suggestion that making more corporate and/or business history available would facilitate a wider inheritance. His underwhelming reply was:

I do not believe that historical context is especially useful to students in understanding wealth creation and the position of industry and commerce in the economy and society of the 21st century. It is vital that we look forward to the entirely different way in which these processes will work during the working lives of current students and not backwards at how they used to work in the past.[3]

Then, even higher up the educational hierarchy there was the following response by Dr Nicholas Tate, a former chief executive of the UK's School Curriculum and Assessment Authority's commentary to the same suggestion:

Pupils study the industrial revolution in some detail and look at the implications for the economic growth of the 19th century. They thus receive an introduction to some important business issues. The

Open University also uses the Battle of the Somme as one of its case studies for its MBA course. It provides an interesting method of helping managers draw upon the lessons of the past.[4]

Why experience is relevant only if it is at least 100 years old was not explained.

Management education has been a professed priority for professional organizations for as long as I can remember, yet the government's Council for Excellence in Management and Leadership's study[5] acknowledged an almost universal lack of management and leadership skills among the professional classes. That was in 2002. Ironically, most *claim* to employ experiential learning techniques, yet will conveniently overlook, or attribute non-educational reasons, for the continuing criticism of their members' unimproved perform-ance. I recollect contributing to the Royal Society of Arts' 1993 Inquiry on 'Tomorrow's Company', the Economic and Social Research Council-commissioned study on 'Manage-ment Research' and the Confederation of British Industry's deliberations on 'Flexible Labour Markets', yet their reports were singularly deficient in anything to do with experiential learning.

To me, all this is very strange in the face of positive feedback from other sections of education and industry.

For my early ideas on corporate and business history's unutilised applications, I have always valued Professor Alfred Chandler's appraisal of my work. The generous estimation of this Harvard-based doyen of the genre – 'I'm indeed impressed by your work and methodology' – has provided me with much sustenance, as has Cranfield School of Management's Professor Malcolm McDonald's 'I am fascinated by your approach and originality'. Sir Peter Parker, one of the UK's top managers, whose experience of industry over the tumultuous post-Second World War period has given him a unique view of its distinctive character, was also generous with his appraisal of my early ideas on how to improve decision-making ('I am struck by the innovative ideas of what you are doing'). In our correspondence he was unequivocal about business history's – and, through it, experiential learning's – untapped potential: '... business history is a missing dimension throughout the educational system. We need to build back into the business school approach the significance of a historical perspective'.

Alongside these, my thanks go to all those who have responded to one or other of my recent academic papers for the University of Nottingham Business School. They have been published on the Web[6] in the hope that they might generate some action, even discussion, among institutional conduits. One includes a 20-point plan to galvanize experiential learning for the twenty-first century while another – a forerunner of this book – focuses on how both, long- and short-term organizational memory can be utilized to improve decision-making. Both papers have fallen on stony ground in the UK even though one of their main recommendations – to formulate a code of conduct for corporate and business history's authors, publishers and their subject companies – was immediately picked up and discussed by the USA's Business History Conference, the sister organization to the UK's Business History Association. With the exception of Nottingham University's Professor John Wilson, all the British academic business historians who were invited to respond, failed to do so.

I will mention some of the individuals who did reply because their responses – all voluntarily given – also illustrate the widespread neglect of, and the perceived requirement for, experiential learning. Instructively, the individuals are all successful in their own right but are 'non-institutional' and thus with no official organizational axe to grind or, unfortunately, much wider political clout. I have long wrestled with whether this last factor is in any way relevant to experiential learning's dogged struggle. Are 'establishment' officers inherently less sighted to organizational needs? Do their bigger budgets or wider spotlight obfuscate priorities? Are the observations of non-institutional individuals considered too inconsequential? How about their stated interest in learning and improving productivity? Is it genuine or is it just lip service? Alternatively – dare I suggest – are establishment officers intrinsically lesser managers? Frankly, I remain undecided, but I raise these questions because of the positive reception about experiential learning from, among others, Bob Garrett, a senior associate at Cambridge University's Judge Institute. Mr Garrett, who is also a Visiting Professor in Corporate Governance at Imperial College's Management School in London, a consultant on director development and a prolific author on human resource management, confirms that experiential learning:

… is a hugely misunderstood and neglected aspect of business and business education, which is a puzzle to me. Effective boards of directors and senior executives need greater intellectual rigour in formulating policy and especially in their strategic thinking skills and this approach to better decision-making through understanding business history is both obvious and highly recommended.[7]

From someone who spans the business and academic worlds, I thank Professor Cyril Levicki, late of Manchester Business School and Reading University, whose observations about management education and industry have provided me with continuing confirmation of their shortcomings. Over the years, we have tut-tutted our way through a train of discreditable anecdotes that have also given oxygen to experiential learning's unused potential. His unwavering encouragement to develop my ideas on organizational memory against the appalling cost that its loss inflicts on organizations and individuals has been sustaining. This management consultant and author of several books on strategy similarly believes that:

We are currently destroying our own value and wrecking the future for the lack of the small amount of efficiency it would take to preserve and apply organisational memory. It's amazing to think we have so little regard for our experience.[8]

Clare Lorenz is also someone who overlaps with the academic world. An Ofsted inspector and founder chairman of an education charity, she admits that:

Business history is not an area I have thought about much – but that is MY fault. It is certainly one that deserves consideration. The link between the past, now and the future and the continuities therein are all important. I am heartily fed up with hearing about organisations re-engineering – i.e. probably throwing the baby out with the bath water in an effort to look modern (as distinct from becoming more efficient). There are of course changes (ICT and global trading revolutions for example) that profoundly affect organisational change but there are also very harmful management fashions that are purely destructive and counter intuitive. Why would a company wish to get rid of its IP wisdom by outsourcing? Why are cheap youngsters hired and then huge training money poured into them to make them viable earners when everyone knows their company life expectancy is no longer than 2 years? Organisations certainly have a lot to answer for.[9]

Another academic to whom I owe thanks is Bruce Lloyd, Professor of Strategic Management at South Bank University, also a constant supporter. Like me, he is studiously aware that understanding the past is an essential prerequisite for making progress:

Despite the widespread acceptance of the concept of case studies, more needs to be done. What is now needed is to more closely integrate these ideas into 'Learning Organisation' and 'Knowledge Management' developments. A Knowledge/Learning approach only makes any sense if we understand our history and put the insights that come from serious reflection on it, into more effective action than would otherwise be the case. Without this integration of past, present and future, there is little chance that the pressure for change into society today will end up by being anything remotely close to what we would all like to define as progress.[10]

My gratitude, too, to Dr John Peters, an academic author on knowledge management and a director of the MCB University Press, whose group has published several articles about experiential learning under my name. His take on the subject is that the fields of management theory and management practice need to come together more effectively:

Too many management theorists for my liking seem determined to make the discipline into a science – using quantitative analysis to 'prove' where there is patently no proof, or to 'prove' where proof is an irrelevance. We can, for example, 'prove', pointlessly, that 46% of large firms in Albania practise centralisation. But we cannot 'prove' that centralisation works better or worse or the same as decentralisation. In reaction to this introspection, real managers faced with real problems fall back on feel, anecdote, political expediency, procrastination and more when trying to make decisions rather than the body of pseudo-scientific knowledge. The action learning approach which seeks to capture the learning gained whilst experience is taking place has moved a few small steps towards bringing the worlds of theory and practice closer. The expansion of management theory from pseudo-science to social anthropology, philosophy and history move us a few more steps closer, in trying to do the simple yet difficult task of capturing stories and making contextual sense of them.[11]

Moving on to industry proper, specifically the public sector, I am grateful to Dr Barry Blain, retired deputy director of the National Automated Fingerprint Identification System (NAFIS), a quango formerly attached to the Home Office. His observations about his own working life reinforced my own views about managers' non-reflective instincts as well as government's role (by neglect) in championing poor decision-making and the massive wastage of resources for which we, the public, end up paying. As an aside I have much sympathy with Prime Minister Tony Blair's exasperated admission in 2000 that he had scars on his back from trying to persuade the public sector to change but little faith in his government's ability to heal his wounds. Not that his predecessors were any more successful. Over the years, their collective efforts to raise output have seemed like a grinding treadmill on which one has to sprint with ever more expensive running shoes just to stand still.

Dr Blain's recall of his own working life is rare for a senior civil servant and is also educational in its candour, no doubt due to his retired status:

… the lack of any attempt at continuity or learning from the past has been screamingly obvious to me throughout my career in the Civil Service. My own tiny area, that of technology support to the emergency services, suffered major structural upheavals several times over the years. … The

management wheel was reinvented over and over again. The cost benefits of any of the changes were never evaluated, and the idea of a business case failed to enter anyone's head. And, frustratingly, each change was put forward as a brilliant and novel approach, and at no time was any previous restructuring acknowledged. An interesting sideline is that after one of the changes, the retiring Director was kept on as a consultant in order to write a history of Home Office research and development in support of the emergency services. He was never allowed to complete this work, and as far as I know his initial contributions were quietly filed away. Of course they do not look at any history of their project (usually because none exists), and certainly not at projects elsewhere in government. And the suppliers rub their hands with glee as they happily charge for the alterations to the specification and for the extra work they must do during the months of delay.[12]

Mike Pedler is a pioneer practitioner of action learning, an enterprising attempt by Professor Reg Revans to introduce experiential learning proper into industry in the early 1980s. A full working life later, he is still amazed 'how we forget what happened even 20 years ago and what little understanding there is of "new ideas" as new wine in old bottles. Loss of corporate memory is a serious blow and is a key issue in the learning organisation.'[13]

Carol Kennedy is one of those corporate historians who academics like to discount – because she's a non-academic. A management writer and business commentator, her view confirmed to me how business history's famine was contributing to the UK's lack of business inheritance:

Could it be that Britain's wilful lack of interest in its rich business and scientific history is linked to the general – and I think criminal – downgrading of history in the educational system? Today's news story about the abysmal levels of knowledge of major historical events and figures in secondary schools is nothing short of a national disgrace: we are short-changing the next generation's knowledge and wasting assets that few other countries can match.[14]

John Emanuel, Chairman of Pax Technology Transfer Ltd, has spent a lifetime trying to do what experiential learning is partly all about – share 'experience' in the form of technology. Perceptively, he pointed out why productivity is probably such a lowly rated priority among many companies and countries. If they see a healthy turnover and/or gross domestic product, they reason: 'Well, we can't be all that bad at what we're doing.' His observation highlighted for me how companies and countries mistake the quantitative aspect of production alone for accomplishment in much the same way as many socialist countries did for most of the twentieth century, albeit in a more politicized and formalized way. In practice, low-productivity organizations have to throw much more unnecessary money at their enterprises. In reality, it is in the quality of production – the ability to do things efficiently – that real wealth resides.

Says Mr Emanuel:

You point out the obvious – so obvious that it has been almost invisible. Without history, what perspective can we have of ourselves to help us understand the present and to grapple with the future? We have plenty of history covering almost every aspect of life except the practical side of co-operative work – the initiation, structuring, operation and development of business and other corporate enterprises. Our school culture and much of our university culture has little or no place for the study of enterprise or enterprises. Indeed I have the impression that many teachers and academics regard 'business' as something alien and disreputable, unworthy of serious attention. In my work I regularly meet good inventors with entrepreneurial instincts but who are ignorant of the simplest business methodologies and strategies they might apply. I also meet directors of established companies who behave as if the enterprise is stuck in a rut without means of change or escape. Educational exposure to simple business methodology and business histories would be invaluable to them, giving them the intellectual tools and role models which they could adapt for their own use, to the benefit of themselves and our society. I would like to see the study of corporate history taken seriously at universities. I would hope that, in time, an understanding of enterprises would become 'common sense', part of everybody's general knowledge.[15]

His wish might just be forthcoming if a research study[15] by four British academics with an interest in corporate and business history doesn't – like several other studies into the subject over the years – fall on deaf ears. Their project, which is part-sourced on my work into experiential learning, is examining my assertion that if the precepts of knowledge management are accepted, then corporate history should be seen as an important repository of organizational memory. The two-year study, due in late 2005 or early 2006, will examine the symbolic significance of history and how businesses learn from their pasts, in particular my contention[16] that British firms miss the opportunity to learn from their own rich histories because of their reluctance to look back. Whilst I'm delighted that the subject is getting some attention (and particularly that someone else has at last made the connection between organizational memory, corporate history, knowledge management and experiential learning), why the Economic and Social Research Council, the academic funding agency for management research, would want to throw another £102 416 – what it's costing – to confirm the blindingly obvious defeats me. All I can deduce is that we're in big trouble if we're still trying to decide in the twenty-first century whether hindsight is valuable or not.

Thanks, too, to Mike Keoghan at the Department of Trade and Industry in the UK. As one of the number-crunchers of the annual *Competitiveness and Productivity Report*, he was able to steer me towards the Groningen Growth and Development Centre and The Conference Board's *Total Economy Database*, the compilers of which he describes 'some of the best operating in this field, so it is credible stuff to use'.

Next, I want to thank my out-of-Britain supporters.

Brian Berman has followed my ideas from the outset and helped me with my conceptual thinking. As a former World Bank economist, as chief financial officer of Paradigm Geophysical, a NASDAQ company with several UK subsidiaries, and latterly as a senior executive for D-Pharm, a drug discovery company, his perspectives have continued to be invaluable:

Our most important asset is our people. High-tech companies are 'mind-ware' companies even more than they are software companies. Managing and maximizing our returns to our accumulated internal corporate knowledge base is critical for our success. Knowledge is nothing if it is not the collective corporate memory, but making sure that memory is refreshed and that lessons are learned is therefore critical to give this knowledge tangible and operative value rather than just passive value. We need to put these lessons into sound management practices to unlock the value of our own corporate knowledge and to learn the lessons from experience.[17]

I have had an enormous amount of help from academics in the US, whose knowledge of the criticisms of business education helped me put my own critique into a wider and more authoritative context. In Los Angeles, Josh Sharfman spotted the importance of organizational memory and asked me to co-supervise his doctoral thesis on how to make workers more receptive to this important component of intellectual capital. With an acquired interest in knowledge management, marketing specialist Professor Al Goldberg at HAIFA Technion – the Israel Institute of Technology – helped me brainstorm the name experience-based management (EBM). He also regularly passed to me relevant academic material to examine. Over in Australasia, the Universities of Auckland and Queensland in Brisbane have responded to local concern about high staff churn by asking me to run local workshops on how experiential learning can still take place in environments where labour turnover is approaching northern hemisphere levels. Elsewhere 'down under', the Western Australia Ministry of the Premier and Cabinet referred to my work on oral debriefings[18] in their 1999 review of how to manage succession in the public sector. And in South Africa, an independent review of the University of the Witswatersrand's decision in 2000 to restructure through retrenchment and outsourcing used my work on corporate amnesia to help them conclude[19] that the university's senior executive team's outsourcing proposals would 'tend to reproduce the legacy of apartheid for both the workforce and the student body'.

And finally, I must thank the British Broadcasting Corporation for a radio programme that first put me on the road to this important subject in the early 1980s. I was listening to an interview with a 1930s heavyweight boxer who was explaining how he had beaten his opponent. One of his throwaway lines in the archive crackle was that he had spent time examining the newsreel footage of his opponent's previous fight and, from that, was able to conceive a strategy to beat his adversary. It struck me that the film clip he had seen was, to all intents and purposes, the equivalent of corporate organizational memory and that the boxer was using experience – this time someone else's experience that wasn't distorted by time or ego – as a learning tool. My imagination then took flight. Was not the boxer the forerunner of hundreds of thousands of other sportsmen and women who, in the relatively short period since then, have enhanced their performances to an extent greater than in any previous period in history? Yes, training techniques have improved, as have athletes' diets, medical procedures (all experiential learning in their own right) and that prime incentive, money, but – I asked myself – could not their employment of 'memory' in this way also be a factor in the dramatic improvement in performances over the entire range of sports? The fact that film and video usage in sports reporting has been around for almost the exactly the same time and that most top sportsmen and women routinely use the medium to examine their own and each other's performances seemed not uncoincidental. If this *was* the case, why, then, could not commerce and industry apply the same principle to equally good effect?

To reiterate, I must thank all those people and organizations that provided the fount evidence for *Corporate DNA: Using Organizational Memory to Improve Poor Decision-Making*. Without them all – allies, detractors, the disinterested, those who tried, those who didn't and the people and organizations that have given me the necessary source material to support experiential learning's unexploited potential – this book would have read very differently. Indeed, it may well not have been written at all. In full appreciation, I blame them entirely.

Notes

1. Henry Thoreau, 'Economy', *Walden*, 1854.
2. DTI research with www.startups.co.uk, published in *Evening Telegraph*, Peterborough, 5 April 2005.

3. Correspondence with author, 1994.
4. Correspondence with author, 1994.
5. Council for Excellence in Management and Leadership, *Final Report*, May 2002.
6. www.nottingham.ac.uk/BusinessHistory, go to 'Research', then 'Discussion Papers'.
7. Correspondence with author, 2001.
8. Correspondence with author, 2001.
9. Correspondence with author, 2001.
10. Correspondence with author, 2001.
11. Correspondence with author, 2001.
12. Correspondence with author, 2001.
13. Correspondence with author, 2001.
14. Correspondence with author, 2001.
15. Correspondence with author, 2001.
16. Arnold Kransdorff, *Corporate Amnesia: Keeping Know-how in the Company*, London: Butterworth Heinemann, 1998.
17. Correspondence with author, 2001.
18. *Passing the Torch*, Ageing Workforce Discussion Paper Series, Western Australia Ministry of the Premier and Cabinet, 1999, at www.psmd@mpc.wa.gov.au.
19. Glenn Adler, Andries Bezuidenhout, Sakhela Buhlungu, Bridget Kenny, Rahmat Omar, Greg Ruiters and Lucien van der Walt, *Support Services Review: A Critique*, internal report commissioned by the University of the Witswatersrand, June 2000.

The Boiler is Running out of Steam

We live in a world where amnesia is the most wished-for state.[1]

John Guare, US playwright

What on earth has the intangible subject of organizational memory got to do with the very tangible matter of productivity? For most managers, they have an incongruous relationship given that memory of any kind is lifeless, merely a remembered record of events past and deeds done. Their characteristic view is that they might have had a hand in how things were done previously, but today, in our fast-moving business environment, circumstances are different and time too short for indulgencies such as *history*. Consequently, what went on in the days, months and years past is of little relevance. Wrong. This book will contend that for any established cooperative venture, from a private company's endeavours to a public-sector institution's activities, the individual establishment's organizational memory is not only the reason for its being but also the key to its continued existence. And for that, productivity, which is contingent on management's good decision-making, is not an optional factor of production.

By way of explanation, we all know what happens when businesses are unproductive. They become uncompetitive, get taken over or go bust. That's serious enough for individual companies but what happens when whole countries lose their edge? Take a deep breath. The productivity growth of five developed countries has entered negative territory. And the rest's average growth is a paltry 0.8 per cent. This is the first time in modern industrial history that so many have crashed through industry's own Maginot Line at any one time with so many others so close behind. Back in 1939 the Maginot Line, coincidentally sited just a short train ride from every one of the negatively-measured economies, was a barrier that was considered impenetrable at the time.

Productivity is critical in several ways. It is the ability to do things efficiently, and particularly more efficiently than others, that, at the end of the day, determines wealth. It is also one of the main requirements for businesses *staying* in business.

The US has held the top position for much of the twentieth century and, even today, is way ahead of the Organization for Economic Cooperation and Development (OECD) pack by a significant margin. With a few exceptions – mainly the countries that have come up from a low productivity base – the rest are mostly struggling to inch ahead (see Figure I.1 and Appendix 1). The inside story *across the board* – that includes the US – is one of declining annual growth rates, indicating that the developed world is rapidly running out of steam. Individual governments could do their bit by introducing extra defensive macroeconomic measures such as subsidies, import duties and interest rate cuts but, as history shows, this still can't detract from the underlying failure of managers to ensure that all the corporate resources at their command are used more efficiently. In the multifaceted world of productivity, this untrumpeted collapse is a late warning sign of systemic trouble for First World industry and commerce. It is now also an eleventh-hour alert that has been threatening for decades, with all remedial measures giving the patients only provisional respite.

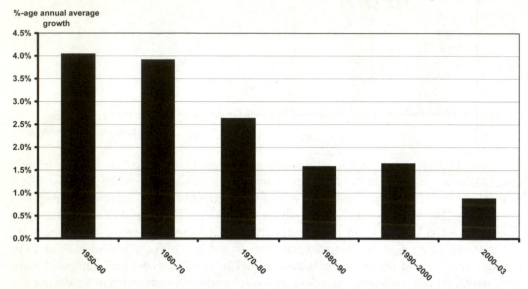

Source: Groningen Growth and Development Centre and The Conference Board, Total Economy Database, August 2004, http://www.ggdc.net.

Figure I.1   OECD countries: productivity per capita

When profit margins crumple

When productivity growth is in the red, employers are getting less than added value from their endeavour. New investment in many areas makes little sense and margins in existing businesses become increasingly difficult to achieve, as Italy, Luxembourg, Holland, Spain and Switzerland will be finding out (see Figure I.2). For their profits, employers increasingly have to depend on a reduction in inputs such as employees, raw materials and capital. Given that the developed world is now predominantly service-oriented, the usual areas targeted are the workforce – the reduction of which automatically affects the quality of service – or prices, or both. And we all know what happens when price increases are not supported by real productivity: that demon inflation kicks in. When higher prices are not supported by corresponding higher value to the consumer, the result is a further loss of competitiveness and a downward spiral towards bankruptcy.

Another possible scenario was indicated in June 2005 when the giant HSBC banking group sounded the first establishment warning of impending disaster in circumstances of shrinking export revenues among many OECD countries, a direct consequence of uncompetitiveness and its main cause, declining productivity. Its chief European economist, Peter Wandesford, said precipitously: 'We're not looking at the doomsday scenario quite yet: but it is a question of when, not if.'

The report[2] on which he was commenting said that Eurozone growth in gross domestic

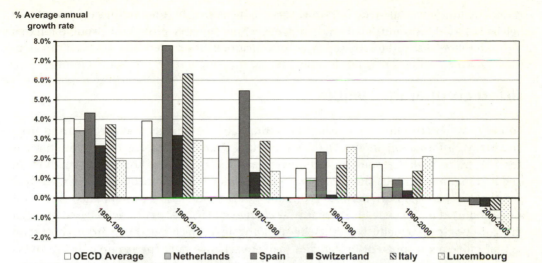

% Average annual
growth rate

Source: Groningen Growth and Development Centre and The Conference Board, Total Economy Database, August 2004, http://www.ggdc.net.

Figure I.2   Productivity growth not sustained

product (GDP) was likely to 'grind to a halt' as exports weakened. With Italy in 'dire straits' after a collapse in productivity and negative growth for five out of the past nine quarters, Germany perilously close to deflation as its exports to China fall away, a 3.9 per cent drop in Italian retail sales and Holland in equal danger, HSBC forecast a meagre 1.1 per cent growth across the Eurozone in 2005 and warned that the bloc may tip into recession as the global trade cycle turns down. The report explained that, as countries struggle to cool down property booms, the European Central Bank's (ECB) one-size-fits-all interest rate is effectively driving Germany and Holland deeper into slump, and added that it could be difficult to hold monetary union together unless the ECB cut interest rates before the downturn became unstoppable. It concluded: 'The dangers of a liquidity trap are rising in the region.'

The so-called liquidity trap to which the report was referring is the scenario painted by economist John Maynard Keynes in the 1930s when traumatized consumers and investors refused to spend, pushing prices lower and lower. The result? Deflation. It is a condition that renders conventional monetary policy largely impotent as it is impossible to cut interest rates below zero. Inflation-adjusted rates rise as the crisis deepens, causing mass bankruptcy. With their core inflation around 0.7 per cent on a downward trend, Germany and Holland may now be slipping into this trap, the report warned. As evidenced by Japan, deflation is hard to stop once it becomes lodged in the system. Japan is now in its eighth year of falling prices, despite zero interest rates for much of the period.

Like HSBC, I should firmly signal that I am not predicting Armageddon just yet because the major industrial countries do not compete with each other in the same way as corporations do. They are, for example, each other's main export markets and each other's main provider of useful imports. Also, computing productivity – like all number-crunching – is an imprecise science, especially when making international comparisons which typically involve judgements by human compilers and self-protective politicians. The wider picture moreover depends on which formula and database is used. For example, OECD figures based on 'per-hours worked' show that negative growth rates have been recorded several times in various countries at different times over the past 30 years.[3] However, using 'per-person' figures adjusted for countries' living standards, which arguably provides a clearer picture of the underlying reality, the current picture looks distinctly wintry.

Using comparative values

To back my observations, I am using the authoritative Groningen data set[4] derived from underlying information in the OECD's Structural Analysis database, which, in turn, is derived from national sources. Groningen applies the Elteto-Köves-Szul method of calculation (I have used its latest 1999 EKA $ rate), which is a measure of exchange value that permits direct comparisons between economies. Called 'purchasing power parity' (PPP), it is a method used to calculate on alternative exchange rate between currencies based on what the currency can actually buy, thereby avoiding inaccuracies deriving from short-term capital movements inherent in standard market exchange rate. For example, PPP conveys how much a euro would buy in London or in New York, allowing the figures to reflect living standards. A good example of a PPP-type measure is the Economist's 'Big Mac Index'.

Normally, small changes in data comparisons are not significant, but the flagging growth figures I have extrapolated from Groningen's productivity databases are not just confined to the early 2000s. The downward drift is evident over a 40-year period, closing with a negative score in five developed countries at the same time. The wider trend can also be clearly corroborated in other databases.

My point is that overall productivity growth among many developed nations is now dangerously low and the upside prospects that might come from pipeline products in the form of nanotechnology's molecular manufacturing and genetic engineering are still a decade or two away. As we all know, timing is everything in business, so until these developments kick in, it's going to be an uncomfortable ride for many. In terms of competitiveness, China, for example, is looking very threatening, as are Brazil, Russia, India and Korea. These five are the so-called BRICK countries that many forward-looking investors have designated as prime investment areas. For these fast-learning emergents, the opportunity to overtake has never been greater, for the aspirants also host one of the other most valuable of all commercial needs – captive markets that span more than one-third of the world's population.

Drucker's productivity challenge

For management guru Peter Drucker, the urgency of the productivity challenge is great. 'The country that does this first will dominate the twenty-first century economically. Unless this challenge is met, the developed world will face increasing social tensions, increasing polarization, increasing radicalization, possibly even class war.'[5] The noteworthy aspect about Drucker's remarks is that they were made more than a decade ago and, since then, progress in the productivity stakes has earned only slim pickings. Although his class war prediction seems to be hyperbole – most developed countries are democracies – polarization in the form of international terrorism has already manifested itself strongly. Some of his other predictions are already apparent in low-productivity countries.

In recent years management has emphasized maximizing the efficiency of capital investment, specifically in technology. These tactics, however, have now virtually played themselves out. Whereas workers employed in making and moving things accounted for a near-majority of employees in the 1960s, they now number less than one-fifth of the typical workforce,[6] which means that there are now too few employees in such jobs for their productivity to be decisive. We've squeezed employee numbers to the point where the human element of doing business seems to have become almost mechanical and certainly disposable enough not to be missed when it moves on. Interest rates in many developed economies may have come down from the high levels of the early 1990s but the capital factor is now so big that providers are demanding shorter- and shorter-term returns. And although technology improvements look endless, the initial momentum that they provided for savings is ebbing fast.

The responsibility for this is traditionally ascribed to workers, or more precisely workers' apparent lack of skills. In reality, though, their skills base has never been higher, opening up the more credible alternative that it is managers who are not giving full value to their employers. The way in which they are making their determinations is conferring virtually no upside potential, which means that it is the decision-makers who are leaving the OECD wide open for experience-poor competitors to step into their experience-rich shoes – exactly as Japan did in the 1960s.

Against the reality that all economies – whether OECD or not or however efficient – depend on productivity growth to sustain their wealth, why? And where next?

Where the blame lies

I am going to part-blame two related constituencies – education and organizations themselves.

Within the former, I will identify a widespread neglect in business instruction of both a subject that characterizes managers' most important skill and a proven teaching methodology that is widely overlooked. They are decision-making, which is – astonishingly – still not a dedicated subject in the way business education and training teaches managers to make their employer's determinations, and experiential learning, self-evidently the process of learning from experience, out of which comes the knowledge variously called 'wisdom', 'hindsight', 'insight', 'good judgement' and '20:20 vision'. This is despite enveloping research[7] that acknowledges that an organization's ability to collect, store and use knowledge generated through its experience can have important consequences for its performance. Ironically, much of the development work into how people learn from experience and how they could be better taught has already been done. In fact, the work has been going on for more than 80 years, carried out by small bands of academics and practitioners to whom management education's mainstream have been paying little regard for years. Its pervasive absence buttresses business education's theoretical bias and, oddly, ignores the single biggest influence on decision-making excellence – institution-*specific* experience.

Within the latter – inside organizations, that is – there are also the unexpected effects of the single biggest change in workplace practice for more than a century – the actively encouraged flexible labour market. Although employers think it is universally beneficial to them, high job turnover has allowed organizations to, literally, lose their organizational memory (OM) and make it difficult for transient managers to learn from their employers' own experiences.

The collective result? The pandemic of repeated mistakes, reinvented wheels and other unlearned lessons and inefficiencies across industry and commerce that is ultimately responsible for correspondingly massively higher-than-necessary investment costs, lower profits, elevated taxes and a poorer quality of life.

These serious-enough consequences aside, flagging productivity also masks a deeply uncomfortable question for business schools and management trainers. In the US, business schools started out in the 1950s, which would suggest that they would have begun to make an impact within a decade. In Europe and Japan, the onset of prescribed business education was around a decade later, signifying that their benefit should have been manifested in the 1970s. If one accepts that business education is there to enable managers to produce their employer's wares more efficiently, the worrying question for management educators is why productivity growth scores are lower today than they were prior to formalized business education.

Knowledge dispossession – the unnoticed revolution

In industry and commerce the flexible labour market has imposed an even more serious problem that has passed unheralded, even unnoticed. Simply stated, it has allowed the ownership of knowledge to pass from the corporate body to the transient individual, condemning almost every organization to running on *others'* experiences.

Because of the intimate relationship between knowledge and power, the corporate body in the form of companies and other kinds of organization, quite deliberately and entirely unwittingly, has allowed its command to be displaced. No longer are individuals an aggregate *part* of an established institution; individuals *are* the institution for as long as they remain *in situ*. Then, when the face changes – as it's doing on average every four or five years in many developed economies – the institution changes or, more accurately, tries to change, bereft of its continuity and at the mercy of new brooms. Ordered evolution has become a shapeless revolution with little regard for the one corporate asset that represents the organization's life form – its institution-specific knowledge and experience. This presages a mercurial world, with such things as corporate culture, ethos, values and tried and tested usage struggling to maintain an even keel, its sponsors adamantly insisting that the more flexible labour becomes, the more beneficial it will be. What has happened is that the motor of Western society's wealth machine has largely disempowered itself, inflicting what footballers describe as an own goal and soldiers see as shooting themselves in the foot. Organizations have consciously chosen to operate in isolation to their own hard-won and expensively acquired experience, which is an inefficient way to evolve and, specifically, learn.

Alongside dispossession of knowledge, institutional disenfranchisement is going to have profound impacts on the wider social order. Arguably, it already has – an explanation, perhaps, for Western society's widely evident and acknowledged institutional breakdowns? When the flexible labour market reared its head in the 1970s, I remember being puzzled by the reaction: the bosses cheering their loss and the workers being highly resistant to their gain.

The three ways of acquiring knowledge

In any dialogue about learning and the acquisition of knowledge it is important to point out the different ways in which learning becomes apparent. One is accidental, with knowledge arriving quite unexpectedly and, usually, unplanned. This was the case in 1928 when a spore drifted on to the culture dish in the laboratory of Scottish research scientist Alexander Fleming while he was on a two-week holiday. It spawned a blue mould that semed to be able to kill off a harmful bacterium. It was penicillin, one of the medical world's most beneficial discoveries.

Then there is the innovative means, the labour of true genius. Into this grouping would fit the work of people such as Leonardo da Vinci who, in the late fifteenth century, conceptualized cutting-edge ideas like the aeroplane, the parachute, cranes, submarines, tanks, water pumps, canals and drills. It is this type of learning that leapfrogs the other type of learning and, in Leonardo's case, was so advanced that it had to wait hundreds of years for incremental learning to catch up. Incremental learning is how the rest of us acquire our knowledge and the way in which most learning takes place – the building of one experience on another. It is this type of learning that is the subject of this book.

Straddling the innovative and incremental way is a subgenus, unique to business, that distinguishes the entrepreneurial nature of the whole capitalist system. Like the innovative approach, it is non-conformist and rare, the means – often borne out of necessity but also generated out of direct experience – that sets businesses and other kinds of organization apart from each other. Such originality, which most call enterprise or entrepreneurship, is the type of erudition that starts off being the fabrication of individuals and then becomes mostly incremental when it is institutionalized. It is the wellspring of wealth – the kind of knowledge that business education is supposed to nurture and most governments chase. It is also, of course, the source of much of their revenue.

The many types of learning

But back to decision-making and how this manner of learning is taught. Decision-making is the single most important managerial skill bar none but, as it stands, the marriage of how to distinguish what to do and then how to execute the chosen preference is poorly addressed in business education in any non-theoretical or 'experiential' way. This is not from want of trying by numerous small bands of academics and practitioners. In fact, the wider discipline of 'learning' has received bewildering attention in recent years, among them the design of processes that also include aspects of experiential, and particularly reflective, learning. My observation is that they have not been applied to business in anything other than in an informal, unstructured and tangential way and that the poor record on productivity and decision-making acknowledges their less-than-successful application.

In researching this book, I came across the tally of the different types of learning that an academic acquaintance had encountered over his more than three decades of teaching.[8] The number topped a staggering 30, among them authentic learning, accelerated learning, action learning, adaptive learning, anticipatory learning, appreciative learning, celleration learning, cognitive learning, collaborative learning, competency-based learning, competitive learning, concurrent learning, constant learning, continuous learning, cooperative learning, creative learning, single-, double- and triple-loop learning, experiential learning, high-impact learning, interorganizational learning, interpartner learning, innovative learning, leading learning, mechanistic learning, organizational learning, outcome-based learning, parenthetic learning, programmed learning, self-directed learning, rote learning, situated learning, strategic learning, total quality learning, transformational learning, virtual learning and virtuous learning.

Most are obscure, the creation of inventive individuals whose efforts have hardly ever been given a practical or applied application in industry, suggesting that the universal process of learning has become so fragmented into specialized branches that the practice has become disaggregated. The implication for generalists, such as managers, is that attention is drawn away from understanding the universal principles of learning. In truth, people have become so used to simply having data and information given to them that they have become unskilled at creating knowledge either for themselves or their employers. Learning, and particularly the interrelated way of decision-making, has gone astray, with its 'specialization' paradoxically inhibiting its own organic development. If anything, the existence of all these 'types' of learning signifies the importance given to the process of acquiring knowledge, but their widespread neglect must surely suggest a pervasive corporate confusion about which to use or their perceived ineffectiveness.

Decision-making techniques

The attention to 'learning' doesn't stop there. There is, in fact, another bewildering clutch of macro-level techniques devoted specifically to decision-making, among them methodologies that would be categorized under the broad-based description of decision analysis. These include techniques such as Analytic Hierarchy Process (AHP), Bayesian updating, outranking, subjective judgement theory, utility assessment, matrix, cost–benefit analysis and the decision tree, the last three being the most commonly taught and used - that is, *when* they're taught at all.

Matrix, for example, utilizes a subjective weight assignment for alternative criteria, its main drawback being that it cannot account for interdependence between so-called best alternatives. Cost–benefit analysis, which provides a quantitative format for reckoning the range of benefits and costs surrounding a prospective decision, aggregates the effects over time, using an approach called discounting and arriving at a 'present value' or 'payback period'. In its simplest form, it is carried out using only monetary costs and benefits but a more sophisticated approach tries to put a financial value on intangible costs and benefits, which makes the calculation highly subjective. Other criticisms include the imprecise techniques used to measure diverse benefits and costs and the fact that, to some, environmental concerns fall properly under the realm of ethics rather than economics. Then there is the 'decision tree', an abstract methodology in which alternative decisions and their implications can be evaluated via a genealogy-type visual aid. Its main criticisms include what is called overfitting, when the tree matches random variations of the target values in the training data that are not replicated in other samples, and instability, when the tree fits the data well, predicts well and conveys a good story, but then, if some of the original data is replaced with a fresh sample and a new tree is created, a completely different root'n'branch picture may emerge using completely different inputs in the splitting rules and, consequently, conveying a completely different story.

However loyal followers of any of these techniques might be, the historical shortcomings of industry and commerce confirm that good decision-making is far more complex a discipline than their methodologies can accommodate.

For the more all-encompassing approach to decision-making, there is probably just one up-and-running approach that consciously addresses experiential learning in its purest format, namely action learning, to which I shall refer in more detail in a later chapter. Little used across industry and commerce, it addresses the institutional-specific aspect of decision-making but – like the other macro-level techniques – it does not deal with the problem of departed knowledge and experience arising from modern-day short-tenure working.

In business schools, educators claim that the experiential element is catered for within case studies. When case studies are used, however, they are usually no more than summarized snapshots explaining the workings of some functional management discipline, an approach that inescapably disaggregates their interrelationship with other management factors and influences. The wider contextual picture illustrating the more complex and intimate nature of running a real business and making real decisions is studiously avoided. In many countries the examples used are also more often *other* regions' exemplars, giving any experiential learning a generalized application. In essence, unfamiliar exemplars are less efficient as learning opportunities than home-grown models.

However decision-making's instruction is delivered, it is usually an addendum to generic subjects such as marketing, strategy and leadership. The 'taught' methodology is generally theoretical and informal, with the main technique focused on problem-solving, and encompassing a routine that, in the main, goes as follows: define the problem → gather information → evaluate the options → select the best alternative → implement the best choice. The baseline 'non-problem' decisions are, inexplicably, given only cursory attention, making the whole approach to decision-making a reactive process.

The same applies to the attention given to the less-than-subtle detail of *how* things should best be done, which is probably where most decision-making falls down. Managers have created sophisticated ways of identifying what needs to be done after the event – this is the process called information or data management – but not the *means*. What's more, the process – with the notable exception of action learning and AHP – largely ignores the necessary cognitive requirements of dealing with the increased complexities of business life, leaving managers to gravitate towards conformist linear actions characterized by one-dimensional prescriptions of how to do something. In many cases, instruction even neglects to include an employer's own experience in the appraisal of a determination. Consequently, newly installed managers are typically thrown into the decision-making cauldron dependent entirely on little more than intuition, non-existent institution-specific experience and untested judgement, so that they have to fall back on 'feel', political expediency, subjective thinking, experimentation and delay. Often, decisions are made for change's sake because something isn't working, with the overall process being little more than guesswork coupled with an ability to play the game of corporate politics well. It is commonly called the 'School of Hard Knocks', a process that is costing businesses and other organizations – and because employers always pass on their costs to their customers or clients, us – big time. Much of industry and commerce's output is being inexpertly flushed down the proverbial toilet.

Where new productivity can come from

It is here – in the inefficiencies of the workplace that have been traditionally ascribed to labour rather than management – that industry and commerce can find its next round of productivity increases.

In a nutshell, businesses have to substantially raise the *quality* of their decision-making, what Peter Drucker calls 'working smarter',[9] a catchphrase first coined by the American industrial engineer Frederick Winslow Taylor 125 years ago. To do this, they need to be much better experiential learners. And for experiential learning to take place, companies and other institutions have to better manage their source evidence known as organizational memory (OM), the corporate equivalent of individual DNA.

OM and experiential learning's likeness to deoxyribonucleic acid is not too far removed. All are multifaceted and complex. OM is the knowledge born of experience that distinguishes the corporate body while DNA is a molecule that identifies almost all organisms. Both carry transmissible information from generation to generation. As such, they are – like experiential learning – organic in the sense that they have an embryonic way of developing within an identifiable context.

In the case of DNA, this embryonic structure looks like a spiral ladder where the rungs are formed by pairs of base molecules coiled about the same axis. Its two strands run anti-parallel, which means they flow in opposite directions. Just like experiential learning, where the generation of new knowledge is dependent on the flow of older knowledge in a two-way reflective context, it is genealogical, a derivation thing that links time and deeds. Most experiential learning is diagrammatically depicted as a loop or as a double loop. My conception is that it is more akin to a spiral – like DNA's famous double helix or, more simply, a coiled steel spring.

Although no single accepted definition of OM exists, its collective awareness provides the type of expertise that is both an organization's adhesive and its lubricant – that is, it relates to all the routines and processes (formal or otherwise) that make an organization tick. Its value represents the capability of the firm and is perhaps the main ingredient of its resilience. In broad-brush terms, it includes the individual's understanding and accommodation of their employer's individual corporate culture, management, communications and decision-making style, the contacts and relationships between employees or teams of employees, the detail of job-related events and the knowledge of tried and tested usage as it applies to the organization's own market circumstances and special environment (so-called episodic knowledge). The qualitative application of OM is closely allied to memory, which is most commonly described as knowledge retention or the difference between having acquired knowledge and having to reacquire it. It is what is *not* forgotten – the reconstruction of experienced events.

The three ages of organizational memory

For practical purposes, OM can be broken down into three distinct timeframes. Short-term OM lasts up to about five years; medium-term OM occupies a timeframe of up to around ten years; periods in excess of this constitute long-term OM. Because of its contemporary and contiguous nature, short- and medium-term OM is generally more relevant to operational issues facing the organization, whilst long-term OM is more conformant with strategy and culture.

OM is the type of knowledge that enables a good theoretician to also become a good practitioner. Without it, organizations – even if they employ the most qualified people in their field – run like a gearbox without oil.

Most organizations think that their OM is, or can be, housed in the minds of one or two key individuals. Therefore, so long as there is someone around with long-term tenure, OM is secure. Failing that, there is always the corporate archive or, in its modern format, the company's electronic databanks, electronic bulletin boards or social networks. Sadly, the volume and diversity of OM that individuals can retain is minimal while little of the OM that is really useful for learning or decision-making makes it to archives. In today's workplace most is either forgotten or walks straight out of the front door on a conveyer belt while the quality of recall among the minority of employees who don't move on is affected by both their inherent short and selective memory and innate defensiveness. With flawed recall the institutional ability to learn from experience is dramatically reduced, and organizations have to keep on depending on informal and indiscriminate means to learn from their own and each others' experiences.

This book is not directly concerned with archives as they exist in their traditional format – primarily as a mechanical function that incorporates the collection, classification, storage and retrieval of corporate documentation and other texts, a job that is well-trodden by generations of skilled archivists. Important as conventional archives are to learning and the decision-making function, it is the other less accessible component of OM – the part of the organization's intellectual capital that greases the corporate wheels – that educators and organizations neglect to address. The mind-resident knowledge and experiences, that which is subject to memory lapse and departure as a result of the flexible labour market, is the part of OM that is, ironically, a factor of production that has already been paid for at great expense and which, puzzlingly, is readily discarded.

The critical importance of organizational memory

In fact, because the nature of business has changed to service industries, where individuals' skills and knowledge are now overriding factors of production, OM is even more important than ever. Managed well, it provides the raw material with which rolling generations of employees can use, the rationale being that experience – whether it was successful or otherwise – is a hugely valuable knowledge resource for decision-making. It is already tried and tested in the organization's own environment and special context, probably many times over. Properly applied – the operative word is 'applied', not 'repeated' – it can provide knowledge and wisdom more cheaply than having to relive it again, and again, and again ....

This brings me to another of the observations I will make in this book. The shortsighted are not listening to the longsighted. The result? An institutional deafness that is blinding organizations to their potential. Mixed metaphors aside, I will also assert that it is pointless to apply any decision-making disciplines only to post-decision problems. Instead of confining the exercise to picking up the pieces – that is, engaging in damage control or firefighting – the more rational approach is to apply a suitable decision-making methodology to *all* decisions with the objective of getting the front-end determinations right and then concentrate on improvements, *à la* experiential learning. Equally, whereas management might well be a generic skill, decision-making is more of an organizational-specific competence. To be competent at the former doesn't necessarily make one adept at the latter, so the discipline should be taught and executed within the context of an intimate awareness of an employer's own experience rather than just in a theoretical way. For this to happen, organizations have to ensure that their transient managers efficiently inherit their experiences and acquired knowledge. Finally, any decision-making methodology should include a process to enhance managers' cognitive capacities to substitute for instinct and the absence of judgement and institutional-specific experience. As I've already suggested, business is now too expensive and too complicated to be left to informal methodologies.

The fact that experiential learning, decision-making and the downside effects of flexible working are not effectively addressed by education and companies/organizations, let alone acknowledged as key topics of corporate concern, suggests a measure of scepticism about the validity of these issues on the part of those on high.

The arguments for better management of OM

For these detractors, I acknowledge that I will have to argue a convincing case, so I have devoted a large part of this book to demonstrating the elemental and intimate relationship between discontinuity and impediment, and specifically why the flexible labour market and the hiring of new blood – even new blood with supposedly superior experience – is not necessarily gainful for employers. I will also explain how shrinking productivity is affecting various parts of the fiscal stepladder – expressly how modern economies are taking a step back for every two steps forward.

Just in case highly paid managers won't believe the evidence of their decision-making skills, I have devoted a chapter to illustrating how often they make mistakes, and specifically the same or similar mistakes. The specific choice of organizations in the US, the UK, New Zealand, South Africa and Israel will provide illustrative comparisons over a wide range of modern industry with relevance to most economies, the common theme being the disconnect between experiential learning and quality decision-making.

And for the teachers of business on whom the quality of the next generation of wealth creators depends, I will highlight how they are missing a significant trick or two. All, I will pointedly declare, are the product of a blinkered business sector and a dysfunctional business education system (not only my words) that treats hindsight as largely irrelevant, decision-making as little more than a theoretical numbers game and productivity as incidental to their efforts.

In order not to give the impression that nobody out there learns from experience, I will also describe how some businesses have created their own special ways of utilizing their hindsight. Then, rather than just shouting about the underlying problem, I will suggest how employers – even those who do experiential learning better than most – can better manage their OM, which is the keystone of both experiential learning and better decision-making. This will include explaining how several traditional 'capture' mediums can be restructured to accommodate the fleeting nature of corporate knowledge so that transient managers don't have to rely exclusively on the evidence of unreliable or 'departed' memory and how, if this is done, employers can retain flexible working *without* having to relearn their inherited wisdom.

Explaining experience-based management (EBM)

Finally, I will explain how I have adapted the experiential learning models developed by John Dewey, Kurt Lewin, and others – but particularly David Kolb – to produce a distinctive learning loop called experience-based management (EBM) to apply OM as a powerful decision-making tool. As a teaching/learning tool, it doesn't only address post-decision problems but also includes a facility for individuals to develop their cognitive skills whilst embracing actual experience as the learning medium.

EBM has several other unique features.

Traditional experiential learning concentrates on individuals improving their own performance on behalf of their employers. Against the background of high staff turnover, the methodology's perspective shifts the emphasis so that learning's benefit is corporately centred, a feature of which is a manager-assembled 'learning audit' of lessons that can cross-pollinate better practice across an organization and down the short-tenure generations. Unlike the traditional retro-approaches that rely exclusively on using reflection *after the event*, its schema also allows learners to build into the learning process an anticipatory element for organizations to select learning opportunities *before* their occurrence.

In so doing it reinforces a methodology that encompasses the universal conception that progress is mostly incremental and continuous as well as addressing the long-acknowledged 'short-termism' of many Western managers who – as a general rule – think little of the long past or the longer future but find safety in short views and danger in guesses at future patterns. Moreover, it goes to the heart of the debate between those who think that industry can learn from the past and those who think that old lessons are misleading or irrelevant because times change. Finally, it gives knowledge management an IT role beyond sophisticated data collection and distribution, and corporate, business and management history its long looked-for function as a legitimate source of knowledge outside public relations.

In summary, it is a serious attempt to professionalize the decision-making process in a way that also addresses many of the shortcomings of traditional techniques used in the special circumstances of modern-day business. In any event, and as I've already suggested, any undue reliance on management instinct, however tempered by personal experience acquired in other corporate environments and then misshapen by fickle memory recall, is too imprecise a discipline with which to manage today's high-value and rapid-change marketplace.

Most would expect the answer to a weighty issue such as waning productivity to be both rocket science and expensive. Happily, it's not.

Notes

1. *International Herald Tribune*, 13 June 1990.
2. HSBC report, June 2005. HSBC is the world's second largest bank.
3. http://www.oecd.org/topicstatsportal/0,2647,en_2825_30453906_1_1_1_1_1,00.html.
4. Groningen Growth and Development Centre and The Conference Board, *Total Economy Database*, August 2004, http://www.ggdc.net.
5. P.F. Drucker, 'The New Productivity Challenge', *Harvard Business Review*, November–December 1991, vol. 69, issue 6.
6. Ibid.
7. Fernando Olivera, 'Memory Systems in Organizations: An Empirical Investigation of Mechanisms for Knowledge Collection, Storage and Access', *Journal of Management Studies*, September 2000.
8. A.M. de Lange, Gold Fields Computer Centre, Faculty of Science, University of Pretoria, South Africa, in *Learning-Org-Digest*, vol. 1, no. 3230, 8 October 2002.
9. Drucker, 'The New Productivity Challenge', *Harvard Business Review* November–December 1991, vol. 69, issue 6.

1 *When Experience-Rich Falls Short of Experience-Poor*

Progress, far from consisting in change, depends on retentiveness. When change is absolute there remains no being to improve and no direction is set for possible improvement: and when experience is not retained, as among savages, infancy is perpetual.

George Santayana, US philosopher and poet[1]

Given that most learning is incremental, there is a curious oversight in how organizations are managing their learning function. Whilst they are taking full advantage of flexible working, they seem remarkably unconcerned about the departure of their institution-specific knowledge and how they should compensate for their inability to learn from their own experiences.

In my Introduction, I noted the pervasive shift in the ownership of corporate knowledge towards the transient individual, with the result that organizations are largely managing themselves in isolation to their own experiences. I pointed out that having to depend on new blood – even new blood with supposedly superior experience – is an inefficient way to evolve and, specifically, learn.

To demonstrate the imprudence arising out of this inattention, one can liken the modern organization to one of any building's massive weight-bearing stress beams. These steel reinforcements running inside and along its length are the equivalent of the organization's institution-specific experiences. Now ask any concrete scientist what may happen to the beam if the steel reinforcements are severed?

For my own real-life illustration, take 17 December 2003. A historic date by any standards, it was 100 years to the day since two self-educated bicycle mechanics from Dayton, Ohio, flew a powered, heavier-than-air machine for the first time. Within four weeks, three of its heirs were due to land on Mars.

At precisely the minute, a century later, that Orville Wright successfully lifted off for a flight that lasted just 59 seconds over 852 feet from the fabled sand dunes near the town of Kitty Hawk, North Carolina, engineering Professor Kevin Kochersberger revved up an exact replica 12hp-engine biplane. Looking on to celebrate the historic occasion were 30 000 witnesses, among them a pack of aviation VIPs including Charles Yeager, the first person to fly faster than sound, and former astronauts John Glenn (the second person to orbit the earth), Neil Armstrong and Buzz Aldrin, the first men to walk on the moon.

The meticulous wood and muslin reproduction of the Wright brothers' 'Wright Flyer', built by a Virginian enthusiasts' group at a cost of $1.6 million, trundled down its runway – and came to rest somewhat ignominiously in a muddy puddle. Sadly, Kochersberger was not able to achieve sufficient lift. The re-enactment was a failure.

So, why did experience-rich fall short of experience-poor? Did the century-older

Virginians get something wrong? Or miss something out? Surely it should be possible to reproduce 100-year-old technology that worked? The real-life Wright Flyer was, after all, still in existence, so it didn't have to be reinvented from first principles. With all those additional years of engineering, manufacturing and flying know-how, the constructors were all very highly skilled aircraft builders and the pilot equally well qualified. Officials had even painstakingly cleared the area of seagulls with a trained bird of prey.

The answer is what this book is all about. Not about the failure as such. Such pioneering equipment, sophisticated as it might have seemed in 1903, would have been especially susceptible to weather, however similar the 2003 conditions were to that momentous day so long ago. But it is about experience, specifically why the availability of supposedly *superior* education and practice could not guarantee success in today's much more advanced environment. It is about the many faces of 'knowledge', the component of experience that companies and other organizations *think* is the main ingredient in the pursuit of business accomplishment. It is about how it works and, when it doesn't, what we can do about it – especially when that experience, which is usually paid for at great expense, doesn't yield enough productivity.

Lack of experience was hardly the problem in the Wright Flyer reconstruction. The example is, however, a useful way of illustrating the 'disconnect' factor – *à la* the severed steel in my building analogy – when actual experience is disengaged by time and/or other factors, not least the single biggest knowledge disrupter of modern times, the flexible labour market, which in many countries has imposed an average job tenure across industry and commerce of little more than four years. This level of 'musical chairs' is equally evident among lower-ranking employees as it is amongst managers, including top executives. Few organizations make any formal attempt to pass across their hard-won and expensively acquired knowledge to succeeding generations, preferring to depend on the outside input of new blood. The attrition of institutional-specific 'knowledge' is truly massive.

The phenomenon of corporate amnesia

I've called the outcome 'corporate amnesia', when organizations, literally, lose their memory and can't experientially learn easily. The primary reason why 'superior' knowledge doesn't always work is because of the absence of a part of organizational memory (OM), otherwise known as tacit knowledge – the event-specific, organization-specific and time-specific 'how' of know-how. I will discuss this in more detail later, but it can be illustrated precisely by another US aeronautical example highlighted by the following citation referring to the current predicament of the US National Aeronautical and Space Administration: 'If Nasa wanted to go to the moon again [as it is planning to do by 2018], it would have to start from scratch, having lost not the data, but the human expertise that took it there last time.'[2]

This example is distinct from the US's other, earlier, technological triumph in Los Alamos, where the atomic bomb was born. In the wake of the US government's decision to stop testing nuclear weapons, officials were concerned that the skills it had developed would atrophy, so, in the event that it might one day resume testing and perhaps actually use the weapon again, it undertook a massive programme called the Knowledge Preservation Project[3] to ensure that the expensively acquired expertise that it had accumulated over the years was not lost forever as archives progressively degenerated and scientists retired. As part of the programme, retired weaponeers were brought back to the laboratory for videotaped interviews intended to salvage knowledge about nuclear bombs that could not be gleaned from blueprints and archived documentation. Researchers recorded more than 2000 videotapes. The rationale of John D. Immele, director of nuclear weapons technology at Los Alamos, at the time was that they didn't want to wipe out their memory and return to their position 50 years previsouly.

What Los Alamos was, in fact, doing was collecting as much of the tacit and other 'dislocated' knowledge as possible so that they could rebuild the past without having to reinvent it. And even if they weren't aware of it at the time, what they were also doing was providing the evidence with which they could also build a better bomb (if that's at all possible) in a much shorter timeframe and also more cheaply. It's what experiential learning, productivity and competitiveness is all about. The implications for companies and other organizations are great. For countries, the collective repercussions are even bigger.

Recreating the past seems to be a simple exercise and, given the unsophistication of original systems, relatively inexpensive. However, it's not – even with rocket scientists on the payroll. It needs a dedicated regard for the process known as experiential learning.

The two experiential learning approaches

The term 'experiential learning' is normally used to describe the sort of learning undertaken as self-development through individuals' reflection on everyday experiences. It is the way in which most people learn. The other type of experiential learning is usually sponsored by an institution and might be used on training programmes for professions such as social work, teaching or in field study programmes in social administration. Rather than problematize the notion of experience itself, they are usually concerned with assessing and accrediting learning from life experiences as a means of implementing change, to raise group consciousness or as a way of instigating personal growth and self-awareness.[4] Within these parameters there are two distinct approaches to the discipline – learning from others' experiences and learning from one's own organizational experiences – which, for some inexplicable reason, are not considered interrelated specialities in practice, at least in industry and commerce's limited application. In a formal context, both are widely overlooked, although the former, in the guise of the discipline known as benchmarking, receives slightly more attention, usually as a way of implementing perceived 'best practice'. Even then, a recent example of how easily (and often) the practice is overlooked can be seen in the aftermath of the Barings bank collapse in the UK, caused by rogue trader Nick Leeson running up £791 million of hidden losses while working for the company in Singapore.

Less than a decade later, four traders at National Australia Bank lost A$252 million (£100 million) in unauthorized foreign exchange trades. In 2002 another trader at Allied Irish bank managed to hide almost £700 million of investment losses before being found out. And, more recently, an independent review at the petroleum company Shell found that company executives had knowingly hidden a massive shortfall in oil and gas reserves. Management and infrastructure flaws continue to allow such events to persist. The lessons of Barings had clearly not been learned, with expensive consequences.

Ironically, Shell was consciously leveraging the concept of the learning organization at the time. Faced with dramatic changes and unpredictability in the world oil markets in the 1980s, Shell's planners had concluded that they no longer saw their task as producing a documented view of the future business environment five or ten years ahead.[5] Instead, they reconceptualized their basic task as fostering learning rather than devising plans and engaging managers to ferret out the implications of possible scenarios. By institutionalizing the learning process, this conditioned the managers – or so they thought – to be mentally prepared for the uncertainties in the environment. It provides a classic example of how difficult the learning process is, even with in-built intent.

These are all lessons that should have come out of the short and medium term.

The peanuts and flight syndromes

By way of reinforcement, I venture the following additional examples of others' lessons to evoke the benefits of even longer-term experiences. They also go to the heart of one of management's fundamental deliberations and illustrate how better decision-making could obviate just one of industry and commerce's most common mistakes.

Among the biggest unlearned lessons of all is the way in which organizations consciously choose to undervalue one or more of their prime assets, such as labour or raw materials. The orthodoxy is that market forces – or what they can get away with – dictate the level of recompense.

Undervaluing labour, for example, brings out two inescapable outcomes, the peanut and flight syndromes, the former promoting low levels of service and the latter encouraging little organizational loyalty in today's marketplace, both of which typically rebound on employers and instantly affect productivity. The UK retail industry, whose front-line employees are the essential conduit for corporate survival for many high street businesses, is just one of many examples. History even suggests that this policy was partly responsible for the demise of much of the UK's manufacturing industry in the 1970s, when low-quality products and services enabled experience-poor operators to easily and quickly outperform British businesses. UK managers thought that they were paying too much for their employees' experience-rich labour, which was underperforming and providing employers – and the nation – with social, political and economic problems far in excess of any collective underpayments.

The overexploitation of raw materials is similarly counterproductive. Cod in the north Atlantic, timber in many parts of the world and the oil and gas industry as a whole provides just three examples. Decades of overfishing, overlogging and exploiting the owners of oil and gas reserves have been rebounding on the industrialized world for several generations with ominous impacts. In waiting is most of the Third World, who, when they eventually fully realize the importance of their primary assets to their richer customers or, in political terms, organize themselves more effectively, will have no hesitation in doing to the First World what the First World has been doing to them for years.

Fair trade

Examples of the converse – experiential learning at work – are the organizations involving themselves with the growing phenomenon known as Fair Trade, a movement that ignores market forces to seek greater equity in international trade by offering mainly southern hemisphere producers of foods such as fruit, chocolates/cocoa and wines prices that would otherwise not be available.[6] Ironically their motivation is primarily ethical, although business history suggests that their endeavour will also turn out to be economically advantageous. Hollywood also illustrates how an industry, in nurturing its prime asset – its actors – has been able to survive and prosper. Related examples can be found in many sports, and football in particular.

Although most businesses see inequity as a justifiable market force, experiential learning teaches that business has to see the marketplace in a much less covetous timeframe. Today's chorus may well be 'we can't afford to pay more' but tomorrow's echo – inevitably more deafening in its outcome – will undoubtedly be 'you can't not afford to pay more'. In suggesting that the disparity between the two is the difference between demise and survival, or at least much organizational turbulence, the underlying business lesson is that underrating prime assets is a dangerous game that non-learners invariably lose. The same applies to overrating one's prime assets, although this is a much less common phenomenon. The precarious path between the two is one of the roads that managers need to tread for better productivity and their surefootedness depends on the quality of their decision-making.

Contemporary non-learning

To illustrate how difficult the learning process is for some, I revert to my Mars reference. Two of the 2003 missions – both American – succeeded while the British Beagle 2 project, costing £45 million, including £22.5 million of public money, failed.

Following a UK National Audit Office report[7] that questioned whether public money should have been spent on a project that was generally accepted to be high-risk, the post-project review of the failed project highlighted 'poor management' that 'rushed to launch'.[8] Most space missions take the best part of a decade to plan, but Beagle 2, whose budget was less than a fifth of the cost of each of Nasa's successful Mars rovers, was cleared to fly on its *Mars Express* just 30 months before its blast off, which meant that the British mission had to cut corners in designing, building and testing landing systems. Two other management-responsible shortcomings were also identified – no back-up for the airbag and parachute system designed to slow the craft's descent and cushion its landing, and no ancillary radio on the probe's exterior to enable signals to be sent in the event that its internal radio failed.

These were apparently logical and seemingly straightforward decisions that managers should have made to give the project a better chance of success. Yet the review pointedly found that the project team had always been open about the fact that failure of any one of its features would doom the mission:

> In the written submissions appraising the case for supporting the project, BNSC [the Government's space funding body] *did not discuss the material risks to success alongside costs and benefits. The risks, and steps taken to mitigate these risks, should have been covered in the formal appraisal submissions. Better performance in these areas is desirable if high-risk but high-benefit projects like Beagle 2 are to be fairly appraised and tightly managed in the future.*[9]

It doesn't take a rocket scientist to conclude that the management of Beagle 2 would unquestionably have had a better chance if more account had been taken not only of the prior experiences of Nasa, also but of its own European Space Agency and even the Russian Space Agency. It is equally clear that these external experiences will be helpful if a Beagle 3 mission is ever undertaken. As noted, this would be one arm of any attempt at *real* experiential learning.

The Big Black Hole

The other, more important, part of the process would be to consider this external learning within the broader context of learning from one's *own* experiences, which I identify as the really Big Black Hole in conventional management education and training. That's because outside practice always has to be personalized – made organization-specific – anyway. Illustrations of how prevalent is internal non-learning in this field, even when best outside practice has been incorporated, I will leave to subsequent chapters, save to mention two examples here.

For the first I go back to the UK Mars mission and the response of the Open University's Professor Colin Pillinger, Beagle 2's project leader, who, when asked on television if he would do anything different if he was managing a Beagle 3, said, unhesitatingly and without qualification, 'No'.[10] This would suggest that he would also want to discount the official recommendations of the post-project review. Even if Beagle 2's lessons are ignored by a Beagle 3 Project team, Professor Pillinger's abortive experience would nonetheless still have a learning application for others. Interestingly, no such 'we-would-not-do-anything-different' emerged from the corridors of Nasa, whose Genesis mission to retrieve particles of solar wind crashed in the Utah desert after *its* parachute failed to open later that same year.

For the second example, I refer to the scourge of modern hospitals in many countries – the superbug known as MRSA.[11] Pre-Florence Nightingale, hospital infections were epidemic. Today, when the nature of contagion is presumably better understood, there is still a high chance that hospitals – places that are supposed to restore one's health – will also pass on to their patients complaints other than that for which they were admitted. Research in the US shows that nearly 2 million people per year come down with an infection they didn't have when they entered a hospital and that more than 80 000 of them die.[12] In England and Wales, the superbug, which is directly attributable to the deaths of about 5000 patients a year (probably a gross underestimate) costs the taxpayer about £1 billion annually[13] (also probably a gross underestimate). In South Africa, about one out of every seven patients can expect to become sick from a new illness while in hospital.[14] The reason? Poor hygiene, a key responsibility of hospital management, who credit much of the problem not to themselves but to hospital cleaners. It is common knowledge that hospital cleaners are extremely poorly paid. Is this another example of undervaluing an important corporate asset? And of a problem giving rise to a solution costing far in excess of any combined underpayments?

The quality of management skills

That managerial skills are less than optimal is not in doubt. This judgement is not only that of this book, it comes straight from the horse's mouth – managers themselves. Their own assessment – in this case by senior British managers and/or direct board report positions in companies turning over more than £200 million per year – is that an astonishing one in four of their decisions is wrong. According to a study by the consulting, technology and outsourcing services company Capgemini, the rate in the financial services sector is even higher – nearly one in three.[15] With an average 20 'business critical' decisions taken by each manager every year, the financial impact of which is computed to be worth an average £3.4 million, this equates to a wrong determination every eight weeks by each of every one of an average 33 decision-makers in every organization. I reiterate that these are the decisions that managers themselves *acknowledge* are wrong. Whilst I leave the *actual* cost–benefit ratio of executives to independent accountants, my observation of the activities of managers all over the world tells me that the self-declaration that managers make so many wrong decisions – coming, as it does, from one the most defensive of professionals in the workplace – is *very* conservative. Yet another self-declaration indicative of the scale of managerial failing comes from Adam Crozier, chief executive of one of the biggest and most important UK employers, the Royal Mail. He has estimated that as many as a third of his 15 000 line managers in this public sector organization are 'not up to the mark'.[16] Wider endorsement comes in a study[17] published in the *Harvard Business Review*, that found that 55 per cent of leaders are associated with below-average corporate performance. Just 15 per cent of the individuals studied over 25 years (the period of growing business education) showed a consistent ability to manage innovation and organizational change. And – for an anecdotally overwhelming indicator of the extent of ineffectual decision-making – an entry of 'poor management' into an Internet search engine[18] found 73 million references worldwide, a third of the number for the most popular word, 'sex', on the same search engine.

These 'snapshots' should not detract from the fact that the majority of decisions that managers make are right, otherwise a lot more companies would not survive. My concerns in this book are the sizeable number of decisions that are wrong, their recurrence, the apparent difficulty that individuals and organizations have in the determination-making process and the opportunity that managers and educators are missing to improve the costly hit-rate. Figure 1.1 gives a graphic representation of how business executives throughout the G7 countries rate quality of management. This evaluation is instructive for the relatively low value that managers in the main OECD countries place on their own skills.

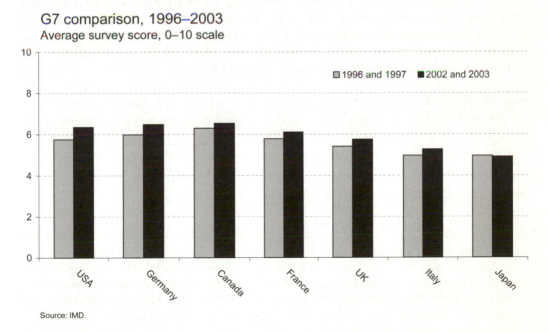

G7 comparison, 1996–2003
Average survey score, 0–10 scale

Source: IMD.

Figure 1.1   Business executive perceptions of the quality of their own management

This evaluation is instructive for the relatively low value that managers in the main OECD countries put on their own skills.

An extra indicator of managerial uncertainty about how executives do their own jobs comes from the Capgemini finding that the most effective individual decision-making styles reveal a strong preference for qualities that support a collaborative decision-making approach while the ability to 'make a call' quickly and stick by a decision, determination to seek out the best possible solution and willingness to take risks are – astonishingly – the least popular characteristics. Managers, the study found, depend on external advice in more than 50 per cent of critical decisions. In fact, the UK central government uses management consultants and other 'advisers' to help its managers push through public sector reforms. According to an analysis[19] of a national newspaper, the cost of proxying its own managerial skills is a staggering £1.75 billion per year. This excludes the money that local councils, NHS trusts and other public bodies spend on consultants outside Whitehall. However these figures are presented, they are hardly an advertisement for the decision-making skills of many managers, whose determinations are often the rubber-stampings of others.

The evidence doesn't stop there. Poor management wastes more than a third of the time every British and US worker spends at work – 87 working days a year in the UK and 96 working days per year in the US.[20] The cost in the UK alone? £56 billion, with an overall cost to the economy of £87 billion. The figures, calculated by Professor Nick Crafts of the London Business School, apportioned 30 per cent of the misused time to inappropriate supervision, 34 per cent to bad planning, 8 per cent to bad communication and 6 per cent to computer problems. An accompanying Gallup poll confirmed that senior executives 'seem to agree' that their poor management was the biggest cause of poor productivity.

A little over a year later an updated study by Professor Crafts indicated how widespread the problem of poor management was. He found that firms in all of the 12 countries surveyed fell short of what was considered to be the optimum use of labour (see Table 1.1).[21] The study's compilers found that the majority of the 800 senior executives surveyed (55 per cent) thought that the key to raising productivity was to increase investment. In the case of the UK, it was suggested that the government was aiming very low in its bid to boost productivity growth and that it had its sights trained on the wrong targets.

Table 1.1   The cost of wasted productivity

	Cost (US$ billiion)	% of GDP
Germany	266.1	9.7
Spain	84.0	8.1
America	888.8	7.6
Britain	158.5	7.5
France	121.3	5.9

Source: Proudfoot Consulting, September 2005.

The study's compilers found that the majority of senior executives – 55 per cent – thought that the key to raising productivity was to increase investment. In the UK's case, it was suggested that the government was aiming very low in its bid to boost productivity growth and that it had set its sights on the wrong targets.

Ironically, these are all outcomes that managers would likely not tolerate among their vocational subordinates. All of which begs the down-to-business poser: Is management too difficult for most managers?

Where organizations fall down

Some clues can be found in some original US research that has a resonance with the flexible labour market and institution-specific knowledge.

The first, in a study by three academics out of Harvard Business School, investigated the phenomenon of corporate poaching,[22] the means by which institutions recruit externally the best and brightest to ostensibly top up their skills and experience. Poaching today represents a large proportion of executive and vocational churn in the mercurial labour market.

The study tracked the careers of high-flying CEOs, researchers, software developers and leading professionals, including 1000 stock analysts. Their findings were arresting. Contrary to the popular belief, they found that after 'stars' moved from their old employer, their performance invariably plunged, as did the effectiveness and market value of their new paymasters. Moreover, the transplanted high-flyers did not stay with their new organizations for long, despite the often astronomical salaries paid to lure them from rivals. And the reason? Most companies overlook the fact that executive performance is not entirely transferable because personal competencies inevitably include company-specific skills. When high-flyers leave the old company for the new, they also leave behind many of the resources that contribute to their achievements. As a result, individuals are unable to repeat their performances in another company – at least not until they learn to work the new system, which could take years. It is a conclusion that shoots down the traditional belief in top-flight infallibility and underlines the importance to good decision-making of experiential learning and institution-specific OM.

The inheritors

The second clue comes in a study of 204 chief executive officers (CEOs) successions between 1993 and 1998 in non-diversified US manufacturing companies.[23] In an effort to confirm the Harvard finding about the importance of an intimate awareness of the new employer's experience, the researchers examined the three main types of succession: relay successions, when an incumbent works with an heir apparent, non-relay inside successions, in which new appointees come from within the organization but had not been the predecessor's heir apparent, and outside successions, where the successor comes from outside the company. Instructively, they found that relay successions led to better corporate performance through several experience-oriented factors, including the knowledge that the heir apparent obtains from on-the-job training, thus reducing the performance risk from any lack of context-specific skills. The researchers also found that, contrary to the traditional wisdom that outside CEOs are better equipped to reverse poor performance, outside successions do not significantly differ from non-relay inside successions, even under conditions of poor pre-succession performance and/or high post-succession strategic instability. Indeed, because outside successors were more likely to lack company-specific knowledge, it was harder for them to formulate and implement appropriate strategic change. In addition, outside successors often disrupted companies and found it more challenging to get support from other senior executive colleagues. It was not surprising, therefore, that outside succession did not always lead to better post-succession firm performance.

In fact, the bigger picture becomes even darker: the researcher pointed out that fewer than 50 per cent of organizations engaged in *any* succession planning and, even when heirs apparent had been designated, a 'significant' percentage did not succeed.

Although both these studies refer to top-flight appointments, their conclusions would not differ materially among other corporate rankings, further endorsing the need for better decision-making processes throughout the corporate hierarchy.

Paying lip service to genuine learning

In the pursuit of decision-making excellence, experience has always been a fundamental imperative, the argument being that those who are practised are more effective decision-makers than those still in rehearsal. Of course, this assumption implies that learning from experience has taken place. However, the reality is actually very different throughout the chain of command, due to the disregard most organizations have towards that wider discipline known as organizational learning in which experiential learning is just one aspect.

The curious characteristic of this disregard is that nearly all organizations claim that they are committed to, and practise, organizational learning. However, in reality, most only pay lip service to the concept, both at an inner institutional level with such aspects as values, behaviours and attitudes and at a wider level with aspects such as policies, practices, materials and resources.

Despite much talk about being participatory and declaring organizational values around education, sustainability and accountability, most organizations maintain a predominantly oral, task-focused culture. With little knowledge-gathering undertaken, few maintain cohesive understandings of past experiences, so information and key insights are soon lost and the opportunity for experiential learning forfeited. The majority labour in historical isolation and, using a transportation metaphor, spend much time and energy running *against* a moving escalator. Although immersed in frenzied activity, many organizations are dangerously stagnant. Few have time to do any detective work before a decision has to be made or to follow up or follow through, with each successive leader intoning the mantra of the difficulties of organizational change. In truth, organizational change is the lifeblood of stable organizations and the staple diet of all management, yet its nature is always treated as something menacing, even unique. When it's not factored creatively into decision-making, the outcome is as 'hit'n'miss' as at least one in four of the wrong determinations highlighted in Capgemini's research.

The ability of managers to make good and better decisions aside, some working cultures make it extremely difficult for decision-makers to effect change. Two examples in Britain's public sector – but not exclusive to the UK or to the public service – illustrate precisely this, both indicative of an inherent proclivity towards workplace inflexibility and, thus, experiential non-learning. It is arguable that this acquired rigidity has supported employer attitudes to encouraging high employee turnover which, in turn, has fuelled even greater workplace intransigence, underlining the importance to organizations of having a formal experiential learning system in place.

The National Health Service (NHS), notoriously unproductive, has long been trying to cut its patient queues. With most critics insisting that the main problem is lack of resources, huge amounts of money have been injected into the system, with little success. In orthopaedics, for example, 1530 surgeons each have about 140 patients waiting three to nine months for surgery.[24]

In 2001, John Petri, an Italian orthopaedic surgeon who joined the NHS in 1994 after working extensively in France, became frustrated at the amount of time he spent 'drinking tea' while patients were being made ready for operations. He persuaded his managers to let him try a new system of working between two theatres. With the help of two anaethetists, he operates on one patient while the next is being prepared next door. When done, Petri immediately moves to the second patient, leaving a junior to finish the first. By the time the second patient is nearing completion, a third is waiting for him in the original theatre. Trial figures show that his five-hour work sessions enable him to perform 270 operations a year, against 225 operations completed by his colleagues using the traditional single theatre approach in standard three-and-a-half-hour sessions. This reduces his 'idle' time by between 40 and 60 per cent. With a waiting list of zero, Petri now operates on patients within two weeks of their first consultation.

Whilst the initiative has been welcomed by his hospital's management – Petri was nominated for the 2005 Medical Futures Innovation Awards by his hospital, the James Paget Healthcare Trust in Gorleston, Great Yarmouth – it is being shunned by his colleagues who, Petri believes, may be deterred by the 'sheer hard work' of the extra one-and-a half-hour session. In a response that was symptomatic of poor decision-making at an even higher level over decades, the reaction by Anne Moore of the Royal College of Surgeons was: 'There is nothing to stop surgeons operating Petri's system. In America surgeons move between as many as 12 theatres but in the UK there are not enough anaesthetists, theatres or other staff to make it work.'

The second example relates to the UK's law enforcement service, where – like John Petri – poor individual performance has been embarrassingly shown up by an overseas-trained professional. The average British policeman makes a derisory 9.5 arrests a year,[25] with the 2003/4 figure for London even lower at 6.7. Enter Diederick Coetzee, a South African police constable who joined the second worst performing force in England and Wales to police Nottinghamshire's Ladybrook estate in Mansfield.

His most recent annual arrest tally is a staggering 309. With his experience gained as an explosives expert and dog handler on the wild streets of Johannesburg, Coetzee is dismissive of many of the traditional excuses for poor performance, among them imposed bureaucracy and supposed stress, the latter of which leads to exceptionally high absenteeism (an average 9.3 sick days a year for every officer in England and Wales).

The Police Federation, the police officer's union, claims it takes four working hours to complete the paperwork necessary for a simple shoplifting offence. For Coetzee, the paperwork 'is not that horrendous. It comes with the job', a comment that gives some credence to the think tank Politeia's suggestion that this may have more to do with officers' poor literary skills.[26]

Instructively, Coetzee has been turned down to become a dog handler, his original skill. And as for another ambition – to work in London – two requests for an application pack have been ignored. He is wondering whether, at 48 years of age, he is over age.

Untrained managers

This book's rationale is simple.

However productive an organization is, none is exempt from poor decision-making. Whilst some managers learn better than others, their real-time performance actually has little to do with the instruction they receive, either in-house or if they trained at a business school. In truth, the numbers of managers who might have had any formal tuition in decision-making, or indeed wider management training, is still negligible, despite the existence of dedicated business schools for up to 50 years. More often than not, the main criterion for their appointment is vocational competence, with the conventional rationaliz-ation being 'If you're the best cook, you're the best choice to manage the kitchen.' The little instruction in decision-making that *is* provided is theoretical, informal and anecdotally included with other generic subjects such as marketing, strategy, leadership and so on; as a core subject it remains strangely neglected.

The experiential learning that does take place is still crudely applied in many organizations, being confined to providing access to external and internal data, information and knowledge through the abundant manuals and textbooks available and companies' own archives, which today are often accessed through sophisticated (and very expensive) electronic databanks, bulletin boards and other OM systems such as social networks. This is known as knowledge management (KM), a discipline that is as youthful (it is barely 15 years old) as it is unexploited to anything like its full potential.

That knowledge management, even in its current unrefined state, is valuable is irrefutable, even in its underutilized form. Among much published evidence, management consultant McKinsey and Co.'s work[27] in the field confirms that more successful companies build a corporate environment that fosters the continual application, distribution, and creation of knowledge. Looking at product development and order generation/fulfilment – two major contributors of corporate value – they found that the better knowledge managers cut throughput time by an average of almost 11 per cent and development time by 4.6 per cent, compared with reductions of just 1.6 per cent and 0.7 per cent respectively at the companies considered to be less effective knowledge managers.

Nevertheless, existing KM techniques are acknowledged to be limiting, as well as little used, even by its most ardent proponents. One limitation is that once data, information and knowledge has been documented, it is no longer living data, information or knowledge anymore but merely dead data, information and knowledge comprising the evidence relevant to old experiences. Although it is all undeniably essential and very relevant, in reality it serves only half the decision-making process, a conception that supports the harsh Koranic analogy that many companies are donkeys loaded with books. Missing is the most valuable component of the decision-making chain that is rarely used because it has either been forgotten or lost forever through high job turnover – I refer, of course, to the tacit and other related lost knowledge comprising the 'how' of know-how, *à la* the Knowledge Preservation Project at Los Alamos. If such knowledge is documented in ways that can be applied to learning, the opportunity arises for the next stage of the decision-making process in which old data, information and knowledge can be transformed into new knowledge – the so-called 'wisdom' that gives people apparent hindsight. The trick is to know *how* to reshape the past to best accommodate the future. This is where reflective thinking, experiential learning and EBM comes in, designed to use existing experiential learning methodology with a number of specific upgrades to make the learning process more relevant to industry and commerce.

Some understandings about management

The long-time evidence of slow change in much of industry and commerce, repeated mistakes, reinvented wheels and other unlearned lessons indicates that many individuals and organizations don't fully appreciate the precise nature of decision-making and, specifically, the importance of retaining evidence. When things go right, most people's instinctive reaction is to gloat, complacently, and reason that success is all about replication. In the learning world this is a fatal disease that goes a long way towards explaining why so many winners one day can so quickly become losers the next. Then, when things go wrong, the most resounding echo is usually 'Hindsight is a wonderful thing'. Rocket science this observation is not, and more erudite people than me have noted that hindsight gives better foresight.

Furthermore, learning from one's own organization's experiences is more effective than just benchmarking on its own, because using others' experience is never *entirely* relevant and has to be adapted to one's own environment anyway. I am not suggesting that learning from others is worthless, or that their lessons should not be accommodated, but rather that it is better for people to become more effective at being Nairobi, Baghdad or Prague businesspeople than for everyone to become more American, British, Japanese or German. This not only permits the retention of individuality and the distinctiveness that brings differentiation rather than homogeneity and less actual choice to the marketplace, but also allows character, culture and operating procedures to improve within their own national confines – always more efficient than trying to be someone else. Putting a political spin on the issue, it might also make fewer Kenyans, Iraqis, and Czechs feel that their identity is being totally consumed.

Another bit of necessary understanding is that good decision-making is proactive; once it becomes reactive for defensive reasons, its excellence is already lost. Moreover, with dedication, both success and failure can be improved upon; decision-making is as changeable as change itself, which, like evolution, is continuous; the flexible labour market is not all good for employers; and, finally, no two organizations are the same, so a decision that might be relevant to one is often inappropriate to another. A better understanding of both change and organizations offers not only a better chance of making better decisions to accommodate the phenomenon of change, but will also increase productivity into the bargain.

The need to teach decision-making

The message of this book is that, with few exceptions, executive decision-making leaves much to be desired, even in the most productive of business environments. It is the single most important skill in any business armoury. Yet managers and other employees are not formally taught *how* to make decisions, least of all good and better decisions. It is time they were. That role is the task of business educators, trainers, management consultants and organizations/managers themselves, whose traditional approach to the subject is largely abstract, unstructured and anecdotally subsumed into other specialities. Without precise attention and teaching, decision-making becomes little more than informed guesswork, where 'informed' is dependent on the awareness of deficient or absent organization-specific memory, and on the input of new blood, however qualified, whose experiences (the recall of which is no less reliable because of their own memory imperfections) are not specific to their new employer.

The role of managers is to get their organizations from 'A' to 'C', preferably via 'B', the proximity of the letters representing the shortest distance between two points and signifying, in business terms, the universal objective of optimum productivity. The trick is to reduce the tendency to reach 'C' via 'Z' by interlinking the various components of experiential learning.

To return to my suggested enquiry to a concrete scientist about what might happen to a single stress beam when its steel reinforcements are severed, now ask what may happen to the whole building ... ?

Notes

1.   George Santayana, *The Life of Reason*, Amherst, NY: Prometheus Books, 1998.
2.   John Brown and Paul Duguid, *The Social Life of Information*, Cambridge, MA: Harvard Business School Press, 2000.
3.   *Los Angeles Times*, 28 August 1995.
4.   S. Warner Weil and I. McGill (eds), *Making Sense of Experiential Learning. Diversity in Theory and Practice*, Milton Keynes: Open University Press, 1989.
5.   Arie de Geus, 'Planning as Learning', *Harvard Business Review*, March–April 1988.
6.   According to John Cavanagh, co-director, Institute for Policy Studies. Currently the business generated by Fair Trade organizations in Europe and the US now accounts for an estimated US $400 million, just 0.01 per cent of all global trade.
7.   Beagle 2 National Audit Office report, March 2004.
8.   Beagle 2 report, British National Space Centre (BNSC) and the European Space Agency (ESA), 24 May 2004.
9.   Ibid.
10.   Interview with Professor Colin Pillinger, *BBC 6 O'Clock News*, 24 May 2004.
11.   Methicillin-resistant *staphylococcus aureus*.
12.   *Let's Live,* June 1995.
13.   *British Medical Journal*, 2 July 2004.
14.   Professor Adriano Duse, a Johannesburg-based infection control specialist, speaking at the launch of a new patient safety plan for African hospitals in Durban, 20 January 2005.
15.   Emma Giles, *Business Decisiveness Report*, Capgemini UK, August 2004 available at: http://www.sinoia.biz/download/Capgemini_BDI_survey%20(2).pdf.
16.   Adam Crozier, chief executive, the Royal Mail, speaking at the UK's Business Insider Elite Leadership Awards, 7 October 2005.
17.   David Rooke and William Torbert, 'Transformations of Leadership', *Harvard Business Review*, April 2005. Rooke is a consultant with Harthill Consulting and Torbert is a professor at the Carroll School of Management in Boston.
18.   Yahoo, 6 April 2005.
19.   *The Daily Telegraph*, 23 October 2004. Figures include £797 million by the Department for International Development, including research, £293 million by the Department for Transport, £2623 million by Ministry of Defence, £10 million by the Department of Health, £15 million by the Cabinet Office, £52 million by the Office of the Deputy Prime Minister, £291 million by the Department for Work and Pensions and £10 million by the Scotland Office.
20.   *Management for Mediocrity*, survey, Proudfoot Consulting, September 2004. The report surveyed workers in 1668 detailed studies undertaken at projects in Australia, Austria, France, Germany, Hungary, South Africa, Spain, UK and the US, based on more than 10 000 hours of observational study in medium- to large-sized firms.
21.   'Treasury Warned Over Productivity', *Sunday Times*, 25 September 2005. Report on a new study by Professor Nick Crafts and Proudfoot Consulting based on 2500 company studies in 12 countries. In the study, Proudfoot considers the optimum use of labour to be 86 per cent.
22.   Boris Groysberg, Nanda Ashish and Nohria Nitin, 'The Risky Business of Hiring Stars', *Harvard Business Review*, May, 2004.

23.   Yan Zhang and Nandini Rajagopalan, 'When the Known Devil is Better than an Unknown God: An Empirical Study of the Antecedents and Consequences of Relay CEO Successions', *Academy of Management Journal*, vol. 47, no. 4, 2004.

24.   *The Sunday Times*, 'French factory surgeon cuts NHS queues', 23 October 2005.

25.   BBC radio and television bulletins, 3 November 2005.

26.   Politeia, *The Policing Matters: Recruitment, Training and Motivation* report, which concludes: 'Poor standards of general education, literacy and numeracy may make routine tasks more time-consuming and the overall job more taxing and difficult than it would be for an abler person.' November 2005.

27.   Susanne Hauschild, Thomas Licht and Wolfram Stein. 'Creating a Knowledge Culture', *The McKinsey Quarterly*, no. 1, 2001, based on a survey of 30 companies in Europe, Japan and the US during the period 1995 to 1998.

2 *How More Equals Less*

A country losing touch with its own history is like an old man losing his glasses, a distressing sight, at once vulnerable, unsure, and easily disoriented.

George Walden, British Conservative politician[1]

For the wider picture of the effects of poor decision-making, it is, admittedly, decidedly confusing to pass judgement on the present if one has any sort of historical perspective. The world has indisputably changed out of all recognition in the last half century: from television to polio vaccinations, frozen foods, photocopying, contact lenses, pantyhose, dishwashers, tape decks, FM, CDs, credit cards and word processors, modern living is undoubtedly richer, thanks in no small way to industry and commerce, which has trailblazed many of these innovations. The presumption is that life has been made easier by all these advances. In reality, however, living and doing business has become more difficult as well as becoming disproportionately more expensive.

Red tape is everywhere, despite determined efforts every few years to cut it back. Computers were supposed to speed everything up, but cheque clearance in many developed countries still takes a baffling five working days, not much better than in pre-digital years. And what about trying to get one's name removed from a computer-generated mailing list? It is slower to get around many metropolitan areas than in the days of horse-drawn carriages, and in many countries, trains were faster and more punctual 100 years ago.

Medical education is supposedly better than ever and hospital equipment never more sophisticated, yet the level of culpable negligence among doctors and nurses is at record levels.[2] In Israel the death rate actually went *down* when doctors went on strike in 1973 and 2000.[3] The same reportedly happened in 1976 in both Bogota, Columbia, and Los Angeles County.[4]

In many areas the more effort we make and the more we spend, the greater the problem. In the UK it is estimated that just 3 per cent of crimes are ever detected, although the official figure is 13 per cent,[5] even with record numbers of police officers in employment. In 2002/3, the declared police success rate was down to an all-time low of 24 per cent of detected crime, a statistic that prompted the admission by Britain's most senior judge, Lord Chief Justice Woolf, that all parts of the criminal justice system – the police, prosecutors and the courts – appeared to have failed the public for years.[6]

Despite the billions of pounds the UK government has spent on its New Deal, there are also now more young people out of work and not studying.[7] And despite serious and very expensive efforts to improve educational penetration and standards in the UK, one in four primary pupils fail basic reading[8] and large numbers of students still leave school unable to read or write.[9] In fact, the same source forecasts that by 2010, one in ten of the total population will, even then, have no form of qualification. The degree to which the UK continues to remain in the educational shadow of many of its overseas peers is evidenced by other research that, in 2001, showed that Britain ranked 23rd out of 29 countries in the number of youngsters staying at secondary school, just ahead of Mexico, Italy, New Zealand, Portugal, Slovakia and Turkey.[10] In another evaluation of the number of children leaving school with top grades, the UK slumped from 13th to 21st among 30 industrialized countries – despite widespread grade devaluation.[11]

In the business world, too, absurdity is not uncommon. Across the world there is a new-found determination to halt the flow of laundered money from crime. In the UK the success rate and cost makes its efforts 'pretty pathetic', according to an expert in financial crime.[12] Over a ten-year period the amount retrieved was just 0.02 per cent of an estimated £250 billion, with the cost of recovering £46 million a staggering £400 million.

Bureaucratic ineffectiveness

Elsewhere, high-priced ineptitude relentlessly dogs large bureaucracies, the European Union being a good example. The EU's Court of Auditors, a spending watchdog, estimates that waste and fraud is running at 5 per cent of the annual budget, which is probably a gross underestimate. The 2001 budget of £62 billion placed this annual figure in excess of £3 billion, and this figure must have risen considerably since ten new members joined the EU in 2004. Yet it was revealed by Jules Muis, the head of the commission's internal audit service who resigned in disgust in July 2003, that the commission was still reluctant to give him the necessary resources to audit the organization's low-quality controls. Muis's description of the EU's accounting system – which is still using a single-entry approach more than seven centuries after the Venetians switched to the double-entry method – was 'chronically sordid' and unable to keep track of its £73 billion budget after a decade of financial scandals.[13]

The office of Neil Kinnock, the commissioner who headed the EU's attempts to cut its waste at the time, said a further three years to implement reform was 'not in the real world',[14] a clear admission of managerial inadequacy. Just months later, investigators for OLAF, the commission's anti-fraud office, confirmed this in a damning confidential report that uncovered an 'endemic culture of unprofessionalism' including 'systemic and flagrant incompetence' amongst management.[15] A further complication is Commissioner Kinnock's retirement in 2004 – an imposed discontinuity that will probably further lengthen and steepen the internal learning curve as someone else is appointed to rein in unnecessary extravagance and profiteering.

Nearly everyone is a supposed 'specialist' but few are professional, let alone reliable. Little ever goes smoothly with the installation of central heating, a house extension, the repair of a car, delivery of furniture, utility services, tax enquiries – the list is endless. Just read the consumer columns in the press or tune into the equivalent programmes on radio and television. Everything is supposed to be geared to make life easier, yet stress levels have never been greater.

I should add that 'progress' is not the issue here – indeed, many of today's developments are both genuinely inspiring and welcome – but however sophisticated we are, the more archaic we ostensibly become in many areas. On the domestic front we've acquired the most time-saving of modern conveniences, yet time is always at a premium. And over in industry, the prevailing scenario is illustrated by several examples. New York's Empire State Building, the world's tallest construction of its day, was erected in the middle of a large city during the 1930s depression. It took exactly one year and 45 days to build. This was when there was no such thing as ready-mixed concrete or the other advanced building techniques available today. Nearly 50 years later, the Natwest Tower in the City of London, which is half its height, took twice as long to construct. And remember when an earthquake at the end of the 1990s downed many of the motorways around Los Angeles? The city was up and running again after just three months. Compare this with time it took to repair the comparatively minimal damage the Irish Republican Army did to the underpass at Brent Cross, the M1 gateway to London, in 1993 – six months.

Higher cost, lower value

Other cases illustrate how expensive some things have become. Somehow, the price of bottled water, certified no less pure than tap water in many countries and indistinguishable in taste, is greater than the volume equivalent of a container of milk. Several of the most popular brands of so-called 'pure' fruit juice would, if not diluted, be more expensive than the equivalent of some of the leading brands of champagne.[16] If you use private telephone service providers, which buy their resource from the large national telephone companies, the cost of overseas calls is often less than the cost of calls to domestic subscribers.

Health treatment for household pets often approaches the fees for private medical treatment for humans. It costs more to accommodate a single prisoner in rudimentary conditions than it costs a businessman to live expensively in a five-star hotel. And prisons have another incongruous facet to their function. They are supposedly secure. Yet however good they are at keeping inmates in, their ability to keep drugs *out* is singularly deficient.

The advent of what is now called information systems (IS) was supposed to have solved most of these problems. In fact, the art of capturing operational and transactional information has been progressive ever since the start of the industrial age, with its biggest advances being achieved during the Second World War. Out of this came a whole range of disciplines, among them information technology (IT), the learning organization, organizational learning (OL), knowledge management (KM) and terms such as change management, continuous learning and continuous performance improvement.

Sharpened by the computer, techniques to identify trends were expected to help managers implement actions quickly. Indeed, organizations have generally developed their information systems to quite impressive heights. With appropriate inputs, High Street pizza companies can quickly monitor telephone orders, compare them with delivery times and speed up any unnecessary delays. Elsewhere, sales at supermarket checkouts can be monitored so that in-store stocks can be quickly adjusted to take advantage of customer demand. In-progress profits or losses can be scrutinized geographically or departmentally, as can customer complaints and new business. The options are endless, the use of targets being just one way of making improvements.

Two steps forward, one step back

The results are often striking – and certainly a huge advance in management practice compared with pre-digital days. However, as the workplace demonstrates – and as the following chapters will also bear out – slowing change, the succession of repeated mistakes, reinvented wheels, unlearned lessons and, ultimately, low productivity reveals that very many managers are, in fact, unable to make better decisions. For nigh on two decades, for example, the computer has identified particular and recurring flaws in the UK's National Health Service, yet all management attempts to radically improve the system (at least 18 have been tried in the last 20 years) have fallen flat on their faces. Over in the private sector (and, before that, the public sector) similar efforts have been made to try to improve the railways – with equal lack of success. All that has happened is that budgets have increased monumentally. IS may well flag up *what* needs attention but it doesn't tell managers *how* to do things. This limitation highlights one of the huge misconceptions that managements retain about their use of the ubiquitous computer. An IS installation is not knowledge management in the true sense of the words. Nor does it automatically make the user a genuine learning organization. In reality, it allows them to be little more than better information managers. The difference is as subtle as it is significant.

Certainly, the axiom about taking a step back for every two steps forward would be an apposite description of our times. Harvard Business School's Professor Robert Hayes – ex-IBM and McKinsey – put his finger on the problem when he noted that business pundits seem to be forever rediscovering the truths known to those who lived two generations earlier. He considered calling this the Hayes Law of Circular Progress until he discovered a similar proposition in an 1843 edition of the *Edinburgh Review*: 'In the pure and physical sciences, each generation inherits the conquests made by its predecessors. But in the moral sciences, particularly the art of administration, the ground never seems to be incontestably won.'

A possible answer – to unlearn or purge beliefs

And the reason? In the learning world, there are several fixed explanations, or part-explanations. From the coalface of industry Dee Hock, founder of Visa, believes that the problem is not how to get new, innovative thoughts *into* managers' minds, but how to get the old ones *out*.[17] John Seely Brown, the chief scientist of Xerox Corporation, puts it another way:

> *The more success you achieve, either as an individual or as an organization, the more difficult it is to change. All of the learning that led to one kind of success becomes implicitly coded and works against your ability to unlearn. The challenge then becomes how to uncover those deeply ingrained assumptions.*[18]

In fact, Brown's reference to 'unlearning' is an imprecise description. Intended to mean that it is the process of changing long-held beliefs, it implies that learning, however correct for one specific occasion, has to be forgotten or somehow deconstructed. In truth, however, no learning should ever be seen as unhelpful, irrelevant or redundant. When individuals or organizations learn they hold their consequential understandings as beliefs, which are statements about reality that are considered as 'the truth'. These beliefs, in turn, shape perceptions that influence thought and determine how things are done. The trouble is that a decision for one point in time is *never* the same for another. In the business of change – that is, the process of learning – the trick is how to amend beliefs, sometimes long-held, into more appropriate beliefs to better suit altered circumstances.

Some practitioners insist that the beliefs have to be purged before change can happen; once you empty the memory of previously held truths, they say, people become open to learning. Others believe that old learning is never redundant. It is a keystone that has to be complemented with newer evidence to allow learners to enrich their mental models – a principle that says that one has to know that milk comes out of cows, not plastic containers, if one is to make its production more efficient. Only when this happens can belief be changed, whether through suspension, expansion or even transformation from disbelief to new belief. It is a diagnostic process that academics describe as heuristic. Amazingly, neither model gets much *applied* house room in practical education, least of all in business education.

The reason for Germany's and Japan's slippage

The downside effects of not being able to learn continuously are not pretty. Taking the really long view, there are more than a few national exemplars that have risen and fallen – many into obscurity. Very recent examples are Japan and Germany. For a 50-year period they rose from being bombed out, and in Japan's case from also being mainly agricultural, to the top of the world's industrial tree. Now they are showing signs of slippage. And over in Europe, and despite a dedicated drive launched at the end of the 1990s to overtake the US economy by 2010, the EU had actually *lost* ground by 2004.[19] EU officials listed low productivity as one of the causes of the continuing gap with the US, reporting that output per person employed had been declining in Europe since the 1990s. There was no productivity gain between 1999 and 2003, they reported, whereas the US figures went up. Although some countries – mainly areas that have started from lower base positions – have shown larger than average gains, the rest of the world is trying to play catch-up. The overall picture is one of an apparent dearth of ideas from which to draw the next round of productivity gains.

The explanation for all this is as consequential as it is simple, and is overlooked by almost everyone: in common with quite a few others, these countries are not effectively using their own and others' hard-won experience as a learning tool. The operative word is 'effectively'. Although some do it better than others – and Japan and Germany, notwithstanding their current industrial woes, are just two examples – the experiential learning that *does* take place in the industrial world is largely unformalized, unstructured and rare, even in the relatively more productive countries.

Excuses, excuses in the UK

The UK is a useful example, appearing as it does in the middle reaches of the productivity and competitiveness league tables among OECD countries. It is the world's oldest industrial nation. In theory this should mean that it should have a significant experiential advantage. Yet for over half a century it has steadily become more and more uncompetitive as less experienced pretenders have outpaced this once mighty industrial leader. In Britain the limp explanations vary from 'We were not bombed out during the war' to 'It's the legacy of colonialism'. While the former is not exactly true (a large proportion of housing and industry *was* bombed) the relative logic of both statements has always puzzled me. It is conveniently ignored that countries currently more competitive than the UK were not bombed out and, moreover, also had colonial pasts. These excuses aside, the most plausible explanation for the UK's uncompetitive record is its admitted lack of investment but even this explanation illustrates the country's experiential non-learning disposition; this reason has been cited for at least four decades. It also highlights the wider misunderstanding of what management and productivity are all about.

In the early 2000s, for example, the huge investment in the UK's privatized railways coincided with a succession of serious accidents. At the time, track maintenance – outlay £1.3 billion[20] – was in the hands of private companies, an arrangement that was supposed to be more efficient and cost-effective than having it done in-house, especially when the railway network was a nationalized industry. At the end of 2003, Network Rail, the government-backed spendthrift successor to Railtrack, decided to stop outsourcing maintenance contracts to seven private companies, on the grounds that privatized management was clearly not up to the job and that it could also achieve annual savings of £300 million within three years. Not only did this amount to an admission that the cost of privatized contracts had, in fact, been miscalculated – a management blunder in its own right – but it also overlooked the reality that the 18 500 new people who Network Rail would need to employ would be recycled from the privatized workforce and – significantly – would be no more qualified at making better decisions than their predecessors. This observation has already been confirmed by railway history. Independent analysis, in fact, immediately disputed the cost reduction argument, suggesting that, by switching over, the wage bill alone would need to rise by £72 million.[21]

Just over a month later, it was disclosed[22] that it would cost the taxpayer another £70 million in extra charges for using loans guaranteed by the government-backed Strategic Rail Authority to finance its activities – a tactic to keep Network Rail's debts off the public accounts. And just a few months after that, Jarvis, one of the private contractors whose performance was under investigation, was awarded a five-year renewal contract worth £300 million on the very line on which one of the accidents had occurred.[23] Barely had the ink dried on this announcement when the news broke that Network Rail's directors were to receive performance bonuses of about 20 per cent of their salaries even though, in the previous year, the company had missed its punctuality target on 20 per cent of train departures and arrivals.[24] It was, snapped the chairman, 'irrelevant' what the public thought of the company's decision to award its directors big bonuses.[25]

Network Rail's problems contain another lesson: that the habitual call for 'reform', which is usually perceived in terms of structural change, is no guarantee of improvement. On its own, it is little more than changing the position of the proverbial deckchairs on the *Titanic*. Also, increased investment is no guarantee of better-value service, another example being the infamous National Health Service. Research by the Royal College of Nursing[26] found that much of the massive investment in the NHS was failing to trickle down to the front line, a finding that confirmed the wider calculation by the Office for Statistical Analysis that productivity had dropped by between 3 per cent and 8 per cent since 1995, with the decline actually gathering pace after the government began its drive to boost spending.[27] The study showed that, using 1995 output levels, the NHS could achieve the same results with £6 billion lower than the £69.4 billion it would receive. Nine months later, the nurses' colleagues, the doctors, confirmed that the latest reforms were in 'deep trouble',[28] with James Johnson, the chairman of the council of the British Medical Association, believing that the entire service was under threat unless value for the huge sums of money being invested could be demonstrated. They are commentaries that demonstrate that, without better decision-making, increased investment just swells the cost.

I am also reminded of one of the many other inconsistent excuses offered for the UK's experiential disadvantage: that sterling was too strong – circumstances that didn't appear to worry the Japanese, the Germans or the Americans too much during the 1970s and 1980s. A decade earlier, when sterling was weak, manufacturing exports, which should have benefited, also lost ground. It was that long ago that government and industry accurately identified yet another of the UK's main industrial weaknesses – its foreign language deficiency; yet, with globalism dominating almost every political and economic decision, the deficit still exists in huge measure today,[29] the underlying rationalization being that as most others speak English, why should the British speak anything else? The arrogance label is one explanation but the supplementary 'lost' trade to non-English-speaking nations, massive in its own right, is awkwardly overlooked, as is the imposing record of higher sales by many non-English speaking nations to English-speaking countries.

Many countries, including the UK, also have an additional constraint to managerial excellence – a cultural predilection to avoid finding fault. It is often in national character not to grumble, at least in public. Few diners in the UK, for example, will complain about unsatisfactory meals, preferring to avoid making a scene. According to Postwatch, the industry watchdog, the predisposition not to complain is a contributory factor to poor letter delivery.[30] The result? Few businesses take the trouble to improve their fares or their services. In experiential learning terms, the failure to criticize reduces the informational base with which managers could, if they wished, respond. Equally, the decision-makers who could implement change often portray complainants as 'whingers' or 'whistle-blowers'.

These examples of non-learning are just the tip of the iceberg, all contributing to a dismal productivity score.

Where real 'wealth' resides

To flag up Britain's lack of productivity may seem somewhat at odds with the national picture of apparent 'wealth'. Britain has achieved more than a decade of unbroken growth, unemployment has dropped to landmark figures and interest rates are unprecedentedly low, as is inflation. In addition, foreign investment inflows are generally high in comparison with other European countries, which provides some people with a fair case that, if others want to invest in the UK, the business environment can't be all that bad.

The reality can be argued very differently, however. That others come to the UK to do business can be explained by the fact that they can impose better management on British labour and that the local marketplace is less averse than elsewhere to paying relatively higher prices for goods and services, this latter point being illustrated by examples from motor cars to food to hotel accommodation, clothing, broadband internet, entertainment and public transport and so on.[31] The four more accurate indicators of national wealth creation – the Stock Exchange, national competitiveness, both business and personal taxation, and the effort and expense of setting up the new businesses that create wealth – show how profitless the actual affairs of state are.

Over the seven-year period to 2003, the FTSE 100 Index's real increase was just 1.8 per cent, compared with the German Dax's rise of 18.3 per cent, the 48.2 per cent advance of the US Dow Jones and the 74 per cent equivalent growth of the Italian BCI index.[32] Over the same period, the UK's economy dropped from 4th to 15th place in the league table of global competitiveness[33] while the additional business taxes on dividends to pension funds and charities and the added costs of regulation rose by £18 billion,[34] dwarfing the £3 billion saving from a cut in corporate tax. In terms of personal taxation, there have been 66 stealth charge rises in the seven-year period to 2003, increasing the amount of tax that a middle-earner pays from 35p to 50p in the pound.[35] And despite regular attempts to cut bureaucracy, Britain spends £31 billion per year[36] (up a tenth on 2003[37]) on administrating business regulations, equal to about 10 per cent of all government departmental expenditure. Furthermore, it takes, on average, 18 days to start a business, compared with two in Australia, five in the US and eight in France.

'You've just got to wait'

Indeed, the government itself describes it as a paradox that prosperity has increased alongside subdued productivity growth and little movement to close the productivity gap with major competitors,[38] offering Professor Michael Porter's unpersuasive explanation – 'This process takes a long time … assets must be built, behaviour has to change, and investments have to feed through to generate results'.[39] Notwithstanding the fact that other countries have accelerated their productivity more rapidly than the UK and that successive British governments have been trying to change many of the macroeconomic indicators for several decades, many of the UK economy's long-standing weaknesses remain unchanged. Alongside depressed productivity, the culture of relatively low endeavour in risk-taking, enterprise, innovation and creativity is little changed while the skills gap lingers,[40] leaving property to buttress the corporate and personal bank account. Real estate, it must be said, is a non-productive asset whose value is also fragile. Whether at a high or a low, it camouflages genuine prosperity.

Focusing on productivity specifically, the output figures vary according to which set of calculations are used. Using any of the established formulas, UK productivity is many percentage points behind most of its major competitors, and has been for more than two decades. Using the UK's own calculations,[41] productivity per worker in 2002 was about 26 per cent behind that of the US, about 23 per cent behind that of France and about 22 per cent behind that of Germany. It also trailed Luxembourg, Norway, Ireland, Canada, Denmark, Switzerland, Holland, Austria, Iceland, Belgium, Australia and Finland and was just ahead of Italy, Japan and Sweden.[42] According to Conference Board statistics[43] a year later, UK productivity was still 25 per cent behind the US, 22 per cent behind Ireland, almost 20 per cent behind Belgium, 14 per cent behind Norway, 11 per cent behind France, 9.4 per cent behind Italy and 7 per cent behind all Germany.

The UK's lack of clever systems

It is not as if the problem is not acknowledged by the powers that be. The UK government quietly ranks productivity as the UK's core economic problem,[44] admitting that slack output cannot be explained simply in terms of market failure. In one of its recent reviews of the problem, it reiterates its solution: the improvement of what it identifies as the 'five drivers' of productivity – investment, innovation, skills, enterprise and competitive environment.[45] Elsewhere, organizations like the Work Foundation, the former Industrial Society, recognize that fiscal incentives to remove macroeconomic inefficiencies are only part of the equation.[46] Increasing productivity, says the Work Foundation, means having more effective processing and translating inputs for every hour worked – a combination of clever systems, social capability, high skills, intelligent direction and motivation. The common thread, it says, is that Britain's competitors – whatever their approach to employee protection, the strength or weakness of their trades unions, or overall labour market regulation – all organize their workplaces more intelligently and creatively than the British. It is here that 'Britain isn't working', a deduction that provides a poignant reminder of a comparable election slogan in 1979 that swept one Margaret Thatcher to office. Significantly, in the detail of all this rhetoric, most institutions studiously overlook the importance of experiential learning in the business lexicon, a discipline that could materially help all of the identified areas of sought-after improvement. To me, this illustrates unambiguously Benjamin Franklin's famous commentary about how the poor care of horseshoe nails can lose wars.[47]

No one is perfect

All this aside for the moment, the fact that no organization, however efficient, is impervious to poor decision-making and that there are organizations worldwide many percentage points less productive than Britain makes the wider issue of how to improve output a relevant and important topic.

I have already suggested how high employee turnover inhibits the ability of businesses and other organizations to learn from experience. The flexible labour market – corporate longhand for 'swing doors' or 'musical chairs' – started out in the 1970s. Encouraged by industry itself and, in the case of countries like the UK, fuelled by 'corrective' anti-union legislation, its introduction was intended to provide organizations with a measure of flexibility to adapt to rapidly changing conditions in the marketplace. As part of the great historical merry-go-round, it was industry's reaction to the inflexible labour policies advanced by organized labour in the period after the Second World War, which in turn was a response to business management's earlier hire'n'fire policies that earned industry the label 'robber barons'. The interim period was an era in which workers could expect to have a single employer, perhaps two or, if one was really unlucky, three in their working lifetimes. Such is the pace of change that those days, even for those individuals who started their working lives then, are a faded reminiscence. Tables 2.1 and 2.2 show how much the situations had changed by the 1990s.

High staff turnover has had another overlooked consequence that organizations have been unable to address. The enormous amounts they spend on conventional staff training are largely wasted. In reality, it is *other* organizations that get the full benefit, with the previous employer having to treat their investment as a social responsibility. For the funding institution, a beneficial effect is only evident if incoming individuals have been exposed to similar training in their previous employment. The usual result? The organization has to keep on refunding its coaching.

Alongside political factors, it has been the advance of technology and the proliferation of products and services that has fuelled short employee tenure. If change is necessary, then, according to the perceived wisdom of employers, transformation is more easily achieved with a new broom. Under the new order, organizations can have injections of new blood whenever they want. More importantly, they can change their largest investment almost at will. When demand rises, they can hire in the knowledge that, if their forecasts don't come up to scratch, they can simply fire without too much trouble or expense. When hiring is the order of the day, it is called 'upsizing'; the buzzword for firing, on the other hand, is 'downsizing', institutional decisions that have spawned a mega-billion-pound consultancy industry that has been singularly responsible for affecting the personal lives of probably

70–80 per cent of all workers in most of the developed world four or five times over the past 30 years. Alongside this is the regular labour market that has encouraged employees to voluntarily change their employment to increase their salary or move into more agreeable jobs.

In this new approach to workplace practice, however, most organizations don't realize that the knowledge that makes them special – that is, the awareness of their particular markets, their unique circumstances and their singular way of doing things – walks out of the front door under a fashionable cloak that almost everyone still thinks is wholly beneficial.

The effects of rapid job turnover

In reality, the flexible labour market has become so elastic that the US National Bureau for Economic Research reported that by 1983 the average American employee would work for ten different employers during their working lifetime.[48] By 2000 the annual average turnover rate was 16 per cent.[49] And in the UK the respected London-based Employment Policy Institute forecast in 1997 that new entrants to the workplace could expect to have an average 11 different employers in their working lifetimes.[50] The latest study finds that one in three workers now remain in their jobs for less than two years whilst one in five considers changing employers in the first 12 months of their new employment.[51] Given that jobs do not always follow each other directly, my own calculation is that an average 44-year working life will – at current levels – reduce to around 41 years of actual employment for most people. On this basis, individuals at all levels of the business hierarchy will be working for each of their various employers for fewer than four years, with many changing jobs within their organizations every 24 months. The four-year tenure level is not inconsistent with current levels of regime change among senior ranks in many large companies (see Figures 2.1 and 2.2).

The organizations that endorse and encourage the flexible labour market include the companies themselves, their trade organizations, governments, and even bodies like the OECD and the European Union. With the possible exception of trades unions (usually for self-interested reasons), they all classically think that the acquisition of other employers' experiences – through external hiring – when necessary will cover any potential adverse consequences. Just how ingrained the flexible labour market has become can be seen in the attitude of the various stock exchanges around the world: share prices rise when companies announce job cuts. Conveniently, few ever think of computing the true price tag.

The domino effect

However personally difficult it is for individuals to keep changing their employer (in terms of insecurity, pension considerations and so on), the implications for organizations are taxing indeed. With most job change now *not* linked to wider economic circumstances,[52] there is continuous jobs disruption, with the effect that no task carries with it the advantage of much stability any more. Simply stated, no sooner than an individual works up to becoming efficient in their job, they move on, embedding a programmed level of organizational inefficiency. Add to this the departing know-how and knowledge from redeployed and relocating employees to the inherent short and selective memory recall of standing

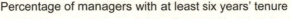

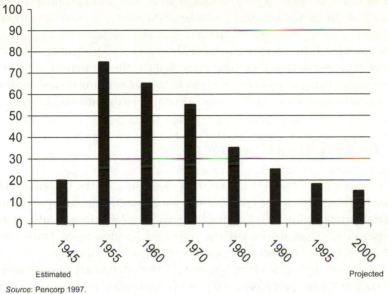

Figure 2.1   The working profile of British companies post-Second World War

A prospect coming to you soon – if it hasn't already. The figure above shows how managerial tenure has progressively shrunk since the Second World War in the UK.

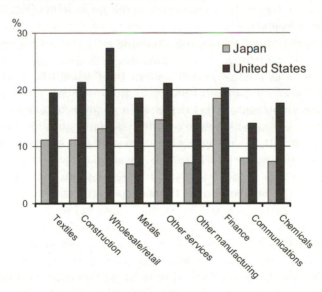

Figure 2.2   Annual job turnover by industry, late 1990s

Across the board increases have occurred since these figures were put together. The figure shows an industry breakdown of jobs churn in two contrasting OECD countries. Despite its recent long recession, Japan's jobs turnover is still much lower than shorter recession-time periods in the West, suggesting that its attitude to retaining institutional experience is little changed.

employees, as well as the questionable nature of their memory as a result of their defensive reasoning processes, and the result is an Alzheimer-like corporate amnesia that imposes an inability on organizations to learn efficiently from their own experiences. The cost of the domino effect of these multiple components – unquestionably the weakest links in any organization's learning chain – is enormous.

Whether staff turnover is due to 'hire'n'fire' policies or to 'itchy feet' on the part of employees, few organizations appreciate that others' know-how and experience is not always relevant. In reality, much of an organization's strength – its know-how and experience – is institution-specific. Collectively known as organizational memory, it marks the establishment's unique capability and is arguably the most important ingredient of its durability. As such it cannot be rehired, only learned, with new appointees generally expected to assimilate it by osmosis. In truth, the flexible labour market is the single biggest source of know-how leakage out of companies, giving rise to a corporate amnesia that reduces the body of evidence that an institution might have at its disposal for better decision-making. Institutional 'forgetting' is one of the biggest constraints to decision-making excellence and a massive contributor to productivity shortfalls.

The cost of lost know-how

But how does one reliably calculate the cost of squandered knowledge? Evidence of short job tenure and corporate amnesia's collective effect on productivity can be seen in several unconnected, but associated studies. In the first, a team of US academics computed the impact of the so-called 'forgetting phenomena' on the learning life cycle of skilled manual tasks in a manufacturing plant.[53]

Using actual learning data on more than 60 individuals undertaking the same task, they imitated the effect of forgetting by subjecting their learning life cycle to a series of interruptions. On the basis that many activities have been described by cyclic models such as the product life cycle and organization life cycle, they reasoned that the same approach would apply to the performance of a task, where each phase of the task could be described as part of a task 'life cycle'. Subjecting their learning cycle model to an interruption after 12 weeks over a 50-week period, their computation was that project performance could be expected to retrogress to 52 per cent of optimum output.

The second study was carried out by the Washington-based Corporate Leadership Council,[54] which put the percentage cost of jobs change at 46 per cent of annual pay for front-line employees, 176 per cent for IT professionals and 241 per cent for middle managers. These included direct expenses associated with replacement hiring and training, the lost productivity associated with a vacated position and the lost productivity of peers and subordinates. Elsewhere, the US actuarial and consulting firm Segal Company calculates that in specialty retailing, for example, which incurs a 90 per cent annual staff turnover rate, the industry has to spend half its total earnings to deal with the problem.[55] A retail store would have to sell 3000 additional pairs of khaki trousers at $35 apiece to compensate for the loss of one worker, it says, and replacing a manager or professional costs much more. The study suggests that employee turnover in the US may double in the next economic recovery.

Some of the unseen costs of staff churn were the subject of another study by a Californian management and training consulting firm specializing in employee commitment and retention.[56] In a survey of several of its Australasian clients, they found that employee

Table 2.1   Jobs: the OECD discontinuity league – average tenure (years)

Country	1992	1995	1998
Belgium	11.0	11.3	11.6
Denmark	8.8	8.5	8.5
Finland	–	10.7	10.6
France	10.4	10.7	11.3
Germany	10.7	10.0	10.4
Greece	13.5	13.4	13.2
Ireland	11.1	10.8	10.1
Italy	11.9	12.1	12.1
Japan	10.9	11.3	11.6
Luxembourg	10.1	10.6	11.2
Netherlands	8.9	9.1	9.4
Portugal	11.1	12.3	11.6
Spain	9.9	9.9	10.0
Sweden	–	10.6	11.9
United Kingdom	8.1	8.2	8.2
United States	6.7	6.7*	6.6
Average	10.2	10.4	10.5

Source: Eurostat, Statistical Office of the European Communities, and national aggregate data from the US and Japan.

* Data refers to 1996

Table 2.2   Annual jobs turnover, by industry, 1990s (%)

Emloyment tenure	Under 1 year			10 years and over		
	1991	1995	1998	1991	1995	1998
Belgium	–	11.6	12.0	–	43.6	46.5
Denmark	–	25.1	22.0	–	29.1	33.5
Finland	11.9	17.6	19.9	34.2	39.6	42.5
France	15.7	15.0	14.3	41.4	42.0	45.0
Germany*	12.8	16.1	14.3	41.2	35.4	38.3
Greece	–	12.6	9.6	–	39.9	51.2
Ireland	–	17.8	18.3	–	33.1	37.7
Italy	–	8.5	9.9	–	45.6	49.2
Japan	9.8	7.6	8.3	42.9	42.9	43.2
Luxembourg	–	11.4	8.9	–	37.8	44.2
Netherlands	24.0	16.3	14.9	26.2	31.7	36.5
Portugal	–	13.4	15.0	–	41.6	43.0
Spain	23.9	35.5	28.4	39.7	34.2	39.8
Sweden	–	14.8	13.4	–	39.7	47.8
United Kingdom	18.6	19.6	19.9	28.9	26.7	32.3
United States**	28.8	26.0	27.8	26.6	25.8	25.8
Average	18.2	16.8	16.1	35.1	36.8	41.0
Standard deviation	6.8	7.1	6.2	7.1	6.2	6.8

Source: Eurostat, Statistical Office of the European Communities, and national aggregate data from the US and Japan.

* Data refer to 1990 instead of 1991.   ** Data refer to 1996 instead of 1995

On jobs turnover, there is a huge divergence between official figures and independent researchers. The US's National Bureau for Economic Research, for example, reported that by 1983 the average American employee would work for ten different employers during a working lifetime. By 2000 the annual average turnover rate was around 16 per cent. In the UK the respected Employment Policy Institute forecast that new entrants to the workplace can expect to have an average 11 different employers in their working life whilst Mintel finds that one in three workers now remain in their jobs for less than two years. Even at 'official' 1998 levels – recorded above – most developed countries breach the point at which academic researchers calculate that their productivity is being affected. Whereas jobs change was previously related to downsizing, it is now a general feature of the labour market, providing endemic jobs disruption and widespread corporate amnesia.

turnover was costing a 400-plus-employee IT services provider more than NZ$16 million per year. Across the Tasman Sea, staff turnover at an 18-employee beauty aids manufacturer and distributor cost more than NZ$2 million in lost sales opportunities annually while the equivalent figure for an 80-store supermarket chain was at least NZ$40 million.

The fourth is a study by the UK's National Westminster Bank[57] that disclosed that more veteran companies in the UK failed in the early 1990s recession than in any other previous economic slump in the twentieth century. A massive 10 per cent of firms that had survived two world wars, the bleak 1930s depression and the succession of subsequent cyclical downturns crashed between 1989 and 1993. Why were they unable to survive this particular recession? Part of the answer – in my opinion at least – lies in the fact that the recession coincided with the height of the downsizing boom. This led to massive jobs discontinuity and an OM that provided individual companies with little awareness of how they manoeuvred their way out of previous crises. No actual figure was placed on the collective effects of all these corporate deaths.

On a national basis, low productivity is no less damaging. In addition to requiring more investment than might otherwise be necessary, it contributes to increased taxes and higher prices coupled with poorer value for money and the erosion of the quality of day-to-day life. The simple reality for lower-productivity countries is that their managers extract less juice out of the same-size corporate orange than higher-output countries. In 2002, for example, UK organizations took around 11 per cent more time, money or employees to achieve the same output as French institutions and a massive 25 per cent more time, money or employees to achieve the same output as US firms.[58] Using the US as the benchmark, another way of putting it is that up to 25 per cent of every pound sterling spent was unnecessary, as was 19 per cent of every Euro in Germany and more than 15 per cent of every euro in France.

Western philosophical differences with the East

The situation is not helped by several philosophies that demarcate workers in the West and the East. The first underlines the differing attitudes towards industry, with the Anglo-Saxon economies arguing that flexible labour markets help companies to better respond to consumer demand and the Pacific Basin countries believing that they inhibit both productivity and profitability over the long term. The fact that job change is still substantially lower in Japan's decade-long recession than during similar downturns in the West suggests that this conviction has changed only slightly.

Then there is the differing attitude towards knowledge. The general belief in the West is that it is mostly technological and/or quantitative in orientation.[59] Western rationalism is based on the theory that knowledge comes through deductive reasoning while Eastern empiricism reasons that erudition is derived inductively through actual experience. As experiential learning specialists Professors Nonaka and Hirotaka Tekeuchi confirm,[60] managers in Western economies generally focus on technically-oriented, mainly explicit information encompassing rules, processes and the professional/vocational information codified in manuals and texts, while the emphasis in Japanese companies, for example, is on more implicit and ambiguous tacit knowledge – a characteristic that is deeply rooted in action as well as ideals, values and emotions. It's part of their Zen Buddist heritage.

In the world of decision-making, the difference is as subtle as it is significant. The importance of tacit knowledge, an essential part of the evolutionary process of applying prior experience to new circumstances (in Nonaka and Tekeuchi's words 'turning old knowledge into new knowledge'), is barely acknowledged by Western managers. Few will even know how to define it, let alone show any concern when it walks out of the front door.

An explanation for non-reflection

The other unhelpful characteristic of many Western managers is that they are not especially reflective in their business lives, which also inevitably affects the quality of their decision-making. This can be blamed on the teaching establishment and industry itself against a background of contemporary Western thinking that society's problems are best solved through technology and psychology-oriented procedures. The resulting shift in educational emphasis means that there are fewer arts/history graduates among senior business leaders than there were 50 years ago, with the not too unsurprising result that learning through historical precedent and association has been largely replaced with hi-tech approaches to management solutions.

This trend can clearly be seen in education, where subjects like political, military and social history are an integral part of many general curricula. Elsewhere, musicians study music history, artists art history, architects architectural history and soldiers military history but for the people who have to go out and earn their living in other ways – that is, almost everyone else – corporate and/or wider business history is virtually non-existent in the education system, even in business schools. The only history that does feature in business education, albeit in declining measure, is economic history, which deals with macro-fiscal issues as they affect national and international constituencies – a discipline that is only remotely associated with the day-to-day running of a business. Harvard is the only business school where business history is a compulsory component of all first-year teaching and where company case studies are explicitly taught alongside wide-ranging country case studies.

Industry is similarly remiss. With the exception of cosmetic induction processes, few companies make any formal effort to pass down their experiences from one generation to the next. The few attempts to learn from experience, such as mentoring and post-project reviews, all suffer from the same structural defect – the highly selective and unreliable memory recall of the know-how and experience passed across by knowledge owners and the equally erratic recollections of the knowledge receiver. Quite simply, the indefinite evidence that springs from either of these approaches automatically flaws any potential experiential learning. If experiences cannot be recalled accurately and in context, they might as well never have happened and the opportunities that might otherwise provide for learning are forfeited. US author Russell Hoban puts it better: 'If the past cannot teach the present and the father cannot teach the son, then history need not have bothered to go on, and the world has wasted a great deal of time.'[61]

No inheritance

Without a conveyed and faithful inheritance, new entrants to the workplace virtually have to start from scratch while those who move laterally across the workforce have little opportunity to learn from their new employer's tried and tested experience. Thanks to short job tenures, a good corporate performance one year can be overturned in another. The workplace has never been more mobile – or so mercurial.

Strictly speaking, experiential learning is a discipline that is included within the broader field of organizational learning, but, in practice, it is largely overlooked in favour of narrower education incorporating skills training and the like. Its true character is left to a few high-profile academics and practitioners whose theory, though admired, is rarely practised by managers. Lip service reigns.

Experiential learning is a discipline as confusing as it is embryonic, and often also comes in the guise of the learning organization, adaptive learning, generative learning, single-loop learning, double-loop learning, or even knowledge management. To Chris Argyris, who developed the concept of double-loop learning in the 1970s, organizational learning is the process of 'detection and correction of errors'.[62] Peter Senge defines the learning organization as an 'organization with an ingrained philosophy for anticipating, reacting and responding to change, complexity and uncertainty'.[63] To Michael McGill and John Slocum the learning organization is 'a company that can respond to new information by altering the very "programming" by which information is processed and evaluated'.[64] It is the ability to gain insight and understanding from experience through experimentation, observation and analysis, as well as a willingness to examine both successes and failures. To me, the measure is all about how organizations learn *not* to be bound by their past experiences.

Adaptive learning, which is associated with single-loop learning, is about coping. A reactive process, it focuses on solving problems without examining the appropriateness of current learning behaviours. So-called adaptive organizations concentrate on incremental improvements, often based on the past track record of success; significantly, they do not question the fundamental assumptions underlying the existing ways of doing work. The essential difference is between being adaptive and having adaptability. Senge observes that increasing adaptiveness is only the first stage of learning. Companies, he says, need to focus on generative learning or double-loop learning. Generative learning emphasizes continuous experimentation and feedback in an ongoing examination of the way in which organizations go about defining and solving problems. In his view, generative learning is about creating; it requires 'systemic thinking', 'shared vision', 'personal mastery', 'team learning' and 'creative tension'.[65]

Curiously, few aficionados mention experiential learning specifically although G.P. Huber refers to some of the field's integral constructs – knowledge acquisition, information distribution, information interpretation and organizational memory. As if to confirm the discipline's emergent character, he also says that such learning need not be conscious or intentional and – surprisingly, given that it defeats the objective of all learning – that it does not always increase the learner's effectiveness, or even potential effectiveness. Taking a behavioural perspective, Huber notes that 'an entity learns if, through its processing of information, the range of its potential behaviors is changed'.[66]

As a field of practice, experiential learning is vast – it ranges from personal growth to conflict resolution.[67] Except in business, that is, where active models are both rare and, where evident, mainly theoretical.

The history of experiential learning

I shall deal more fully with the history of experiential learning in Chapter 10 but, briefly, the concept first emerged in the fields of psychology, philosophy and physiology through the early work of Jean Piaget among children and R. Gagne with intellectual skills. Their work was then refined by the likes of Jack Meizirow, who introduced the concept of transformative learning, Paulo Freire, whose methodology introduced 'dialogue' into the learning process, John Dewey, whose concern was with 'interaction, reflection and experience', Kurt Lewin, who brought to the table the concept of action research (a form of collective self-reflective enquiry) and, more recently, David Kolb, who is probably experiential learning's most prominent proponent.

Most models of experiential learning are cyclical and have three basic phases: an experience or problem situation; a reflective phase within which the learner examines the experience and draws erudition from that reflection; and a testing phase within which the new insights or learnings, having been integrated with the learner's own conceptual framework, are applied to a new problem situation or experience. The concept's starting point is that individuals or organizations seldom learn from experience unless the experience is assessed and then assigned its own meaning in terms of individuals' and/or organizations' own goals, aims, ambitions and expectations.[68] From these processes come the insights and added meaning. The end product is better decision-making.

The reason for decision-making's neglect

On the basis that good decision-making characterizes good management, why is this critical business skill not a dedicated subject in business education and management training? My own explanation is that business academics and trainers, both of whom still see decision-making's instruction in its established theoretical context, have not yet devised a suitable reflective technique because the evidential base is either non-existent or too unreliable for rigorous application. Alongside this, the perception mistakenly persists that good business practice is all about 'leadership' coupled with a macro-environment that encourages high levels of skills and innovation, low taxation[69] and minimal red tape. It is, but the most important factor of production of all – the ability of managers and other workers to make good decisions – appears to be disassociated from the critical performance measure called productivity and somehow misplaced in the multifunctional package of skills called business education. Overriding all this is the fact that most teachers have no hands-on business experience, so anything they impart is dissociated from reality, which no doubt explains their theoretical bent and inspired playwright George Bernard Shaw's cynical opinion of the teaching profession: 'He who can, does. He who cannot, teaches.'[70] Put simply, it doesn't matter how congenial is the business environment or how high is the level of vocational skills. If individuals don't know *how* to make good decisions, progress is slow whether the rate is good or bad.

This observation is part of a growing and wider concern about the effectiveness of established business education that suggests it is arrogant to assume that unaccompanied theory can teach practice efficiently. Led by distinguished academics such as Harold Levitt and Henry Mintzberg, the criticisms are that business curricula, including that for degrees such as the flagship MBA, overemphasize analysis 'at the expense of both integration and developing wisdom as well as leadership and interpersonal skills'.[71] It is a subject that I develop in the next chapter among other themes that – in Levitt's and Mitzberg's words – suggest that traditional business education teaches 'the wrong things in the wrong ways (and perhaps to the wrong people, or at least at the wrong time in their careers)'. From the available data, their conclusion is that business schools

... are not very effective: Neither possessing an MBA degree nor grades earned in courses correlate with career success, results that question the effectiveness of schools in preparing their students. And, there is little evidence that business school research is influential on management practice, calling into question the professional relevance of management scholarship.[72]

In the UK, for example, where business education has experienced a meteoric rise in the past 15 years, the uncomfortable verdict by the Council for Excellence in Management and Leadership is that 'current management and business leadership development is a dysfunctional system'.[73] From an investigation described by the government as the most comprehensive study ever conducted into the supply of and demand for management and leadership capability in the UK, the indictment could not be more damning.

Instinct is not enough

However effective (or ineffective) past performance has been in using existing teaching methodologies, it is now clear that – against the background of growing pressure on modern industry, politicians and civil servants to deliver better-value products and services in both the private and public sectors – new approaches to teaching business, and specifically decision-making, need to be devised.

The management debate about how to improve competitiveness has conventionally yo-yoed between apportioning higher investment and, when the outlay starts looking too high or the benefits less than worthwhile, cutbacks, usually in manpower. Throwing money at products or services does not automatically bring about changes for the better, as many parts of the public sector in the UK and elsewhere demonstrate. Nor do lay-offs. Enhanced productivity does bring change for the better, but this involves making good and better decisions.

For too long managers have been flying in the face of experience. Instead, we need to let experience – real-life experience, experience that can be recalled rigorously and with purpose – help us with this basic but vital managerial process. Enter business education and management training.

Notes

1. George Walden, *The Times,* London, 20 December 1986.
2. One out of every 300 patients worldwide will die from a medical 'mistake', according to the World Health Organization (WHO). On 7 February 1991, the *New England Journal of Medicine,* quoting a Harvard research project analysing hospital records from the state of New York, estimated that, over a one-year period, more than 13 000 New Yorkers were killed and 2500 permanently disabled as a result of flawed medical care. They attributed more than 51 per cent of the deaths to negligence. According to the *Wall Street Journal* on 13 January 1993, between 150 000 and 300 000 Americans are injured or killed each year because of medically mistreated diseases, surgeries, drug reactions or incorrectly prescribed drugs. In 1999 *The Medical Journal of Australia*, quoting a Quality in Australian Health Care Study (QAHCS) together with a Harvard study on which it was based, reported that, each year, 50 000 Australians suffer permanent disability and 18 000 die at least in part as a result of their healthcare. And on 30 June 2003, the National Health Service reported that almost 8 per cent of the UK's total National Health Service budget was used to fund compensation claims in 2001, with another £5.25 billion of outstanding claims due to be settled over the next ten years.

3.   *British Medical Journal*, 10 June 2000.
4.   Ibid.
5.   According to the Home Office, 21 October 2003.
6.   Lord Woolf, *The Times*, 23 April 2004.
7.   According to a report published by the Office of National Statistics on 13 October 2004, 1.1 million people under 25 are unemployed and not in full-time education, 25 000 more than in 1997 and up by 54 000 in the three months to August, 2004. See 'Unemployed Youths Rise by 25,000 under Labour', *The Times*, 14 October 2004.
8.   UK Ministry of Education, 19 August 2003. Ofsted reported in December 2004 that at least 35 per cent of pupils in 10 per cent of the UK's primary schools still cannot read by the age of 11, despite the introduction of a compulsory reading hour in primary schools seven years previously. See 'One in Three Pupils Aged 11 Cannot Read, Says Ofsted Report' *The Independent*, 15 December 2004.
9.   *Working Capital. Intangible Assets and the Productivity Gap*, The Work Foundation, 2002.
10. OECD, 2001. See 'Lagging Behind Korea, Greece and Ireland. British Schools Slide Down International Table', *The Independent*, 17 September 2003.
11. In the UK pupils have been awarded a B grade in a maths GCSE exam despite scoring only 17 per cent. Previously, pupils sitting GCSE maths had to achieve about 40 per cent to get a B grade. But with the new exam, designed by the Cambridge-based exam board OCR, those who got as little as 17 per cent were given a B grade, while those scoring 45 per cent were awarded an A grade. The move, reported by *The Daily Telegraph* on 16 January 2005, was revealed just days after government ministers hailed record achievements at GCSE level. The pass marks for the new exam, which was taken in 2004 by 7500 children from 65 schools and due to be introduced nationwide in 2005, were an all-time low.
12. *The Times*, 15 March 2005.
13. *The Daily Telegraph*, 15 March 2004.
14. *Sunday Times*, 13 July 2005.
15. OLAF report, reported in *Sunday Telegraph*, 19 October 2003.
16. Food Commission, 'Parents Beware: Juice in Juice Drinks Costs up to £34 per Litre', 30 April 2004 at: http://www.foodcomm.org.uk/lowjuice_04.htm.
17. Dee Hock, *The Art of Chaotic Leadership*, San Francisco: Leader to Leader Institute and Jossey-Bass, 2000.
18. John Seely Brown, *Appreciative Inquiry Newsletter*, issue 10, August 2000.
19. European Commission report, 21 January 2004. See 'Europe's Dream of Overtaking US Collapses in Failure', *The Independent*, 22 January 2004.
20. Network Rail, 'First Anniversary: Focus on Improvements Continues', press release, 2 October 2003.
21. According to Michael Donnelly, Bridgewell Securities, as reported in *The Daily Telegraph*, 3 October 2003.
22. *The Daily Telegraph*, 2 December 2003.
23. *The Daily Telegraph*, 25 March 2004.
24. *The Independent*, 12 May 2004.
25. *The Daily Telegraph*, 22 July 2004.
26. MORI poll for the Royal College of Nursing, May 2004.
27. According to an analysis by the Office for National Statistics, October 2004.
28. *The Daily Telegraph*, 5 February 2005.
29. According to the Centre for Information on Language Teaching (CILT), November 2004, two-thirds of state secondary schools no longer make foreign-language lessons compulsory.
30. Report, Postwatch, May 2004.
31. According to a *Sunday Times* survey reported in the newspaper on 7 November 2004, BA was charging British residents twice as much as those in continental Europe for the same business class flights to New York. Compared with French prices, Hertz was charging British motorists more than 16 per cent more for three-day car hire, a New York hotel booked through Thomas Cook was priced 25 per cent higher while Sony charged 7 per cent more for one of their laptops.
32. John Littlewood, Paper, Centre for Policy Studies, April 2004. See 'Labour is Destroying the Wealth of Britain', *The Daily Telegraph*, 30 April 2004.
33. *League Table of Global Competitiveness*, World Economic Forum, 2004.
34. John Littlewood, Paper, Centre for Policy Studies, April 2004. See 'Labour is Destroying the Wealth of Britain', *The Daily Telegraph*, 30 April 2004.

35. Research study, Smith & Williamson, UK independent financial services group, September 2004.
36. *Doing Business in 2005*, World Bank survey, September 2005.
37. British Chamber of Commerce quoted in *Daily Mail*, 24 June 2004.
38. *UK Productivity and Competitiveness Indicators 2003*, DTI Economics Paper No 6, November 2003.
39. M.E. Porter and C.H. Ketels, *UK Competitiveness: Moving to the Next Stage*, DTI Economics Paper No. 3, 2003.
40. *Working Capital*, op. cit.
41. *UK Productivity and Competitiveness Indicators 2002*, DTI Economics Paper No, 5, 2002.
42. OECD, *Annual Report*, 2002.
43. Groningen Growth and Development Centre and The Conference Board, *Total Economy Database*, August 2004 at: http://www.ggdc.net.
44. Treasury/DTI, *Productivity in the UK: The Regional Dimension*, 2001 at http://www.hm-treasury.gov.uk/97F/66/REGIONAL_POLICY.pdf.
45. *UK Productivity and Competitiveness Indicators 2003*, op. cit.
46. *Working Capital*, op. cit.
47. Benjamin Franklin: 'For the want of a nail, the shoe was lost; for the want of a shoe the horse was lost; and for the want of a horse the rider was lost, being overtaken and slain by the enemy, all for the want of care about a horseshoe nail.'
48. Quoted in Richard Bolles, *What Colour is your Parachute?*, Berkeley, CA: Tenspeed Press, 1983.
49. BNA Inc., publisher of analysis and reference products, 2003.
50. Employment Policy Institute, London, 1997.
51. *British Lifestyles*, Mintel survey, November 2004.
52. OECD, *Annual Report*, 1994.
53. J.G. Carlson and A.J. Rowe, 'How Much Does Forgetting Cost?', *Industrial Engineering*, vol. 8, no. 9, 1976. The researchers work for the University of Southern California.
54. *Employee Retention: New Tools for Managing Workforce Stability and Engagement*, Washington, DC: Corporate Leadership Council, 1998.
55. Gerry Ledford and Matt Lucy, *The Rewards of Work: The Employment Deal in a Changing Economy*, The Segal Group, 2003.
56. KASE Consulting Group Ltd. and Integral Training Systems, Inc., study into staff turnover costs, 2003.
57. *Review of Small Business Trends*, National Westminster Bank, 1994.
58. *UK Productivity and Competitiveness Indicators 2003*, op. cit.
59. J. Yates, 'For the Record: Embodiment of Organizational Memory, 1859–1920', *Business and Economic History*, Second Series, vol. 19, 1990.
60. Ikujiro Nonaka and Horotaka Tekeuchi, *The Knowledge-Creating Company*, Oxford: Oxford University Press, 1995.
61. R. Hoban, *The Lion of Boaz-Jachin and Jachin-Boaz*, London: Jonathan Cape, 1973.
62. 'Double-loop Learning in Organizations', *Harvard Business Review*, 1977.
63. Peter Senge, *The Fifth Discipline: The Art and Practice of the Learning Organization*, New York: Doubleday, 1990.
64. Michael E. McGill and John W. Slocum, *The Smarter Organization: How to Build a Business That Learns and Adapts to Marketplace Needs*, Chichester: Wiley, 1994.
65. Senge, *The Fifth Discipline*, op. cit.
66. G.P. Huber, 'Organizational Learning: The Contributing Processes and the Literatures', *Organization Science*, February, 1991, pp. 85–115.
67. Susan Weil and Ian McGill, 'Meaning and Practice in Experiential Learning', in Susan Weil and Ian McGill (eds), *Making Sense of Experiential Learning*, Milton Keynes: SRHE/Open University Press, 1989.
68. Albert Wight, 'Participative Education and the Inevitable Revolution', *Journal of Creative Behaviour*, vol. 4, no. 4, Fall, 1970.
69. Stephen Dorgan and John Dowdy, 'How Good Management Raises Productivity', *McKinsey Quarterly*, no. 4, 2002.
70. George Bernard Shaw, *Man and Superman, Maxims for Revolutionists: Education*, London, 1903.
71. Jeffrey Pfeffer and Christina Fong, 'The End of Business Schools? Less Success Than Meets the Eye', *Academy of Management Learning & Education*, vol. 1, issue 1, September 2002.
72. Cited in ibid.

73. Council for Excellence in Management and Leadership, *Managers and Leaders: Raising Our Game*, London: CEML, May 2002.

3 The Gaping Holes in Business Education

In a time of drastic change it is the learners who inherit the future. The learned usually find themselves equipped to live in a world that no longer exists.

Eric Hoffer, US philosopher[1]

This book is written against the background of a perplexing aspect to business. Despite its importance to everyone's national prosperity, its stock in trade – the practice of business – has yet to assume the status of a full-blown profession in most parts of the world, including many developed countries.

Taking into account all cooperative work from high street shops to large institutions, relatively few companies or other organizations are administered by trained managers. The rest are run by people who may or may not be vocationally trained at something, but have had no bona fide business or management education. In fact, most entrepreneurship does not come out of universities at all, although nearly all of the resources into its teaching are still targeted on the tertiary sector.

Even now, schools and universities in many countries treat business as an after-thought, whilst dedicated business schools, although they have mushroomed in numbers over the last 40 years in many countries, still seem detached from traditional education.

One of the yardsticks for most other professions – for example, music, architecture, art, soldiering, politics, and so on – is that their generic history is recognized as a discrete academic field of learning. In most business curricula, both corporate history, which is the memoir of individual companies or other institutional bodies, and wider business history, the more general historical study of the subject that builds a general appreciation of the contribution of single enterprises to the wider sector, industry and national economic context, is studiously avoided as a teaching tool. The only exception is economic history, which is the application of economic theory to historical study using econometric measuring techniques called cliometrics, a combination of mathematical economics and statistics. Its purpose is to provide economic interpretations of history, like Adam Smith's eighteenth-century theory about free trade which played an important part in the Industrial Revolution. Although economic history provides a valuable macro-perspective of how financial systems work, which may be practical for economists and important to academics, it is only of peripheral benefit for sharp-end businessmen and women having to deal with the micro-issues of running a company or other type of organization. Nevertheless, economic history is, for some inexplicable reason, seen as more valuable to managers than corporate, management and business history.

Even in industry, corporate, business and management history is rarely seen as 'experience' or used as an applied field of study, in which its inventory of tried and tested practice is a knowledge resource that is part of a natural process of progress and change. If anything, its nature is more commonly seen as immutable rather than evolutionary, and as little more than public relations.

In most other professions – and trades, come to think of it – teachers are practitioners first. It is a curious anomaly that few business academics ever put their toe into the world of industry and commerce, least of all make any money in it. Even fewer become captains of industry.

In many countries, management is still considered a trade even though its instruction is elitist. Moreover, academics are still not certain whether the wider practice of business is a science or an art. And despite the fact that the business of trade and industry is the world's second oldest profession, no-one has generated any big theories to explain its being.[2] It is widely accepted that it is the leading driver of change and wealth creation, yet all that has emerged after more than two centuries of scholarly attention is the mixed bag of limp beliefs that it is an idiosyncratic activity of singular individuals, that it is the result of social norms and that it happens because of the concentration of capital and resources from ongoing activities, and even – in some politicized quarters – that it is something genetic. The fact that most people get little or no business 'inheritance' in schools or universities is unstudiously ignored. In 1995, for example, the University of Derby's Centre for Applied Social and Organizational Research found that students could name only one successful British company and had no idea what the acronyms of the country's representative bodies for industry or the trades unions – the CBI (Confederation of British Industry) and the TUC (Trade Union Congress) – stood for.[3] The more recent observation of *The Financial Times* is that curricula in the UK are still not providing business graduates with commercial awareness.[4]

More relevantly, however, there is clear evidence that calls into question the effectiveness of traditional business education and management scholarship. While these statements will immediately raise the defences of the business teaching establishment, I should hurriedly add that this is not only my view, which comes not from the coalface of business education, but rather from the user end of the educational trail – industry itself. Through my work in, first, business journalism with *The Financial Times* in London and latterly in knowledge management and business itself, it is evident that managers and the organizations for which they work do not seem to be learning very much from experience. In theory business education should help make business more efficient. Instead, the evolutionary curve for this driver of prosperity seems as flat and as long as it has ever been for much of industry, raising the uncomfortable reality that, if some more statistics that academics themselves research are right and the critics are not wide of the mark, business teaching is not working very well.

Failures in start-ups and acquisitions

For example, more than 10 per cent of new companies in the UK, which are the lifeblood of the wealth-creating system we've developed, fail within 12 months of registration,[5] rising to one in three new companies in the first three years of operation.[6] By year seven, two-thirds of the remainder fall by the wayside. And of those left, only three out of ten will reach the second generation – figures that have not improved much over decades.

Research also points to a truly massive failure rate of acquisitions and mergers worldwide – and also that the 'flop ratio' has changed very little over at least a 20-year period. Statistics from the London Business School[7] and international accountants Coopers & Lybrand[8] (now Pricewaterhouse Coopers) in 1993 showed that around half of all acquisitions fail. In 1996 the Economist Intelligence Unit[9] put the figure at up to 60 per cent while, in 2001, KPMG, the international management consultants, raised this elevated number to a staggering 83 per cent.[10] The figures worldwide are truly spectacular, even when they embrace just foreign-based purchases. In the first nine months of 1996, for example, the value of international cross-border mergers and acquisition targets totalled $181.7 billion, up from $173.7 billion in 1995.[11] Given the enormity of the sums involved, it is instructive to put the figures into a more understandable context. If a 50 per cent failure rate is applied to just the UK's 1996 figures, the cumulative total of unproductive or loss-making assets is equal to the amount raised by a charge of 27p on the basic rate of national income tax or to a figure just short of Denmark's 1993 national budget. The bottom line is that acquisitive companies are wasting shareholders' funds on a truly massive scale – and have been doing so at an unchanged rate for years.

At another level, Chicago University's 1995 Nobel prizewinner Professor Robert Lucas's most influential work tested out the implications of individuals' ability to learn from their mistakes. His insight – which is that countries are full of people trying not to repeat the past – has served to underline the propensity for experiential non-learning and undermine the confidence in the ability of governments to fine-tune their economies.

Then there's my productivity observations around the Groningen Total Economy Database (Figure I.1, p. 2) that show an annual decline in productivity growth from more than 4 per cent per year in the decade to 1960 to just 0.8 per cent in 2002/3 and my discomforting question for the system that purports to groom the inheritors: namely that if business education is supposed to help managers sell their employer's wares more efficiently, how is it that 1950s and 1960s managers totted up higher productivity growth scores *without* any formal business education?

Although these examples alone demonstrate a good deal of fortitude on the part of countries, companies, individual entrepreneurs and all their bank accounts, it does little to recommend the effectiveness of business teaching overall. If it did, fewer start-ups would fail, valuable capital that otherwise is dissipated into failed corporate marriages could be utilized more effectively elsewhere, business would have been more successful at solving the 50-year-old productivity predicament and countries would not have to endure the full effects of the four-year Kitchin wave, the nine-year Juglar wave or the 54-year Kondratieff wave. All I am doing is following the likes of Professors Henry Mintzberg and Harold Leavitt, who have been leading a small, but growing, band of critical observers of the way in which the education system teaches the practice of business.

The lip service treatment of corporate and business history

For my part I've highlighted two interrelated and glaring omissions in the educational package – the widespread absence of experiential learning and, specifically, the non-existence of any *dedicated* instruction into how managers can make better decisions. There are some universities that even think the former has something to do with providing students with real-time exposure to industry rather than giving them a way to learn from experience. In the practice of business, both are so blindingly obvious as a teaching methodology and critical management skill that the long-time resistance to their implementation – or even consideration as curricula inclusions – has always puzzled me. Just the mention of corporate or business history, which is the evidential base of all long-term business experience, causes eyes to cloud over. From most business academics, the suggestion that corporate or business history might be usable as a teaching tool typically generates disinterest at best and hostility at worst. In industry itself, the characteristic response ranges from the parroting of Henry Ford's pronouncement that 'History is more or less bunk'[12] to 'Old lessons are misleading or irrelevant because times change' and 'One must only look forward, not backwards'. If the 'history' and 'lessons' are replaced by 'experience' or 'organizational memory', or the suggestion made that these components may be useful in the wider application of experiential learning, some acknowledgement of its importance may follow, then lip service prevails.

Two other disregarded subjects

Experiential learning and decision-making are not the only subjects to be overlooked. Two other equally valuable (and just as puzzling) exclusions in the curriculum were highlighted by a recent discussion on the Internet when an academic, A.M. de Lange, raised the related subjects of creativity and imagination, both of which are coincidentally also vital ingredients in any decision-making process.[13] What premium, he asked, was placed on the subject of creativity, without which all progress is tentative? Copernicus, he observed, changed science forever with his creativity whilst the father of modern science, Albert Einstein, indicated that this mysterious subject was his key to success. Yet the academic could find only one university in the world – the Aichi Shukutoku University in Japan – with a dedicated department of creativity. He asked:

Why does it [creativity] *not figure administratively in our educational systems? Is creativity a too nebulous subject? Does creativity undermine beaurocracy? Perhaps we do not appreciate enough how much creativity has to do with authentic learning. I don't know. But what I do know is that a lack of creativity is the most important stumbling block in the path of success of students … pupils who do best at school are also the most creative in their learning … Yet our educational systems do not embrace creativity formally.*[14]

The same applies to imagination. Education in many countries, claimed de Lange,[15] is falling apart, mainly because universities do not impart information imaginatively. He quoted Alfred North Whitehead's 1929 book on education, *The Aims of Education and Other Essays*, in which he stated that a university which fails in this respect has no reason for existence. Quoting from Whitehead again, he writes:

The tragedy of the world is that those who are imaginative have but slight experience, and those who are experienced have feeble imaginations. Fools act on imagination without knowledge; pedants act on knowledge without imagination. The task of a university is to weld together imagination and experience.[16]

De Lange continues:

People are so deluged by external information that they do not distinguish it any more from personal knowledge which dwells within them. And would they have done it, perhaps they would have realised what Einstein once wrote:

'I am enough of an artist to draw freely upon my imagination. Imagination is more important than knowledge. Knowledge is limited. Imagination encircles the world.'[17]

'There is no relation between business education and success'

As a foretaste of the broader censure of established business and management teaching, which today extends beyond business schools to consulting and training companies, e-learning and in-house company programmes, I tender a range of random observations and critical views about how the subject (including the MBA – the standard international qualification for senior managers) is taught in the US and the UK. The US is the leader of business education in the Western world and the UK is a significant exporter of management teaching (its business schools are among the country's top 50 overseas earners, attracting a revenue of more than £640 million per year[18] and another £500 million in foreign students' fees[19]).

I should temper these commentaries with the early rider that although they apparently imply that conventional business teaching is not particularly successful at what it is designed to do, the practice of business has nonetheless achieved desirable standards of living in both these countries, albeit substantially more so in the US than in the UK. Whilst defenders of the systems would no doubt claim that this reflects the relative worth of current business teaching in their regions, the other possible explanation is that businesses 'succeed' *despite* current business education. In the words of Stanford University's Professor Jeffrey Pfeffer's and Christina Fong's critical review of business education and its flagship, 'Possessing an MBA neither guarantees business success nor prevents business failure.'[20] They reached two other, equally sobering, conclusions. The first was that possession of neither a business degree nor grades earned in other business courses correlated with career success. The other was that there was little evidence that business school research was influential on management practice – findings that further question both the effectiveness of business teaching as well as the professional relevance of its management scholarship. Indeed, the authors found that business practice and management thought was principally being led by non-academics such as journalists, consultants and people working in companies – practitioners that business academics traditionally (and not without some condescension) hold at a professional arm's length.

This observation is given some weight by Lord Sharman, a former international chairman of KPMG and a member of the exclusive 'The Times Power 100', which ranks directors of FTSE 100 companies on the strength of their boardroom connections. He cannot recall any book on management that made him stop and say, 'My God'. Interestingly, the texts he says *were* useful were history books of the military kind, among them Sun Tzu's *The Art of War* and Nicolo Machiavelli's *The Prince*.[21]

Even though I believe that business is not rocket science (otherwise, why are so many of the untutored so successful?) I subscribe to the systemic premise of a direct relationship between teaching and national prosperity. Given that business education worldwide is broadly predicated on the US and, to a lesser extent, the UK models, if their formats are not all they're cracked up to be, then the versions of lesser-competitive nations are even more suspect. Imagine, then, if business instruction was actually good?

The shortcomings of business education

On this basis, the following commentaries, selected at random from a short search of academic research studies, newspapers and the Internet, should be instructive and also have wider relevance.

Of the four American CEOs people most often named when asked who had accomplished great things, none had a business school degree and two – Galvin of Motorola and Gates of Microsoft – didn't even finish college.

Professors Henry Mintzberg and Joseph Lampel[22]

Most of the best ideas in management over the past decade or so did not originate in business schools.

Professor Gary Hamel[23]

We have built a weird, almost unimaginable design for MBA-level education that distorts those subjected to it into critters with lopsided brains, icy hearts, and shrunken souls.

Professor Harold Leavitt, on business's premier qualification[24]

The industry is overbuilt.

Professor Robert Hamada, ex-dean of the University of Chicago's business school, on the MBA[25]

… fuzzy, irrelevant, and pretentious.

Richard R. West, ex-dean of New York University's graduate school of business, on management school research[26]

Business schools appeal to one another as scholarly communities through a plethora of academic journals that are utterly divorced from the challenges of everyday management.

James Bailey and C. Ford[27]

In today's prestigious business schools, students have to demonstrate competence to get in, but not to get out. Every student who wants to (and who avoids financial and emotional distress) will graduate. At Wharton, for example, less than one percent of the students fail any given course, on average … the probability of failing more than one course is almost zero. In effect, business schools have developed elaborate and expensive grading systems to ensure that even the least competent and least interested get credit.

Professor J.S. Armstrong, an MBA teacher for 30 years[28]

The mark of a true MBA is that he is often wrong but seldom in doubt.

Professor Robert Buzzell, Harvard Business School[29]

Business schools are not a major source of books that directly influence management thought, whether measured by sales or by more subjective assessments of the value of the books.

Jeffrey Pfeffer and Christina Fong[30]

The research done in business schools only makes a modest contribution to management practice and management thought when compared with research produced by non-academics such as journalists, consultants, and people working in companies.

Jeffrey Pfeffer and Christina Fong[31]

Any leaders Britain does have are a result of accident, not design.

Professor John Adair, Exeter University, on the UK's managerial abilities[32]

It stinks.

Professor Michael Porter, Harvard University, on Britain's poor showing as a generator of wealth[33]

Business schools dampen entrepreneurship.

Anita Roddick, founder and managing director of Body Shop International[34]

When you compare Britain's adult workforce, from top management down, with those of our main competitor countries, we emerge as a bunch of thickies.

Sir Bryan Nicholson, a former chairman of the Post Office and ex-head of the Manpower Services Commission[35]

For all too many years people went to schools which despised the world of work and went to universities which totally rejected it.

Lord Young of Graffam, former Secretary of State for Trade and Industry under Margaret Thatcher[36]

The experience of several large US management consultancy firms, traditionally major hirers of business graduates,[37] is particularly edifying. Although such firms have always also recruited non-business professionals such as lawyers, doctors and philosophers, the proportion of non-MBAs they've been hiring has increased in recent years. In 2000, for example, 20 per cent of the consultants hired by the Boston Consulting Group did not have MBAs, Booz Allen and Hamilton planned to hire one-third without graduate business degrees, and more than half of the consultants at McKinsey and Company did not have an MBA.[38]

All the new non-MBAs were given special training on three- or four-week programmes to learn the basics of business. How did they fare? Internal studies conducted by the firms found that the non-MBAs did no worse and, in some cases, better than their business school counterparts. The London office of the Boston Consulting Group, for example, reported that the 'non-MBAs were receiving better evaluations, on average, than their peers who had gone to business school', while a study at McKinsey of people on the job for one, three and seven years found that at all three points the people without MBAs were as successful as those with the degree.[39] Another internal study by an outside consulting firm also 'determined that the people ... hired from high-end business schools were no better at integrative thinking than the undergraduates... hired from top-notch liberal-arts programs'.[40]

'Dangerous' MBAs

Equally instructive is Mintzberg and Lampel's observation that getting to the top does not mean succeeding at the top. Their interest in MBA performance began when they noticed only two out of *Fortune* magazine's '10 most admired CEOs' in 1998 had MBAs. When *Fortune* later ran a list of 33 failed US chief executives, they discovered that 40 per cent had MBAs. What's more, three of those failed chief executives had previously been celebrated by *Harvard Business Review* as examples of 19 Harvard graduates 'who had made it to the top'. Intrigued by such conspicuous failures, Mintzberg and Lampel examined the performance of these top Harvard graduates and discovered that more than half had failed.

Their conclusion? MBAs are largely dangerous. Like many critics of business teaching, they say that MBA graduates reach for too many off-the-shelf solutions:

Looking over the tales of these 10 [failures] *suggests an often fatal tendency to pursue a formula – some kind of generic solution. Pretending to create managers in a classroom setting is wrong-headed at best and, as our evidence suggests, dysfunctional at worst.*[41]

Criticism of American business instruction, which now turns out more than 100 000 MBAs per year,[42] has been around for almost as long as business schools started. In the 1950s, they were described as 'a collection of trade schools lacking a strong scientific foundation'.[43] This prompted a change in approach, and the schools moved under the arts and social sciences umbrella, with an initial emphasis on the use of quantitative and statistical analyses.[44] This immediately provoked concerns about business teaching's relevance to management,[45] specifically that it overemphasized analysis and theory at the expense of developing wisdom, leadership, communication skills, problem-finding against problem-solving and implement-ation,[46] and being insufficiently integrative across the various functional areas.

Illustrative of life on the business school campus are the commentaries of two graduate students attending Stanford's Graduate School: 'Learning is not an explicit goal'[47] and 'the core curriculum taught at business schools is irrelevant, and … the utility of a business school degree is to provide a pedigree rather than learning'.[48] In fact, business school curricula have changed little over time. Course materials have been upgraded and some class offerings have changed, but the 1960s product was still quite recognizable in the 1990s.[49]

These criticisms, which have persisted through to the present day, have been repeated time and time again by the likes of Michael Porter and Lawrence McKibbin,[50] the Graduate Management Admissions Council[51] and Professors Henry Mintzberg and Jonathan Gosling, who noted that 'contemporary business education focuses on the functions of business more than the practice of managing'.[52]

In these observations, a key reproach is the method of instruction.

Mintzberg's and Lampel's position is that teachers

cannot replicate true managing in the classroom. The case study is a case in point: Students with little or no management experience are presented with 20 pages on a company they do not know and told to pronounce on its strategy the next day.'[53]

Elsewhere, Bailey and Ford argue that although a scientific approach may be useful for the study of management, it is not at all clear that it helps in teaching management: 'The practice of management is best taught as a craft, rich in lessons derived from experience and oriented toward taking and responding to action.'[54] But, as Leavitt noted, 'business schools have been designed without practice fields'.[55]

Mintzberg's view is that the MBA programme claims to be creating managers when it is not:

The MBA is really about business which would be fine except that people leave these programs thinking they've been trained to do management. I think every MBA should have a skull and cross-bones stamped on their forehead and underneath should be written: 'not prepared to manage'.[56]

His disenchantment with existing business instruction has led to his pioneering what has been dubbed the anti-MBA or 'Real-Alternative MBA', whose acronym, RAMBA, has been described as a 'sort of feminine Rambo'. With the help of Jonathan Gosling of Lancaster University in the UK, he launched his International Masters in Practising Management (IMPM) in 1996 to give more emphasis to encouraging managers to become more reflective. The approach concentrates on the complexity of real managerial and organizational problems rather than specialized knowledge in subjects such as marketing or finance, with students studying issues from within their organizations rather than general case studies. IMPM has also been introduced at McGill University in Canada, INSEAD in France, the Indian Institute of Management in Bangalore, India and with a group of academics from Hitotsubashi University, Kobe University and the Advanced Institute of Science and Technology in Japan. To study for the IMPM, all students must be practising managers and all must be sponsored by their companies, which so far include Alcan Aluminum Ltd., AstraZeneca PLC, Deutche Lufthansa, the International Federation of the Red Cross and Red Crescent Societies, Matsushita Communication Industrial Co. Ltd, Motorola and the Royal Bank of Canada. Their collective penetration is still small.

The history of business instruction in the UK

In the UK, where US-style business teaching and specifically the MBA were introduced in Britain in 1965 amid concern over the economy's apparent inability to keep pace with America, criticism has been equally vocal but less high-ranking. Although sharing a belief that there was a direct relationship between economic performance and managerial capability, a schism developed almost immediately between those who supported the notion of formal education for management and those who went further to insist that such education should conform to externally verifiable and rigorous standards in order to ensure the credibility of management qualifications.[57]

Just six years later, in 1971, surfaced what became known as the Owen Report[58] into business schools, which focused on the views of manufacturing industry before its near-disintegration in the 1980s. Notable for its transparent attempt to evenly balance criticisms with praise, it voiced the now familiar tension between theoretical and practical approaches to management instruction, with one main criticism being that postgraduate education emphasized academic qualifying criteria, a bias that ensured, at least in the eyes of industrialists, that successful applicants were generally of lower calibre than they otherwise should be. Underlying the report's imposed 'balance', there was clear hostility towards business schools and their postgraduate product, a sentiment emphasized by commentators on the report.

In the wake of the Owen Report, business schools attempted to revise their offerings in line with the perceived interests of industry. Part-time or modular MBA programmes and MBA courses for specific industries or organizations were introduced. Average levels of work experience prior to the commencement of the MBA increased, but such shifts in emphasis continued to cause dissent.

A decade later, in the 1980s, the two most influential reports into business education, which identified the requirement of management education initiatives to adapt to different national contexts, continued to position the American-inspired MBA degree at the pinnacle of their educational solutions to British management weakness.[59] The result? British business schools developed as hybrid institutions attempting to appease the divergent interests of the academic culture of the universities in which they were placed and of a diverse consumer market of business people. These conflicting interests ensured that British business schools were caught in a tug-of-war between practical and academic approaches to management education.

Just in case I am accused of being selective in my choice of critical commentaries, a 1992 government survey[60] of 52 companies and leading business schools in the former polytechnic and college sector uncovered widespread doubts about local MBA courses in terms of quality, language and information technology training and personal skills development. The MBA provision received support from only a minority of employers, most seeing it as irrelevant to the needs of their companies. It was felt that some teaching staff lacked relevant business experience. Of 116 institutions offering MBA programmes, only 27 UK business schools were recognized by the Association of MBAs. The UK has no accreditation body like the American Assembly of Collegiate Schools of Business.

What appears to have happened – in my view at least – is that the pressure for more 'experience' in the curriculum was misinterpreted as a plea to raise the entry qualifications. Few business schools saw it as direct criticism of their course content or the way in which they taught the business of business.

In fact, as early as the 1970s it was observed that there was virtually no experiential learning where, in David Kolb's words, 'concrete experience is the basis for observation and reflection'.[61] According to Kolb, students learned to talk about business, but it was not clear that 'they learn business'. The voices of those other few who emphasized the importance of experiential learning and the practical application of academic knowledge simply got lost in the system.

Now, more than 30 years later, their disregard shows.

Business schools' record at turning out top-flight managers for UK companies has not been good. Nor has British management's record been particularly helpful in producing top-flight companies.

By 2002, for example, just four British or Anglo-Dutch-owned businesses appeared in Fortune's list of top 100 companies.[62] By 2004, 17 of the 50 largest British firms were being run by foreigners, compared with five in Germany and the US and three in France.[63] Non-Britons – the Rothschilds, Kleinworts, Hambros, Barings, Schroders and Warburgs – created the powerhouse called the City of London; today, few of the large financial service companies they created are British-owned. By 2003, the top eight earners among legal firms based in the UK were US-owned,[64] with their in-house lawyers and partners easily out-earning their British counterparts. Car production, which represents a significant proportion of UK manufacturing, is now almost entirely foreign-owned, with MG Rover, the last UK-owned mass-producer, going into receivership in 2005, having been humiliatingly rebuffed by Chinese and Iranian would-be purchasers. Just months later the company was picked up from the administrator PricewaterhouseCoopers by Nanjing Automotive, China's oldest car maker, for an opportunistic price after employees had been dispersed – a ploy not without its own managerial adroitness learned, no doubt, from others' experience.

Other experience-*rich* industries in the UK such as shipbuilding, steel, textiles, motor cycles and bicycles and so on have, in many cases, surrendered almost entirely to experience-*poor* operators supposedly on grounds of high labour costs, although in some cases – for example, shipbuilding in Germany and Italy, steel in the US and Japan – wage regimes are higher than in the UK. Nor is the management of much of British sport exempt from non-UK leadership, football and cricket being notable examples. In the media world, when the then director-general of the BBC wanted to top up his managerial skills, the business school in which he chose to do it was Harvard.

The unprepared professionals

With the number of business schools having risen to 120 by the late 1990s,[65] the body that described current management and business leadership development in the UK as dysfunctional concluded that the recent quantitative leap in management education had not resulted in the development of the kind of practical management and leadership skills most conducive to entrepreneurial-led economic growth. The government-appointed Council for Excellence in Management and Leadership's view was that business schools and other training providers were 'light on leadership development and, in general, insufficiently flexible to customise themselves to match organisations' or individuals' needs'. Conflictingly, it said that the MBA degree had 'succeeded as a qualification but has not necessarily developed future leaders'.[66] In fact the demand for MBA graduates fell by a fifth in the first half of the 1990s.[67]

Among its specific criticisms are the untrained state of the many individuals in the professions who exercise management responsibilities, with few professional associations having mandatory management and leadership specifications for membership. And much of the money spent on management training – both in the public and private sectors and in the professions – has little impact on outputs. It concedes that, overall, around 4.5 million individuals in the UK – about 14 per cent of the workforce – have significant management responsibilities, yet 36 per cent of enterprises report that their managers are not proficient,[68] a polite way of saying 'less than competent'. Some 140 000 new managers are required each year but at the current rate of progress only 20 per cent will achieve management qualifications, however useful.

Two cases in point are the nation's company directors, whose activities include the key decision-making role of originating strategy for private-sector companies, and human resource professionals, who are themselves usually responsible for others' skills development. For the former, George Cox, director-general of the Institute of Directors (IOD), is adamant: 'We feel that far too few directors in the past have been properly prepared for their entry into the boardroom and that too little has been done continuously to develop directors thereafter.'[69] This is despite a full range of around 40 IOD courses, including Board Decision Making, part of its Company Direction Programme, which is centred on standard problem-solving models applied to themes/issues, and Directing and Leading Change courses based on Harvard Business School Professor John Kotter and Kurt Lewin models. For the latter group, the verdict of its professional association, the Chartered Institute of Personnel and Development (CIPD), is that 'current management development practice is disconnected from the business challenges in many organisations'.[70] Like the IOD's efforts, this is despite efforts to promote various forms of learning through its research reports and its professional development activities advocating a form of experiential learning called the 'Thinking Performer' model. By their own admissions, both these examples unequivocally confirm that existing educational approaches are lacking. Either more has to be done or the advocated methodologies to enhance performance need to be improved.

Since these comments were made, business education continues to concern, with little apparent improvement. The view of *The Financial Times*, for example, is that the local MBA is of limited value.[71] Productivity – business instruction's bottom line – continues to languish while politicians, educationalists and industrialists carry on a never-ending debate about the system's shortcomings.

'World-class UK management researchers are as rare as world-class UK managers'

One such instructive volley that puts the whole problem into a cogent context surfaced in *The Observer* newspaper in 2002. One of its senior commentators, Simon Caulkin, pointed out that in 2001 more undergraduates studied business and management – 227 000 of them in fact – than any other subject. With the speciality accounting for 15 per cent of university activity, he asked the no-nonsense question: 'Why is British management so bad?' All those business graduates 'have not made the slightest dent in the UK's persistent 20–30 per cent productivity shortfall compared with rival countries'. Despite the runaway growth of business education, 'we still can't run a railway, telephone or a car company, or indeed any large-scale private enterprise outside oil and pharmaceuticals'.

He added, rather sadly:

We are notably inept at rejuvenating our national institutions, the wrecks of which clutter the landscape like decaying hulks. As for the public sector – let's just whisper 'NHS' and pass on in silence. It may be no coincidence that British theory is no better than its practice. World-class UK management researchers are as rare as world-class UK managers.[72]

Caulkin's particular complaint at the time was the poor quality of local business and management research. In particular, he turned on the Economic and Social Research Council (ESRC), the funding agency for management research, and the Research Assessment Exercise (RAE), the government's own audit process of academic research quality, quoting a business school head who didn't want to be named – 'The reason we're in the present mess is that the ESRC has failed to provide leadership in management education' – and one who didn't mind,Professor Leo Murray, head of Cranfield Management School – 'the RAE encourages mediocre research for research's sake rather than the creation of usable knowledge'.[73] His instructive criticism aside, he – like most business educators – bizarrely avoided mentioning the very discipline and business skill that could teach future businessmen how to proceed more effectively - namely the coupled fields of experiential learning and non-theoretical decision-making, to which I have already referred. Both areas are the stuff of reflective thinking on past experience, the blind spot of business teaching.

The aftermath of the Enron and other corporate scandals also illustrates how little the art of reflectiveness is even considered as a teaching tool. Many critics in fact attributed the events to business school teaching, saying that business schools do not adequately prepare people for the real world of management. Most vociferous was London Business School's Professor Sumantra Ghoshal, who said:

Business schools do not need to do a great deal more to help prevent future Enrons; they need only to stop doing a lot they currently do. They do not need to create new courses; they need to simply stop teaching some old ones. But, before doing any of this, business school faculties need to own up to their own role in creating Enrons.[74]

In Ghoshal's view, business schools have 'actively freed students from any sense of ethical responsibility'.

The importance of reflectiveness

Elsewhere, Professor Jonathan Gosling, director of the Centre for Leadership Studies at Exeter University, said that business schools have to shoulder their share of the blame for Enron and other ethical lapses. Business schools, he says, are guilty of teaching management as a purely technical subject. His next comment on how business ethics are taught also highlights the disregard of experiential learning as a teaching tool. The ability to reflect on these sorts of dilemmas, says Gosling, is vital but is often neglected. In his view, 'Reflectiveness is one of the more crucial elements in the MBA curriculum and people need the skills and vocabulary to be able to do this.'

Coincidentally, the neglect of both ethics and business history in the business school curriculum was pointed out just a year earlier by the *British Journal of Management*.[75] It said that there was a justification for adding both components to a fully relevant business education. When the two were combined, the result could be a highly rewarding combination that provided insights that might not otherwise be possible.

Across the Atlantic, Harvard's Professor Shoshana Zuboff also weighed in against business schools for 'the pandemic of corporate narcissism, greed, rigidity, and sheer cluelessness', likening the reaction of business schools laying on more ethics courses to 'ancient emperors fiddling while Rome burns',[76] a commentary that came after the conclusion from a management education task force of the Association to Advance Collegiate Schools of Business that the MBA curriculum was, indeed, out of step with business needs.[77] Their report also questioned the relevance of other business school courses.

So far as the British experience is concerned, it is noteworthy that, since Victorian times, the institutional choice in Britain has been to shift responsibility for technical training from the educational system to employers – in contrast to, for example, the German model.[78] Although this might suggest that the wider system would then be correspondingly better attuned to experiential learning, the actual record demonstrates the opposite. For much of the twentieth century on-the-job training compared badly with other developed countries, with the mainstay of any formalized experiential learning resting largely on the apprenticeship system that was discontinued round about the time when the flexible labour market was beginning to make inroads into traditional employment practices. Although the institutional view about apprenticeships seems to be reverting, the antipathy towards formal experiential learning continues – Lancaster University being a notable and rare exception.

The dearth of experiential learning

Only a handful of universities, for example, refer to one of the few formal methodologies known as 'action learning', among them Ashridge Management College, which offers a module in its Executive Education programme, Leeds Business School in its Masters Degree in

Company Direction and the University of Bradford as part of an engineering degree. An approach pioneered by Reg Revans in the early 1980s, action learning uses a skilled facilitator to impose a discipline of self-reflection and analysis on team members of individual projects. It is instructive to note that Revans' conceptual thinking is one of the few innovative ideas in management development to come out of the UK during the post-Second World War period, yet its application – like much of the UK's inventive energy – has been relocated elsewhere: Revans University – The University of Action Learning – was set up in Colorado, USA, to offer distance learning worldwide with another US organization, the International Management Centers Association (IMCA), as its sponsor.

There has been no shortage of latter-day attempts to identify and do something about the problems, the most recent initiative being the two-year study by the Council for Excellence in Management and Leadership (CEML).[79] Alongside this, the DTI funded a £17 million initiative through the ESRC called the Advanced Institute for Management. Plugging into this was Professor Porter's study to examine the effect of poor management on the UK's productivity.[80] In another project, a panel of business experts, in a joint DTI/DfES initiative has looked into the problem, all of which triggered the exasperated response by Petra Cook, head of policy at the Chartered Management Institute (CMI), that too much time is spent 'making the link between management and business performance rather then getting out there and doing things to improve performance'.[81]

A story of failure

Coincidentally – and ironically – a small band of Britain's academic business historians have been valiantly trying to introduce their subject into the education system for years. Had they been more successful, the evidential part of experiential learning – or at least part of the evidential package – could have been the launch pad for the wider-based subject. Their story also highlights the ongoing resistance to experiential learning by both the UK's academic and political establishment, as well as their limited vision of their subject's wider application.

The academics' efforts, which date back to the late 1970s, came about through two unconnected events involving two of Britain's best-known corporate figures at the time. The first was advice given by Sir Arthur Knight, chairman of Courtauld, to the vice-chancellor of Oxford University urging the need for a more multidisciplinary approach to business education through the introduction of corporate and business history. The second event concerned Pilkington Brothers, where Professor Theo Barker, one of the doyens of British business history, was working on a commissioned book for the St Helens-based glassmaker on the company's revolutionary float glass process. When it was completed, the company's lawyers became extremely distressed about its possible implications vis à vis American anti-trust laws. There were a number of important court cases pending in which the company was to defend its position worldwide on issues of know-how. Pilkington's lawyers decided that the company could not have a book put out into the public domain where every word and every date would be examined by other lawyers.

Somewhat embarrassed, Sir Alistair Pilkington, who had personally invented the float glass process, went back to Professor Barker and offered to finance a solicitor to help him fight a case against the company that his family had founded. Barker refused and suggested that the book remain on ice until a more opportune time. As a quid pro quo, Sir Alistair asked Professor Barker what else the company might do. He replied that business history had generally been ignored in the UK. Would Pilkington Brothers help get the concept established on a formal academic footing?

Pilkington donated £15 000 and launched an appeal to other businesspeople to set up the Business History Unit (BHU) at the London School of Economics. The sponsors hoped that the unit would eventually be subsumed into the university. On the back of a total £250 000 raised, the BHU was – coincidentally – established just as Mrs Thatcher's government was elected to office with a vision of popular capitalism. As the interest in business history grew among some academics and a few of the larger companies, Downing Street had strong hopes that the unit might make some contribution towards improving the quality of British management and even that it might, by example, further seed the efforts to cultivate the enterprise economy.[82] The academics hoped to shift the emphasis away from narrow-focus company history towards broader comparative studies.

Later that year the newly formed BHU tried to encourage the teaching of business history at a one-day conference on the subject. Like the academics' earlier effort at Cranfield School of Management, this, too, was largely a failure, with the delegates consisting mainly of the country's few fledgling business historians. Attendees remember the conference as mostly preaching to the converted.

With interest at postgraduate level almost non-existent, the next initiative was a top-level investigation into economic and business history teaching in the UK and the US. In 1980 the newly-appointed director of the BHU, Leslie Hannah, who was later to become the UK's first professor of Business History, was despatched to the US by the Social Science Research Council's (SSRC's) Economic and Social History Committee. His report, which highlighted a number of key differences between the UK and the US, suggested that if business history was to be adopted in UK business schools, the research undertaken would need to be modern, policy-oriented and theoretically based. To draw business historians into business schools, he recommended that the SSRC fund several post-doctoral fellowships to provide a model teaching post. The argument was that, once the appointments proved themselves, the universities could take over the funding themselves – in exactly the same way as, it was hoped, the LSE would assume financial responsibility for the BHU. In 1982 the SSRC agreed to fund two such posts at Bath University of Technology and the London Business School, where appointments were eventually made in 1983 and 1984 respectively. Like the other initiatives to introduce more business history into management education, the outcome of the SSRC's – now renamed ESRC – fellowships was also a failure. Neither post was made permanent, and both incumbents left their posts.

Since then, the BHU's pioneering efforts have had to contend with the government's financial strictures on all academic institutions, which has led to the withdrawal of promises of permanent funding. When the Unit ran short of funds in the late 1980s, Sir Alistair Pilkington personally injected a further £90 000 to keep it running. With its survival constantly in doubt, its output – both as a research and teaching body – continues to fall short of the vision of its industrial founders.

Over the years, the penetration of business history in UK universities has been minimal. For example, Manchester University, which was among the first UK educational institutions to introduce the subject, estimates that it exposed just 350 students to business history over a 20-year period to 1990.[83] In 1993 an Association of Business History (ABH) study nationwide found that no more than 1700 students, many of them unconnected with business studies, had *any* exposure to the subject. Across academia as a whole, there is a reported decline in interest in business history subject-matter among higher-degree students.

Grudge, friction and neglect

Business history's existence since then has continued to be grudgingly accepted by universities and business schools generally. Long-held frictions between business historians and both establishment academics and management educators have not been successfully bridged, nor has the difficult relationship between academic and non-academic corporate historians and even between economic historians and business historians.

Whilst there are more than a handful of economic historians who cross the divide into corporate and business history, the generic medium is still a reluctant bedfellow of its overlooked neighbour. Currently, US business historians, for example, are calling for a completely new relationship – what they call an 'interdisciplinary dialogue' – with their counterparts in the economic history world. In the journal *Business and Economic History*, three senior business historians suggested that, despite their very different interests, the two groups have much to gain from the exchange of ideas:

> *We are not calling for a hierarchical conception of scholarship that (Norman) Gay attempted to impose on (Edwin) Gras during the 1930s – we do not see business historians as research assistants for economists who engage in a higher level of thinking. Although we hope that a by-product of this dialogue will be better modelling by economists, our main concern is that the work of individual business historians rebound to the credit of the field of business history as a whole. The recent benefit of recent theoretical developments in economics is that they enable business historians to recognise the essential unity that underlies a great number of the problems with which they are concerned. As a result, studies on one topic can resonate with studies on others, strengthening them all and, in turn, the field as a whole.*[84]

This is a proposition that also got much earlier support in the UK, where Reading University's Professor Geoffrey Jones, said:

> *There is evidence, too, that economists and management theorists want and need the kind of empirical evidence generated by business historians. If business history is made accessible, readable and as intellectually challenging as the subject it describes, there will be no problem finding markets for its wares.'*[85]

The silence from economic history has been deafening, keeping corporate and business history in business education's instructional shadow.

Unlike analogous subjects (for example, politics, art, music, architecture, and, yes, economics), which sustain a healthy research/publishing/teaching base), business history is virtually unknown as an established historical discipline, with their professional reputations in many countries not extending beyond their small business history communities. Relatively few corporate and business histories are done, and their employment both in industry and business schools is studiously lacking in almost every country except the US.

This is exemplified by the attitude towards the official history of ICI, once one of the UK's biggest companies, which was written by a non-academic, the late Bill Reader, who is acknowledged as being one of the UK's finest modern corporate historians. In this work – described even by academic business historians as one of the best and most readable of the genre – there is an account of how individuals speculated massively against the company in the 1930s – a classic account of insider dealing.[86] According to Dr Richard Davenport-Hines, a former editor of the journal Business History: 'Nobody's ever cited it as an event ever since. No one knows about it because few have ever read the book. They can't have done because the documentation in the story that Reader got through is stunning.'[87] And when ICI responds to historical enquiries, it often hands out a commercially produced book entitled *ICI – The Company That Changed our Lives* rather than its official history. Reader once complained to an academic acquaintance that his one professional regret was that companies for which he wrote histories (also Bowater, Birds Eye Foods, Metal Box, the Weir Group and the City firm, Foster & Braithwaite) did not make use of his work in any imaginative way. This disappointment should also apply to the academic community which also resists using corporate and business history as a teaching tool.

A specific methodology to doing business history, or even the adaptation of any of the US approaches (for example, the Chandler model, a systematic and analytical approach which tracks forward from the past to the present and backward from the present to the past), is also glaringly absent. In the UK, for example, the first wider history of British business by an acknowledged academic business historian saw the light of day only in 1995.[88] Indeed, there is still no twentieth-century history of British management on the bookshelves. In fact, the first formal acknowledgement of business history as a core management subject occurred in Reading University's Research Assessment Exercise in 1996. The subject's tenuous embrace on education was reaffirmed when the recognition of business history as a separate subdiscipline under both History and Business and Management units of assessment (UoAs) was reversed after HEFCE (Higher Education Funding for England) dropped business history in 1999 and then reinstated it after successful lobbying from the Association of Business Historians. Disillusioned with the UK's attitude to the university system, Professor Geoffrey Jones, the university's business history stalwart, left for Harvard shortly thereafter.

Although regional research activity is noticeably much greater at the UK's only permanently funded business history centre at the University of Glasgow's Economic History Department, applied teaching from this source – as well as any other – is also still a rare commodity.

Needed – another look at business education

Against this background, how can business instruction be better constructed? On the existing evidence, the business of teaching business needs to be fundamentally re-evaluated (yet again) based on several unequivocal pointers that emerge from the available evidence, and which have not been sufficiently acknowledged in prior reviews.

On the basis of the fact that few entrepeneurs have a university background, it would be clearly more prudent to direct many more resources into the non-tertiary sector, which would necessarily dictate a completely different way of teaching the business of business. And given the shortcomings elsewhere in the system, it would be sensible to re-evaluate how business should be taught right across the educational spectrum.

Like business school education in many parts of the world, management instruction is renowned for its resolute concentration on theory whilst paying only lip service to the empirical. On the rare occasions educators *do* use, for example, corporate and/or business history, the motivation is usually to validate management theory. As a rule – and as the record shows – this approach tends to produce managers who are less practical than they might otherwise be, an observation highlighted in the UK at least by *The Financial Times*'s observation that curricula are still not providing business graduates with commercial awareness.[89] What is needed are more *functional* managers who learn from real experience, with theory occupying a supporting role, and this requires a shift towards an educational teaching policy that incorporates real experience and existent organizational memory, authentic practice, bone fide procedure, even corporate and business history.

In this fundamental reassessment, the value of experience, otherwise known as organizational memory or plain old business history, should be clearly emphasized. Whether the experience has been of failure or success, it is an important intellectual asset for individuals, organizations and the nation, as evidenced by the uncomplicated fact that organizations pay people *with it* more than those *without it*. Pass experience on – and one doesn't have to reinvent it. Learn from experience and decision-making becomes automatically better. On that basis alone, experiential learning – a plainly visible oversight in the learning package – is surely the midwife to a better bottom line.

It might be thought that education, by its nature, would be able to learn from its own experience but, ironically, educational reassessments of traditional practices are tortuously resistant to change, whether they be in business or elsewhere in institutional education. Despite apparently overwhelming evidence that better teaching processes exist, prevailing values seem to be continually reinforced.[90] Dr Mark Smith expresses it succinctly: 'For all the talk of learning amongst educational policymakers and practitioners, there is a surprising lack of attention to what it entails.' Theories of learning, he declares, do not figure strongly in professional education programmes for teachers and those within different arenas of informal education:

Get the instructional regime right, the message seems to be, and learning (as measured by tests and assessment regimes) will follow. This lack of attention to the nature of learning inevitably leads to an impoverishment of education. It isn't simply that the process is less effective as a result, but what passes for education can actually diminish well-being.[91]

Yet, the noticeable omissions to existing business instruction aside, there is a much more compelling reason to re-evaluate the way in which the subject is taught. It is all to do with that small thing called 'productivity' to which I've already referred.

Notes

1. Eric Hoffer, *Reflections on the Human Condition*, New York: HarperCollins, 1973.
2. Claudia Bird Schoonhoven and Elaine Romanelli (eds), *The Entrepreneurship Dynamic: Origins of Entrepreneurship and the Evolution of Industries*, Stanford, CA: Stanford University Press, 2001.
3. *Understanding Industry*, research study into attitudes towards industry, University of Derby's Centre for Applied Social and Organizational Research.
4. 'Unskilled in the Way of Business', *Financial Times*, 29 April 1998.
5. HM Treasury, letter to author, 26 June 2001, referring to 1998 figures.
6. Dun & Bradstreet research, 1992.
7. John Hunt and Stephen Downing, *The Human Factor*, London Business School research study, 1991.
8. *Financial Times*, 3 May 1993.
9. Economist Intelligence Unit study, *Making Acquisitions Work*, reported in *Financial Times*, 26 January 1996.
10. *Unlocking Shareholder Value: The Key to Success*, KPMG, 2001.
11. *Acquisitions Monthly*, 20 December 1996.

12. *Chicago Tribune*, 25 May 1916.
13. A.M. de Lange, Faculty of Science, University of Pretoria, South Africa, 13 June 2003 at http://www.learning-org.com.
14. Ibid.
15. Ibid., 5 March 2004.
16. A.N. Whitehead, *The Aims of Education and Other Essays*, London, 1929, pp. 139–40, cited by A.M. de Lange, ibid.
17. Ibid.
18. S. Crainer and D. Dearlove, *Gravy Training: Inside the Business of Business Schools*, San Francisco: Jossey-Bass, 1999.
19. Professor Stephen Watson, Principal, Henley Management College, in Council for Excellence in Management and Leadership, *Final Report*, London: CEML, 13 May 2002.
20. Jeffrey Pfeffer and Christina T. Fong, 'The End of Business Schools? Less Success Than Meets the Eye', *Academy of Management Learning & Education*, September 2002.
21. Interview, *The Times*, 26 April 2004.
22. H. Mintzberg and J. Lampel, 'Matter of Degrees: Do MBAs Make Better CEOs?', *Fortune*, 19 February 2001.
23. Gary Hamel in Crainer and Dearlove, *Gravy Training*, op. cit.
24. H.J. Leavitt, 'Educating Our MBAs: On Teaching What We Haven't Taught', *California Management Review*, 1989.
25. Quoted in P.O. Gaddis, 'Business Schools: Fighting the Enemy Within', *Strategy and Business*, 2000.
26. Quoted in ibid.
27. J. Bailey and C. Ford, 'Management as Science versus Management as Practice in Postgraduate Business Education', *Business Strategy Review*, 1996.
28. J.S. Armstrong, 'The Devil's Advocate Responds to an MBA Student's Claim that Research Harms Learning', *Journal of Marketing*, 1995.
29. J. Fisk and R. Barron, *The Official MBA Handbook of Great Business Quotations*, New York: Simon & Schuster, 1984.
30. Jeffrey Pfeffer and Christina Fong, 'The End of Business Schools?, op. cit.
31. Ibid.
32. *Financial Times*, 5 March 1997.
33. Professor Michael Porter, Institute of Personnel Development annual training conference, March 1996.
34. *The Daily Telegraph*, 11 November 1987.
35. *The Times*, 21 March 1986.
36. *The Observer*, 6 October 1985.
37. F.H. Norris, 'The Crimson Crop is Plenty Green', *New York Times*, 2 January 1997.
38. D. Leonhardt, 'A Matter of Degree? Not for Consultants', *New York Times*, 1 October 2000.
39. Ibid.
40. R. Lieber, 'Learning and Change: Roger Martin', *Fast Company*, December 1999.
41. H. Mintzberg and J. Lampel, 'Matter of Degrees: Do MBAs Make Better CEOs?', *Fortune*, 19 February 2001.
42. J.L Zimmerman, 'Can American Business Schools Survive?', unpublished MS, Rochester, NY: Simon Graduate School of Business Administration, 2001.
43. Ibid., quoting 1959 Gordon and Howell report.
44. Bailey and Ford, 'Management as Science versus Management as Practice', op. cit.
45. L.W. Porter and L.E. McKibbin, *Management Education and Development: Drift or Thrust into the 21st Century*, New York: McGraw-Hill, 1988.
46. H.J. Leavitt, *Corporate Pathfinders*, Homewood, IL: Dow-Jones-Irwin, 1986.
47. P. Robinson, *Snapshots from Hell*, New York: Warner Books, 1994.
48. S. Godin, 'Change Agent', *Fast Company*, September 2000.
49. S. Davis and J. Botkin, J., *The Monster under the Bed: How Business is Mastering the Opportunity of Knowledge for Profit*, New York: Simon & Schuster, 1994.
50. Porter and McKibbin, *Management Education and Development*, op. cit.
51. R.L. Jenkins and R.C. Reizenstein, 'Insights into the MBA: Its Contents, Output, and Relevance', *Industrial Relations Research Association 36th Annual Proceedings*, 1984, pp. 1–13.
52. H. Mintzberg and J.R. Gosling, 'Reality Programming for MBAs', *Strategy and Business*, 2002.
53. Mintzberg and Lampel, 'Matter of Degrees', op. cit.

54. Bailey and Ford, 'Management as Science versus Management as Practice', op. cit.
55. Leavitt, 'Educating our MBAs', op. cit.
56. Interview with Henry Mintzberg, *New Zealand Management*, June 2003.
57. Joanna Workman, 'The MBA in Britain', paper presented at the British Association of Management Conference, September 2003.
58. Advisory Panel on Management Education, *Business School Programmes. The Requirements of British Manufacturing Industry*, London: British Institute of Management and Council of Industry for Management Education, 1971.
59. Charles Handy, *The Making of Managers. A Report on Management Education, Training and Development in the USA, West Germany, France, Japan and the UK*, London: National Economic Development Office, 1987; and John Constable and Roger McCormick, *The Making of British Managers: A Report for the BIM and CBI into Management Training, Education and Development*, Corby: British Institute of Management, April, 1987.
60. Her Majesty's Inspectorate, 1992.
61. D.A. Kolb, 'Management and the Learning Process', *California Management Review*, 1976.
62. 'The 2002 Global 500: The World's Largest Corporations', *Fortune*, 22 July 2002.
63. *Companies: 'The International Who's Who'*, Thompson Datastream, 2004. In 2002, BA was being run by an Australian, Marks & Spencer by a Belgian, Barclays by an Irish Canadian, Bank of Scotland by a Kenyan educated in the US, the Dome by a Frenchman, Pearson, Siebe, London Transport, Go and Covent Garden by Americans, Safeway's UK operation by an Argentinean and Selfridges by an Italian. An American, a Dutchman and Kenyan-born Asian help to set Britain's interest rates. By 2004, Frenchmen were running Glaxo SmithKline and the Anglo-Dutch Unilever, an Indian was running Vodafone, Americans were running Cadbury-Schweppes and other pure-bred native institutions like English Heritage and the Royal College of Nursing, as well as the bid by London to host the 2012 Olympic Games.
64. Annual statistical review of the legal profession, *The Lawyer*, September 2003.
65. *The Economist*, 1996.
66. Council for Excellence in Management and Leadership, *Final Report*, op. cit.
67. *The Economist*, 1996.
68. Council for Excellence in Management and Leadership, *Final Report*, op. cit.
69. Correspondence with author, 2 June 2003.
70. *Developing Managers for Business Performance*, survey, Chartered Institute of Personnel and Development, September 2002.
71. *Working Capital. Intangible Assets and the Productivity Gap*, London: The Work Foundation, 2002.
72. 'A Mess in Theory – A Mess in Practice', *The Observer*, 13 January 2002.
73. Ibid.
74. Times Online, 2 October 2003.
75. R. Warren and G. Tweedale, 'Business Ethics and Business History: Neglected Dimensions in Management Education', *British Journal of Management*, 2002.
76. Quoted in 'MBAs Deny Link to Climate of Corruption', *The Times*, 2 October 2003.
77. *Management Education at Risk*, Management Education Task Force, Association to Advance Collegiate Schools of Business, 2 August 2003.
78. Michael Sanderson, *Education and Economic Decline in Britain*, New York: Cambridge University Press, 1999.
79. Ended May 2002.
80. M.E. Porter and C.H.M. Ketels, *UK Competitiveness: Moving to the Next Stage*, DTI Economics Paper No. 3, May 2003.
81. *Sunday Telegraph*, 24 November 2002.
82. *Business History Newsletter*, 1986.
83. Author research.
84. N.R. Lamoreaux, D.M.G. Raff and P. Temin, 'New Economic Approaches to the Study of Business History', *Business and Economic History*, vol. 26, no. 1, Fall 1997.
85. *Business History Newsletter*, October 1986.
86. Bill Reader, 'Dictatorship in the '30s, Barons Revolt', in *Imperial Chemical Industries: A History*, London: Oxford University Press, 1970, 1975.
87. Interview with author, October 1997.
88. J. Wilson, *British Business History 1720–1994*, Manchester: Manchester University Press, 1995.
89. 'Unskilled in the Way of Business', *Financial Times*, 29 April 1998.

90. R. Havelock and S. Zlotolow, *The Change Agent's Guide* (2nd edn), Englewood Cliffs, NJ: Educational Technology Publications, 1995.

91. M.K. Smith, 'Learning Theory', *Encyclopaedia of Informal Education*, 1999, 2003, 2005 at www.infed.org/biblio/b-learn.htm. Dr Smith specializes in the field of informal education and lifelong learning. He is the Rank Research Fellow and Tutor at YMCA George Williams College, London and Visiting Professor in Community Education, University of Strathclyde, Glasgow.

4 Productivity – The New Corporate Imperative

The disadvantage of men not knowing the past is that they do not know the present. History is a hill or high point of vantage, from which alone men see the town in which they live or the age in which they are living.

Anne Brontë, English novelist and poet[1]

Of all the business skills, the most important is decision-making. On it depends everything – from product quality to profitability and even continued organizational existence. Nevertheless, within this chain of interrelated links, there is one key building block without which organizations don't get very far. This is productivity, the ultimate measure of efficiency and, through it, the most important source of sustained growth for businesses and, in turn, the host country's wealth and survival. In business terms it is the rate at which goods or services are produced.

Productivity is usually expressed in terms of output per unit of labour, giving the impression that labour is the predominant factor in productivity's performance. In fact, of all the statistics that organizations use to evaluate their performance – from gross margins, return on capital employed to market share – productivity is probably the most accurate indicator of policy-making and decision-making skills. As such, its computation is more a gauge of management than just labour. I've often mischievously suggested that it should be expressed in terms of output per unit of *management*.

How productivity is calculated

Productivity is calculated in a number of ways, not all of them straightforward. For national productivity statistics, one formula is to take an estimate of aggregate output such as real gross domestic product (GDP) – the total unduplicated value of economic goods and services originating within the boundaries of a country – and divide it by the number of workers or the number of hours worked. These estimates are often described as 'labour productivity', a computation muddied by issues such as national working hours, numbers in employment and strike rates. Using this form of calculation, it is tempting to conclude that productivity is automatically enhanced if working hours are increased, more people are employed or work stoppages reduced. Not necessarily. The British work the longest hours in Europe,[2] yet Britain's productivity falls substantially below many of its competitors in Europe and North America.

A second formula uses a more comprehensive definition of inputs into the production process; the result is referred to as multifactor, or total-factor, productivity. The statistic is estimated by dividing the product of a broad sector by an input index that is a weighted average of two indexes, one of labour inputs and the other of capital inputs. The former – a quality-adjusted labour index – is a calculation of a weighted average of employee-hours for several groups of workers defined by sex, level of education and experience while the capital input index is a weighted average of capital services from many different categories of structures, equipment, inventories and land.

Many economists construct their own numbers. In the GDP-divided-by-population formula, employment or employee-hours are sometimes used instead of population. In calculating estimates of multifactor productivity, some analysts also distinguish between skilled and unskilled labour or between privately-owned and government-owned physical capital. At the industry level, estimates are often constructed from figures representing value added rather than gross output.

The simplest formula

But productivity's most straightforward measure, at least at the individual company or organizational level, is probably the more simple calculation of dividing sales or operating budgets by employee head-count on a departmental, regional or group basis. On its own, the number is meaningless. It only becomes helpful if the calculation is compared with prior data, and it becomes even more valuable if it is measured against the organization's competitors. A lower comparison, for example, means that the organization's contenders are doing the same thing more effectively and/or more cheaply. When a rival is more competitive, an organization's durability, and even survival, is threatened.

Although this statement may seem obvious, its importance as an appraisal of accomplishment cannot be underestimated, a view endorsed by management guru Peter Drucker's vision of its urgency,[3] which I've recalled in the Introduction. For most, Drucker's observation carries a curious misunderstanding of productivity's attainment that can be seen in the responses of many businesses and, in particular, governments in the provision of public services. To them, improved productivity is mostly directly related either to cutbacks, usually in the form of redundancies, or to the provision of more working capital or higher budgets. Unfortunately, the relationship of productivity to both these approaches is tenuous without the ability to do the same things more efficiently. Without efficiency the result is just higher-than-needed levels of capital or lower-than-necessary levels of service.

In the quest for productivity, many governments see their wider role as improving the macro-environment for business – for example, by giving business more agreeable tax incentives, reducing red tape or providing improved training facilities. These measures are clearly expedient but it is in the micro-environment – the activities of organizations themselves and the individuals within them – that productivity's main potential resides. This is a view endorsed by Drucker's notion that it is managers, not nature, economic laws or governments, that make resources productive and confirmed by McKinsey Global Institute (MGI), whose research into the manufacturing sector shows a strong correlation between national productivity rankings and management practices.[4]

Productivity down the years

Looking at the longer term, productivity's past performance has been uneven across both countries and industries. The UK held the top slot for most of the nineteenth century with an annual productivity growth rate of 1.2 per cent from 1820 to 1890.[5] In the twentieth century, the laurels went to the US, with an annual growth rate of 2 per cent from 1913 to 1989. From 1950 to 1973 it was Japan's turn; its productivity increased by a factor of almost six, which resulted in an 8 per cent annual rate of productivity growth. But it is perhaps Ireland that has been the most impressive and consistent performer from the lowest base over the longest period of time; over the last four decades its productivity growth has averaged an impressive 3.4 per cent per year, closing the productivity gap with the US from 37 per cent to 89 per cent in 2003 (see Appendix 4). When compared with the US over the same period, the other most improved OECD countries have been Australia (from 68 per cent to 78 per cent), France (64 per cent to 86 per cent), Germany (60 per cent to 71 per cent), Italy (from 54 per cent to 75 per cent), Japan (from 34 per cent to 71 per cent), Spain (from 35 per cent to 65 per cent) and the UK (59 per cent to 74 per cent), all of which have been losing ground since 2003. The worst performer is New Zealand, its productivity gap widening in three shallow waves from 80 per cent in 1965 to 58 per cent in 2003, with Holland's divergence against the US virtually unchanged at 70 per cent and now static.

On both competitiveness and productivity growth,[6] the average EU economy receives worse ratings than the US and the group of other OECD economies in every area bar social inclusion. As a general rule, weak and mediocre performance is country-specific while high performance is issue- or organization-specific, a picture that bears out the added advantage of the management-led approach to productivity. In the global picture, industries like manufacturing, farming, mining, construction and transportation have shown an annual increase in wealth of 3–4 per cent – a 45-fold expansion overall[7] – over the last 100 years. Because of the relationship between productivity and wealth, some would claim this to be impressive; others – me included – would not.

The enormous potential still in hand

For a world that has seen man fly, split the atom, walk on the moon, reproduce in a test tube and even clone animals, the wastage of resources by low-productivity activity is still incalculably enormous, suggesting that there must be very many opportunities for doing things better and cheaper. In fact, my historian's view is that productivity's potential has hardly been scratched – an opinion that tomorrow's history will no doubt confirm in exactly the same way as today's history points out yesterday's immeasurable inefficiencies.

Although ongoing productivity increases are still being achieved, my concern is not just with the veiled day-to-day waste of resources but also with the even less visible aspect of this central component of wealth, productivity's intrinsic growth. The conventional way of thinking is that so long as productivity is evident, everything is fine and dandy. But what happens when productivity growth, the ability of businesses to keep on upping the ante, hits the buffers? I call it industry's Maginot Line after the Second World War fortifications erected on the eastern border of France by André Maginot, Minister of War. It was considered impregnable but easily flanked by the Germans in 1940. As Figure I.1 (p. 2) and Appendix 1 show, in reality the post-Second World War cycle of productivity growth is coming to an end. To use a railway analogy, the train is running at less than a quarter of the rate it did in the 1950s. The US, the first-class ticket-holder, is travelling at slightly more than half the pace, with almost all the second-class ticket-holders at crawler speed, while Luxembourg, Italy, Holland, Switzerland and Spain are already in reverse gear. This is the first time in modern industrial history that the momentum has reversed among so many developed economies at the same time and with so many others in stalling mode. In the Introduction I suggested what will happen when the train stops moving forward.

Ironically, the situation is more serious for the more productive countries. However bad, for example, are Zimbabwe's decision-making skills and productivity, its prospects for improvement are still huge. In contrast, many of the more productive countries may have the edge at the moment, but without productivity *growth*, there's no forward potential. I think that my schooldays instructor in boxing had a point when he tried to reassure me that the bigger my opponents were, the harder they would fall. What we have to do is find a way of rolling with the incoming punch, at least until the inherent advantages of nanotechnology and genetics – or something else – are realized.

The history of productivity

The effort to produce products and services more efficiently can be traced back to a young American industrial engineer called Frederick Winslow Taylor who developed the system that became known as the time and motion study. When he became foreman of a steel-making company in 1878, he developed detailed systems to determine the best methods for performing tasks in the least amount of time. The systems involved minute analysis of actions to reduce production time and raise output from workers and machines.[8] It was Taylor who first coined the terms 'scientific management' and 'working smarter', which are still in use today. His work was later refined by Frank and Lillian Gilbreth who developed more systematic and sophisticated methods that took account of human physical and mental capacities and physical environments, and, later, by Harvard's Elton Mayo, whose work in the electrical industry later came to be called 'human relations'.

Their approaches, which were mainly top-down – that is, manufacturing workers were *told* how to make improvements – took a quantum leap after the Second World War when it was realized that workers themselves might have views on how their productivity could be improved. Out of these collaborative approaches came new methodologies such as total quality management (TQM), quality circles and Douglas McGregor's 'Theory X' and 'Theory Y', all imposed on the back of the other stimuli to productivity – capital, new technology and job-cutting.

But, as pointed out earlier, the gains that industry has been experiencing are now coming to an end as fewer and fewer employees are employed in making and moving things,[9] their non-manufacturing occupations now being classified as 'knowledge' or 'service' work.

Over the 30 years while this has been happening, the cost of almost all employees (except management) has always been considered too high. Hence the deliberate shift to technological alternatives to production. The trouble with this move was that the reallocation of resources from labour to technology was illusory in many industry sectors due, no doubt, to underlying social and political considerations led by demand because of social and political pressures which demanded lower employment as well as increased demand. With employment being kept higher than anticipated, wages continued to rise, often in excess of inflation and, in many cases, out of step with productivity. Consequently, the effect has not been to diminish the relative weight of labour in the production computation; instead, labour continues to be a key factor – often the most important constituent – in the modern workplace. Yet, although most organizations know this, they still only pay lip service to its importance.

The arrival of hire'n'fire

Alongside the rapidly changing profile of the workforce came the arrival of flexible working in the 1970s to disrupt job continuity and dispose of OM. The significance of the new work model can be illustrated by figures that reveal that Britain's top 12 companies – from BT to Racal Electronics and Pilkington – cut their workforces by an average 44 per cent between 1990 and 1995,[10] a rate of attrition that was largely matched by much of the rest of industry during the same period. W.H. Smith, for example, cut its staff by 30 per cent in 1993 alone.[11] In many City of London companies, employees stay just four years on average. A three-year study published in 2005 found that annual teacher turnover rates in British secondary schools were as high as 40 per cent while 160 primary schools had staff churns of 100 per cent; in one case, a London primary replaced its entire staff, only to see their successors all leave within 12 months.[12] In a poll of 25 companies across the UK, just 16 per cent of managers had been with their current employer for more than six years.[13]

Job churn 'above recognized danger levels'

Even though the widespread perception persists that the flexible labour market is wholly beneficial, the rate at which old employees leave and new ones arrive is now above recognized danger levels in many industry sectors, including wholesale/retail, finance, textiles, chemicals, tourism, health, advertising/marketing and IT, and some industrialists are beginning to question the wisdom of this seemingly unstoppable trend.

By the mid-1990s the American Management Association found that cutting the labour force failed to improve product quality in most companies.[14] Furthermore, less than half the companies that had cut jobs since 1990 had seen a rise in profitability. In fact a number of companies that refused to downsize during the 1993–96 wave – among them Gillette, Hewlett-Packard, United Airlines and Ford Motor Corporation – all showed significant stock price appreciation relative to the rest of their industry.[15] Shortly afterwards, the man who first touted downsizing as a way of improving productivity – Stephen Roach, Morgan Stanley's chief economist – reversed his opinion, saying that the tactics of open-ended downsizing was a 'recipe for industrial extinction'.[16] In the UK, organizations such as the Institute for Personnel and Development were reporting that too many companies were unable to differentiate 'fat' from 'muscle' and that companies were generating workforces unable and unwilling to make the most of new opportunities as they arise.[17] This was a perspective supported by Martin Bangemann, the EU's industry commissioner, who endorsed the Pacific Basin approach that more stable workforces improve company competitiveness in the long run.[18] Paradoxically, it is a view that is not supported by wider EU policy, which prefers to encourage the 'flexibility' of short job tenure at the expense of productivity and competitiveness. Several years later, researchers at the University of Auckland Business School found that even a 10 per cent labour turnover per year was likely to affect an organization's productivity.[19]

Some European countries have responded with a so-called downsizing tax.[20] In France, for example, any company that fires over 40 workers must file in writing with the labour department, pay hefty severance fees, lose exemption from many payroll taxes, contribute to an unemployment fund and submit a plan to the government outlining how it will retrain its displaced employees for future employment. Many companies also find themselves out of favour when bidding for government contracts. Elsewhere, whilst lonely industrialists such as Sir Christopher Gent, a former chief executive of Vodafone, may also have recognized that productivity is the key to growth,[21] improving yields are not yet generally perceived as being a big enough issue among companies and countries, with high labour turnover still being the preferred option.

Redundancy and the inability to grow

Just one example of how high staff turnover makes it difficult to innovate and grow can be found at ICI, once Britain's largest company, where corporate downsizing resulted in a cut in head office staff from 1200 in 1976 to just 240 in 1996. It was a rationalization that eventually cut the top executive team to just four executive directors. A senior manager admitted shortly afterwards that the smaller head office function had made it extremely difficult to 'seed' new markets.[22] The company also found it difficult to present to potential clients a suitably qualified employee of the expected seniority. Seven years and three chief executives later, the 77-year-old company, whose executive team had by now been upsized, was issuing a low profits warning, thanks to shrinking market share, loose cost control and customer misgivings. The outgoing boss, who had joined the company five years previously, gave the following telling – and brazen – explanation: 'The changes made in ICI were absolutely the right thing to do. What we have with some people are fractured customer relationships … . This is a problem, not a crisis.'[23] The company, a constituent of the original pre-Second World War FT30 list of blue chips, was facing possible eviction from the broader FTSE100 Index. Just weeks after the new chief executive took over, the company was announcing major employee cutbacks in its biggest earner – the Dulux paints division – in the first phase of another radical shake-up.[24] It was a decision that also preceded the appointment of a new chairman, whose first pronouncement was that he would spend six months 'getting to know the company'.[25] Regrettably, no up-to-date history of the company exists. If it did, he could have been up and running within weeks. It would be interesting to learn whether or not anyone suggested he read Bill Reader's 1975 work or its later, more abbreviated, 'commercial' version.

Rewarding failure – and its justification

Paradoxically, the decisions of each of the last three ICI chief executives earned them handsome exit payments, a characteristic evident throughout industry which consistently rewards poor decision-making.[26] Other examples selected over a relatively short period of time include senior executives from the communications company Telewest, retail group Kingfisher, insurance company Prudential, supermarkets group J. Sainsbury and, over in South Africa, the banking group Nedcor. Even politicians encourage the discounting of good decision-making by rewarding failure – witness Prime Minister Tony Blair's 2004 New Year Honours to the bosses of discredited government agencies.

In all of the debate about high reward and failure, it is interesting to gauge the mindset of many managers, whose salaries are often the decision of remuneration committees run by fellow managers. Ahead of the decision to award large additional handouts to senior managers of the UK's dysfunctional Network Rail in 2004, Ian McAllister, the company's chairman, argued that a decision not to pay bonuses would indicate that the board lacked faith in senior management and would send a message to the outside world that the company was failing.[27] On the other hand, Jim Cornell, the chairman of the company's remuneration committee, insisted that bonuses should be paid to the executives only when performance targets had been hit. McAllister's view won the day.

Instead of serving to buttress the organization, the tidal flow of experience within individual companies is taking no prisoners, with longevity and/or size no longer giving businesses much experiential advantage. In today's fast-moving world, businesses can dominate one day go under very soon thereafter. Alongside ICI and Telewest are companies like Invensys, which was formed from the merger of front-runners Siebe and BTR, Corus, the former British Steel, Marconi, previously the mighty GEC, and Cable & Wireless, the one-time thrusting telecoms group – to name but a few. Indeed, an inspection of the top 100 companies in any of the main industrial countries even a decade ago will look very different to the list of today.

World ranking in staff turnover

The US heads the world discontinuity league[28] (see Table 2.2, p. 40), followed by Denmark, the UK, Holland, Spain, Ireland and Finland. Since these rankings were published in 1998, overall job tenure has further declined – in some geographical areas, quite markedly. In the UK, for example, the number of different employers that new entrants to the labour market will have over their average 44-year working lifetime is put at 11,[29] giving organizations a typical four-year tenure for their employees; this is confirmed by research from the Chartered Institute of Personnel and Development (CIPD) in 2001 that overall labour turnover is 25 per cent on a year-on-year basis. This churn is equally evident in the boardroom. The average tenure of chief executive officers in British blue chip companies is just 4.6 years.[30] More than a third of CEOs are in office fewer than two years and a further 30 per cent leave the boardroom within four years. Just one in ten stays for a decade or more.

For confirmation of the relationship between higher staff turnover and lower productivity, one can turn to the Japanese experience. Historically, Japan has had a low staff churn (in fact, the industrialized world's lowest) with a productivity to rival that of the US – until the early 1990s that is. Since then, its employee turnover has risen in tandem with its recession, albeit not as rapidly as employee turnover in prior recessions in Western countries. Nevertheless, Japan's productivity has fallen away to the point where it now ranks just below the UK's, with my part explanation of its woes being that it is not as good at experiential learning as previously.

The US: an exception to the rule

Although this diminished ability to benefit from hindsight illustrates the relationship between employee turnover and productivity, the US experience is the clear exception. The US has the developed world's highest rate of employee turnover, which would, using my thesis, suggest a low level of productivity. In fact its productivity outranks all, with the explanation for this paradoxically endorsing the wider and more important direct liaison between legacy and the ability to benefit from hindsight. In short, American managers are better equipped to be experiential learners for a variety of very pertinent reasons.

Uniquely, the US has been formally providing successive generations with a business inheritance since the 1920s, when both corporate and business history were first recognized as separate scholarly disciplines. Pioneered at Harvard Business School, where the well-known preoccupation with the practical study of change is focused on putting business in its historical context, business history has been one of business students' most popular curriculum options for at least a decade and is a compulsory component of all first-year teaching. There is a dedicated core community of around 400 academic business historians across the country. The subject is considered important enough to be a separate functional division of America's Academy of Management.

Further evidence of the value of providing an inheritance can be seen in the related science sector, which is the world's leader in its field. The broader-based history of science was also acknowledged as an independent discipline in the 1920s. Alongside the enormous number of US-produced books now available on the history of science, there are more than 60 American universities offering dedicated higher degrees in the history of science, technology and medicine. In addition, many colleges offer a concentration in history of science at the undergraduate level. More than 70 years after its importance was first recognized, the History of Science Society, which promotes US teaching in the field, describes the subject as a bridging discipline that involves exposing students to more than the technical skills and theories of the natural sciences. It takes the view that scientific literacy is a necessity in a culture pervaded by scientific values and crucially dependent on the applications of scientific knowledge – 'one that students, parents, educators, and political leaders in the US all demand'.[31]

This formalized attitude towards the provision of a business inheritance contrasts with the situation in almost every other industrialized country except Japan, whose interest in business history was triggered in the early 1970s when, on the instructions of the then Crown Prince, a business historian was appointed to every faculty of business and commerce in the country.[32] Today, Japan's core community of business historians equals the numbers in the US. In contrast, the UK supports just four professors of business history (by the early 2000s, one had left Britain for Harvard and another for the University of Tokyo) within an academic community of around 40, with the use of corporate and/or business history in the business curriculum virtually unknown. British companies also make little effort to pass down their knowledge and experiences from one generation to another.

Alongside the formalized endeavour to provide continuing generations with a business legacy, US society nurtures and values the enterprise ethic, which also gives individuals a much more responsive attitude to experiential learning. In addition, Americans talk among themselves about business and money more than most other national groups, a characteristic that annoys many other population groups. This is not an insignificant factor. In Britain, for example, discussing work in the home environment is considered less than polite, a distinguishing national trait that Richard Branson, the Virgin CEO, mentions in his autobiography as being unhelpful. When the practice of business is not common conversational currency, there is automatically less scope for learning from experience.

Finally, there is the immigration factor. The US has an exceptionally high proportion of immigrants. Because immigrants feel inherently insecure in the unfamiliar environment, they have an additional incentive to learn.

Nevertheless, this explanation is not to suggest that US organizations are immune from poor decision-making; only that their decision-making skills are comparatively better than anyone else's.

The other agents of OM dispersal

In the wider world, the changing profile of workers and the flexible labour market are not the only factors to affect organizational decision-making capabilities and workplace productivity. Three others are inherent short and selective memory recall, and the attribute known as defensive reasoning. Although short-stay workers have a huge impact on short- and long-term organizational memory these two aspects apply in general, although not exclusively, to longer-term employees.

Short and selective memory recall

In respect of short and selective memory recall, Harvard scholar Alan Kantrow observes that 'When we go to work, we forget.' To Kantrow, managers' choices and actions may find a ready place in memory but the reasons and the intended significance of their deeds quickly float away out of reach and beyond recall. He observes that, while all organizations have some form of recall, their memory is frequently inaccurate:

The style of a business presentation, the kinds of evidence that tend to sway decisions, the shared sense of what constitutes relevant information about a new market or product, the deep-seated visceral preference for certain lines of business – all these characteristics, and a thousand others like them, are the subtle products of memory. In no two organizations are they exactly the same, nor in any two parts of the same organization. Intuitively we know this. But on the job we usually disregard it. In particular individuals forget both the density and duration of the activity underlying the surface facts. We forget that, like an iceberg, nine tenths of the mass lies hidden, well below the normal waterline of vision. And we forget that the part we can see is not just 'there' but is very much something built, something constructed or pieced together over time.[33]

How this forgetting extends to the corporate level is corroborated by international management consultants McKinsey & Co., who observed in the context of one business area:

Companies without practical mechanisms to 'remember' what worked and what didn't in the past are doomed to repeat failures and rediscover successes time and time again. As the industrial battles of the past decade have shown, competitive success often rests on world-class manufacturing – and that, in turn, on engineering capability. All too often, however, that capability is both poorly leveraged and poorly maintained. Companies regularly 'forget' what they have learned in earlier generations of product design. Worse, they do not organise to build, capture, or make easily accessible their hard-won store of engineering expertise.[34]

An example that goes back many years is recalled by Australian academic Alan Cotterell,[35] who was responsible for introducing the first process specifications into a local defence manufacturer, where he worked for 13 years during the 1970s and 1980s. In one particular year, 11 foremen with an average 35 years tenure each retired. 'How much knowledge do you think left with them?' asked Cotterell. Between them, they led a 900-strong workforce. During the Second World War many had been in charge of engineering workshops but were told that they had to accept qualified engineers into the shops. As a result, many of them became little more than progress checkers but, nevertheless, were theoretically in charge. The factory, Cotterell recalls, was effectively managed to extinction by 1989.

A more recent example of the effects of lost memory is Cordiant, the former Saatchi & Saatchi advertising agency that, at one time, was capitalized at £1.6 billion. Less than a decade after the bitter ejection of Maurice Saatchi, who founded the company with his brother Charles, it was on the auctioneer's block after two years of loss-making. The reason? The new managers, whose instructions were to cut costs, forgot that the mainstay of advertising is creativity.

The significance of accurate recall as part of the experiential learning process is confirmed by Gabriel Szulanski and Sidney Winter in an article in the *Harvard Business Review*. They wrote: 'Businesses often fail when they try to reproduce a best practice. One reason: in-house "experts" don't truly know why it worked in the first place.'[36] In reality, copying others ignores the context of both place and time and disregards the dynamic of one's own organization-specific circumstances. It kills both innovation and the learning opportunity. Most organizations only learn from worst practice.

Defensive reasoning

The other contributory factor to decision-making abilities – defensive reasoning – is reinforced by a substantial body of academic research into organizational learning, much of which confirms the reluctance of companies and their managers to objectively examine their performance, especially their mistakes. Harvard's Professor Chris Argyris explains that whenever a manager's performance comes under scrutiny, the individual begins to feel embarrassed, threatened and, because they are so well-paid, guilty:

> *Far from being a catalyst for real change, such feelings cause most to react defensively. So, when their learning strategies go wrong, they become defensive, screen out criticism and put the 'blame' on anyone and everyone but themselves. In short their inability to learn shuts down precisely at the moment they need it the most.*[37]

This is why, says Argyris, we all tend to collude in admiring the emperor's new clothes, and why we feel such a sense of chagrin when we realize that the emperor is, indeed, unclad.

This is attributed to a particularly well-developed managerial ego. Commenting on the difficulties of teaching managers how to learn, a top US industrialist describes the apparent amnesia evident in many of his top employees: 'For many years I have been troubled by the inconsistent attitudes of high-achievement professionals who have superb intellects yet appear not to learn from experiences or colleagues,' he observed. His explanation is that professional service companies in particular attract what he calls

> *the stereotypical self-motivated, supercharged MBAs whose past successes build their defences against being incorrect, hence against any need to learn or change. I suspect that the defensive reasoning process is well developed early in the life of a high-achievement person.*[38]

In fact, Argyris's defensive reasoning highlights one of a series of regional differences that give Eastern managers an important edge over their Western counterparts in decision-making.

Making mistakes – the East–West difference

Rare is the Western manager who will admit to a mistake. A success, yes. But a blunder? Only very occasionally, usually when the evidence is irrefutable. Otherwise, the characteristic reaction is defensiveness, a mechanism which in psychoanalysis terms allows individuals to protect themselves from feelings of anxiety or enables them to modify reality to make it more tolerable. It is also called denial, an attribute in which the individual rejects or represses the facts, or – as Argyris has observed – passes the blame across to others. Many are the occasions when individuals will twist and dodge every which way to avoid acknowledging that their performance is less than rigorous. In the West failure is considered irremediable and unforgiveable. It marks one out. If it happens, it is something to be forgotten. Typically the result of insecurity or arrogance, it is one of the biggest constraints to experiential learning.

In contrast, Eastern businessmen are widely socialized to be far more humble, with public self-effacement not an uncommon occurrence in boardrooms when things go wrong. What is seen as humiliation in Wall Street or the industrial parks of Manchester is dignity in Japanese boardrooms. In the world of experiential learning, this is crucial. To the Eastern manager, their preparedness to concede to shortcomings potentially makes them very good experiential learners. To them, failure becomes delayed success.

Denial in politics

These characterizations are different in the political world, with neither Western nor Eastern decisions-makers being particularly eager to admit to any sort of failure. If anything, Eastern politicians are more defensive than Western politicians although, at times, the difference is unclear.

At the beginning of 2003, for example, the Chinese government avoided announcing the flue-like SARS virus for months beyond the point when it might have been prevented from spreading around the world. In addition to the death toll – more than 800 people died – the effects on regional tourism and investment were substantial. In 2003, Libya agreed to pay billions of dollars as compensation for the terrorist attacks on US and French aircraft over Scotland and Niger, yet refused to publicly admit that its operatives were responsible. The payment was to facilitate the lifting of United Nations sanctions, imposed nearly 20 years earlier by the global community for Libya's support of terrorism.

Another good example of denial occurs in the home borough of British Prime Minister Tony Blair, where employees had to 'whistleblow' to a local newspaper the intelligence that children in the care of London's Islington Council were being exploited by pimps, paedophiles and drug pushers, and were moreover being groomed for the sexual gratification of men, often council employees. The then leader of Islington Council, Margaret Hodge, who initially ignored social workers' alerts, also dismissed the *Evening Standard*'s exhaustive investigations as 'gutter journalism', even reporting her complaints to the Press Council. She eventually admitted that she had made a mistake when an inquiry was launched to establish the facts.

The issue was then further highlighted when the government announced in June 2003 that Mrs Hodge, who by then had become a member of parliament, had been appointed the first UK Minister of State for Children in the Department for Education and Skills. Against a tirade of opposition ('We cannot know how many children she condemned to a period of further abuse by not acting immediately'[39]), her defence was that her experiences made her an ideal candidate for the job. *The Independent*'s comment incisively reflected the issue of whether or not prior denial and associated inaction over a prolonged period qualified as demonstrating an aptitude for experiential learning:

Mrs Hodge argues that, far from rendering her an inappropriate person to be minister for children, the failures of the past have made her an ideal candidate. How much can Mrs Hodge really have learnt, though? Not enough to understand that the people who fell victim to her decisions – both abused children and frustrated social workers – remain understandably bitter. The outrage that these people still feel after the passing of a decade or more is perfectly understandable. It is worrying that neither Mrs Hodge nor those who appointed her were able to understand that this sort of response was inevitable. As for the idea that Mrs Hodge has learnt from her mistakes, one can only regret that the government is stretched so thin that it has to rely on these people, instead of those who have learnt from their successes.[40]

Hostile defensiveness

Defensive reasoning can be manifested in several other forms. In addition to straight denial, when individuals deny that an 'experience' actually occurred, there is an aggressive form, one example being the reaction of senior European Union officials suspected of fraud. Robert McCoy, the Commission's internal auditor of OLAF, the European Anti-Fraud Office complained that he had been threatened with disciplinary proceedings if he continued to ask awkward questions. As part of their assertive response, he was taunted with cries of 'Gestapo' by members of the Committee of the Regions.[41]

Alongside this is the type of learning or, to be more precise, non-learning, that I call lip service learning – when individuals and/or organizations identify a problem, spend time and money importing the necessary experience to solve the problem and then do nothing. This was the case after the 1990 Manjil earthquake in Iran laid waste to cities and villages, when a number of experts arrived to advise under the United Nations Development Programme. Roy Taylor, a steel construction consultant from New Zealand, a country also subject to earthquakes, said that, although the Iranians seemed interested in advice on seismic design, they did not apply it, 'no matter what we did or what advice we gave'.[42] Collapsed structures were replaced, he said, with similar styles in the same vulnerable materials. His comments were made 13 years later after the country's latest earthquake in Bam, which killed around 30 000 people.

Often, when the accusation of lip service learning is impossible to avoid, managers defensively change the way in which productivity is measured. I call this variation 'massage' learning, the inventive nature of which is often politically very sensitive. One example is the British government's efforts to change the figures that measure value for money in schools, hospitals, pensions and economic growth.[43] In 2004 ministers confirmed that the Office for National Statistics was exploring how to change the decades-old system of measuring productivity to avoid giving the impression that that up to £20 billion of taxpayers' money was failing to reach its targets. Illustrating how productivity can be intentionally distorted, the argument they use is that the traditional system simply counts the numbers of patients treated or pupils educated rather than the extra time – the inefficiencies inherent in non-productivity – spent by nurses and doctors with patients, or on the prevention of crime or illness. Within months, the country's statistic watchdog, the Statistics Commission, criticized the figures, saying that they undermined public confidence and that some of the revisions could have been avoided by better management in the past.[44] The new figures raised NHS output to more than 4 per cent a year between 2001 and 2003 from early estimates of between 1.9 and 2.6 per cent.

The culture of deception

Targets are also a managerial device to improve productivity, the rationale being that a clear objective provides an added incentive. Introduced in the US in the 1980s, they are a useful spur for management to become more inventive in their decision-making. In many cases, however, their application has also brought about an imaginative culture of deception, which is another form of 'massage'. In the UK, for example, where the latest Labour government has taken to the idea with gusto across the public sector, targets for recycling waste are now statutory for local authorities. To meet their goals, some councils have suddenly started running schemes to collect grass and hedge cuttings that could easily be composted at home.[45] In the health service, deception is even more deliberate. In an employment tribunal hearing in 2003, the finance director of the UK's tenth largest NHS organization in Tooting, south London, recalled the story of a colleague asking a junior member of staff to send incorrect figures to the Department of Health that indicated there had been no cancelled operations in a particular week in 2001. When the statistics were checked, he discovered that his colleague knew that there had been 28. For the prior week, zero had also been imputed when there had actually been more than 40 cancellations. Ian Perkin, who claimed that finance directors in other trusts had confirmed to him that the culture of deception was endemic across the NHS, said that NHS trusts were being asked to make huge savings – in his case the figure was £4.5 million during 2001 within his overall budget of £270 million. Told that the information was not his responsibility, Mr Perkin was subsequently dismissed after refusing to take up an offer to 'go quietly' with a six-month salary cheque and another job in the NHS – a deal not denied by the hospital. As a result of having a high rate of postponed operations that year, the trust in question – St George's Healthcare – failed to win the top three-star rating.

The above example also classically illustrates an ethos of experiential non-learning arising out of denial. Perkin's bosses insisted there was no deliberate attempt to disguise the figures, explaining the incident as a computer glitch that affected their ability to give reliable figures. The Trust also denied that he was dismissed for 'whistleblowing' or for 'expressing his views on its financial position'. There was, it said, an irretrievable breakdown in relations between Mr Perkin and the Trust. His position had simply become 'untenable', despite his long tenure of 16 years with the hospital.[46]

The confusion surrounding knowledge management and the learning organization

Collectively, these factors – the changed workforce profile, the flexible labour market, short and selective memory recall, defensive reasoning, lip service learning and 'massage' learning/deception – represent a huge obstacle for organizations looking to continue their productivity gains. There are now just too few manufacturing workers for their productivity to be decisive. The little continuity in employment that exists at all levels of the organizational hierarchy and occupational classification ensures that job disruption is both widespread and regular. Furthermore, corporate loyalty is virtually non-existent and organizations have little ability (or, indeed, opportunity) to learn from their own institutionally relevant experiences. Nor does working harder or longer seem to be the answer, as the British experience bears out.

To keep the productivity ball rolling, industry has since come up with several mantras conforming with the new information age. They are knowledge management and the learning organization, whose popularity is matched only by the confusion over how to put them into practice.

Knowledge management is still a discipline that most businesses find bewildering. It has variously been defined by KM expert Yogesh Malhotra, the founder and chief knowledge architect of the New-York based research and advisory company, the BRINT Institute, as a synthesis of information technology and human innovation,[47] by chief knowledge officer for PricewaterhouseCoopers, Ellen Knapp, as intellectual asset transformation[48] and by Karl Wiig, a former director of Applied Artificial Intelligence and Systems and Policy Analysis at Arthur D. Little, as a combination of perspectives involving business, management and operation.[49] More relevantly, it relates to the collection and application of appropriate data/information/knowledge for competitive advantage, although many organizations neglect to relate to the 'leverage' part of the definition. Specifically, a learning organization has to be skilled at systematic problem-solving, experimentation with new approaches, learning from its own experiences and past history, learning from the experiences and best practices of others and transferring knowledge quickly and efficiently throughout the organization. Of all the learning organization's individual components, it is learning from one's own experiences that is most overlooked by the practitioners, a notion reinforced by Chris Lorenz, the late management editor of *The Financial Times*, whose observation over many years of seeing managers at work was that the drive for better external learning was blinding companies to one of the most valuable sources of insight and added knowledge – their own experiences.[50]

In fact, many who court the wider gift of knowledge management and the learning organization pay lip service to their application. In 1997, for example, just 11 per cent of UK companies were judged to be authentic learning organizations,[51] with only one in ten believing that they genuinely promoted learning. Harvard Business School's Professor David Garvin's view[52] is that the topics 'in large part remain murky, confused and difficult to penetrate, with scholars partly to blame, their discussion often reverential and utopian, and filled with near mystical terminology'.[52] This widespread confusion was confirmed in 2003 by a survey of the educational needs and wants of knowledge management professionals worldwide. It was found that, by their own admission, up to 70 per cent of KM operatives had an urgent need for training in KM tools and methods and techniques to enhance knowledge-sharing.[53]

The result? Much confusion about the role of technologies, especially information technologies, and the difference between information systems (IS) and information technology (IT), with many companies mistakenly believing that the sum total of organizational knowledge can be stored in databanks.

The outcome has financed a huge industry in its own right. In their use of knowledge management and/or 'learning organization' procedures, organizations have mechanically turned to the expensive hi-tech application. Current practice usually involves the installation of sophisticated computer retrieval systems that provide quick access to archival documentation. In fact, their most useful applications are the ability to identify people within organizations with relevant skills and experience who can, theoretically, be consulted and data collection to identify useful trends upon which to concentrate management attention. Unfortunately, the flexible labour market replaces almost the entire employee base of most organizations every four or five years,[54] leaving few individuals to consult. Also, as already pointed out, whilst organizations can well identify *what* needs attention, the computer cannot convey how best, and when, to achieve it. It is the equivalent of providing a novice golfer with the most sophisticated golf clubs and expecting regular holes-in-one.

Drucker's productivity challenge is instructive in several other ways. His reference to service workers includes government and the civil service that today represents an enormous sector of the economies of most countries and which does little or no manufacturing. As a general rule, productivity in this sector is lower than that of private industry – often substantially lower – and mounting pressures to deliver better-value services are now requiring public administrators to also become better decision-makers. And although Drucker was referring specifically to developed countries, his challenge is no less relevant to countless emerging economies, many of which have aspirations to leap into the modern world without the experiential advantage of their predecessors or, in many cases, without the desire to learn from others' experience. Like their First World cousins, the aspiration to learn from their own experiences appears just as remote.

Explains Drucker:

Capital cannot be substituted for labor. Nor will new technology by itself generate higher productivity. In making and moving things, capital and technology are factors of production. In knowledge and service work, they are tools of production. The difference is that a factor can replace labor, while a tool may or may not. Whether tools help productivity or harm it depends on what people do with them, on the purpose to which they are being put, for instance, or on the skill of the user.[55]

The solution, he suggests, is to turn one's attention to service workers and return to the 120-year-old notion of the man who started off the productivity chase to 'work smarter'. Redesigning a job and then teaching the worker the new way to do it, which is what Frederick Taylor did and taught more than a century ago, cannot by itself sustain ongoing learning, he says:

Training is only the beginning of learning. Indeed, as the Japanese can teach us (thanks to their ancient tradition of Zen), the greatest benefit of training comes not from learning something new but from doing better what we already do well.[56]

Drucker's roadmap to better productivity throws up other key regional differences in attitudes to learning and decision-making as well as providing several clues as to how the next cycle of productivity gains can be achieved.

Alongside the different East–West perceptions about knowledge, which I outlined in Chapter 3, and the dissimilar way 'failure' is dealt with by individuals, one other key character variable is how Western managers comprehend modern management. The most common understanding is that management is a science rather than an art. This has come about because of the rapid rate of technological change and the ensuing massive increase in the number of products and services generated, the belief being that their management has therefore little relevance to previous practice. In this I am reminded of the reflective observation by a writer travelling the ancient Great Wall of China: 'What does it mean when smoke signals are replaced by cell phones, but you still have to climb the wall to use them?'[57]

Alongside the realization that the practice of management is little changed is the wide-spread assumption in management that decision-making is like a recipe. Mix the ingredients together and – *voilá* – the cake is necessarily digestible. When the variables – the quality of ingredients, equipment, the consumer and the biggest movable feast of all, the cook(s) – stay the same, the outcome is constant. Unfortunately, the variables never stay the same. Ever.

Herein lies the weaknesses in Western educational approaches to teaching the business of business – the oversight of organizational memory (OM) and its application as a way of benefiting from hindsight.

Part of OM is the experiential component of an organization's intellectual capital. The aggregation of the institution's experiences and knowledge, it is this intellectual asset – hard-won and expensively acquired – that, in today's workplace, goes walkabout. Without it, rolling generations of workers have to keep on reinventing the wheel. If it is not to pass beyond reach – that is, become unusable as a learning medium – it needs to be managed, just like any other corporate asset.

What are data, information and knowledge?

To fully understand the nature of experiential learning, it is necessary to comprehend the distinction between data, information and knowledge, the difference between explicit knowledge and tacit knowledge, and the way in which knowledge relates to decision-making. Data is a fact depicted as a figure or a statistic while data in context – such as in a historical timeframe – is information. By way of illustration, take a typical announcement of a company's annual performance, which is usually published alongside the previous year's achievement. The figure published for either year is data while the relationship between the company's two sets of annual figures is information.

In contrast knowledge – around which OM is constructed – is interpretative and predictive. Its deductive character allows its owner to understand the implications of information and act accordingly. Of an exceptionally esoteric nature, it is variously described by Alvin Goldman as justified true belief,[58] by Bruce Aune as information in context,[59] by Verna Alee as experience or information that can be communicated or shared[60] and by Karl Wiig as a body of understanding and insights for interpreting and managing the world around us.[61]

In its modern understanding, knowledge is made up of explicit knowledge, sometimes called skilled knowledge, and tacit or cognitive knowledge, sometimes known as 'coping skills', a category first identified by Michael Polanyi in 1958.[62] The former is the type of knowledge such as the professional or vocational skills recorded in the abundant manuals, textbooks and training courses – the 'what' of know-how. Tacit knowledge, on the other hand, is the non-technical 'how' of getting things done, what Edward de Bono, the inventor of lateral thinking, calls 'operacy'[63] or the skill of action, and what Drucker identifies in the use of the word *techne*[64] (the Greek for 'skill'). Much of it is implicit and ambiguous and acquired largely by experience that is functional and context-specific. Typically existing only in the minds of individuals, tacit knowledge is normally very difficult to capture. But it is through tacit knowledge that most erudition takes place.

Two of the best descriptions of tacit knowledge's make-up come from New Zealand knowledge management specialist Carl Davidson and David Snowden, Director of the Knowledge and Differentiation Programme, IBM Global Services, UK. Davidson's picture is as follows:

Remember how Grandma baked the best scones you've ever eaten? Maybe you've got her recipe but no matter how many times you tried, your scones never turned out as good ... Grandma gave you only explicit knowledge by writing down instructions. What you also needed was her tacit knowledge of how she worked in the butter and milk, how she kneaded the dough. You would get this only by talking to her face to face, watching her, or making a batch alongside her.[65]

Snowden's depiction is to consider how best to get around London's roads. One could use a map, which contains information with which to navigate using universal symbols and structure to observe, orientate and then decide how to move. Using the services of a taxi is faster, however, because the taxi driver uses tacit knowledge acquired over 30 pre-qualification months cycling round the streets of London, doing 'the knowledge'.[66]

I particularly like Snowden's imagery because it also illustrates the importance of specificity to decision-making. The basic skill of a taxi driver is driving. Driving, though, is not universally applicable, for a New York taxi driver will have to learn another type of driving – left-side driving – to earn a living in the UK. Equally, the additional tacit knowledge that makes the New York taxi driver a better New York taxi driver is quite irrelevant in London. The logic is irrefutable. One decision-maker, however good in one situation, is not necessarily of the same quality in another. Decision-making is environment-specific.

In business terms, tacit knowledge is a passive misnomer for active sharing of knowledge to make an organization more effective. According to A.M. de Lange, the word knowledge comes from the Saxon word *cnaw-lec*. The suffix *lec* has become in modern English '-like'. So knowledge means 'cnaw-like', with 'cnaw' meaning 'emerge'. The best interpretation, then, is that it is an emergent phenomenon, an extension of existing erudition.[67]

This suggests that knowledge has various lives. There is existent knowledge that is historical – knowledge that is already established and recognized. When it is remembered, this type of knowledge immediately reverts to information. It is in the transition to new erudition that knowledge reasserts itself to become new knowledge, what some academics call 'knowledge in action', and where decision-making – the process of making choices – becomes important. By way of a simple illustration, existent knowledge is the established awareness that, because it is hot, it is necessary to avoid sunburn and dehydration. Whether or not a hat is worn or liquid consumed is a decision. Decisions may be good or bad but they are nevertheless predicated on the awareness of knowledge. Where existent knowledge becomes new knowledge is when, for example, a European holidaymaker, more used to wearing a cap in home sunshine, decides to wear a sombrero in a Mexican summer.

The educational neglect of experiential learning

The West's other associated educational weakness – OM's related role in how industry gets to benefit from hindsight – also gets Drucker's attention in his declaration that: 'We often hear it said that in the information age, every enterprise has to become a learning institution. It must become a teaching institution as well'.[68] His observation is the related insight that workers learn most when they teach:

> *The best way to improve a star salesperson's productivity is to ask her to present 'the secret of my success' at the company sales convention. The best way for the surgeon to improve his performance is to give a talk about it at the county medical society.*[69]

Whilst such 'teaching' in the traditional sense would probably be unappealing for most workers, what Drucker is, in fact, advocating is the wider concept of experiential learning, which is what this book is all about.

It is against this background that organizations must find a new route to better decision-making and, ultimately, to improved productivity. Using the experiential learning route, there must, first, be a more sensitive appreciation of the intellectual asset known as organizational memory. Given that the flexible labour market is here to stay, at least for the foreseeable future, organizations must next instigate formalized processes to capture it in suitable formats while it is still fresh in the mind and, importantly, before it walks out of the front door. Thereafter, it needs to be applied through experiential learning's process of critical reflection.

The linking principles are as logical as they are simple, best articulated by sages such as J.G. Pleasants, a former vice-president at Proctor & Gamble, who believes that an organization which understands its own past is able to adapt previous successes, avoid repeating mistakes and acquire knowledge far beyond one single person's experience.   Spanish-born US philosopher George Santayana's famous quote on the subject – 'Those who cannot remember the past are condemned to repeat it' – was used by historian William L. Shirer as an epigraph in his 1959 book on *The Rise and Fall of the Third Reich*. Just as explicit is Winston Churchill's observation that 'the furthest backward you can look, the furthest forward you can see'. My own personal favourite, which rings bells every time an organization makes the same poor decision more than twice, is contained in the dialogue in one of English novelist J.L. Carr's books: 'You've not had 30 years' experience. You have had one year's experience 30 times.'

At risk of fastening down the board with too many nails, the appreciation of organizational memory is like the rear view mirror on a motorcar. Without it, one has to continually crane one's head to make navigational decisions. At best, drivers get themselves a stiff neck; at worst, they can have a fatal accident. Translated into current business-speak, the message is that, in the world of continuous learning, OM is a factor of production that needs management – just like any other business asset. If an organization is losing its OM, it should ensure that there are processes in place to capture it – rigorously. With the evidence in hand, the organization can then impose disciplines to help managers make better decisions.

Without OM, organizations have to keep on starting from scratch in the roller coaster of daily determinations. This can be very, very expensive, as all less competitive organizations can show quite easily – and as the examples in Chapter 5 will confirm.

Notes

1.   Anne Brontë, *Agnes Grey*, London: T.C. Newby, 1847.
2.   Research, Wolverhampton Business School/UMIST, 13 June 2001.
3.   Drucker, P.F., 'The New Productivity Challenge', *Harvard Business Review*, vol. 69, no. 6, November–December 1991.
4.   Stephen J. Dorgan and John Dowdy, 'How Good Management Raises Productivity', *The McKinsey Quarterly*, no, 4, 2002.
5.   Roy H. Webb, 'National Productivity Statistics', *Economic Quarterly*, vol. 84, no. 1, Winter 1998, pp. 45–55.
6.   World Economic Forum, *Global Competitiveness Report*, September 2002.
7.   Drucker, 'The New Productivity Challenge', op. cit.
8.   F.W. Taylor, *The Principles of Scientific Management*, New York, 1911.
9.   Drucker, 'The New Productivity Challenge', op. cit.
10. Hemmington Scott, quoted in *Director Magazine*, April 1996.
11. *Financial Times*, 14 May 1996.
12. *Teacher Turnover, Wastage and Movement Between Schools*, government research by the Centre for Education and Employment Research, Buckingham University, May 2005.
13. Research into employment discontinuity, Pencorp, 1994.
14. American Management Association, annual survey, October 1996.
15. Jonathan Lurie, Princeton University, thesis on downsizing at: www.geocities.com.
16. Morgan Stanley report, May 1977.
17. *Issues in People Management No. 15*, London: Institute of Personnel and Development, 1996.
18. 1996 EC report on competitiveness of European industry, reported in *Financial Times*, 9 October 1996.
19. Peter Boxall and Erling Rasmussen, research study, University of Auckland Business School, October 2001.
20. Jonathan Lurie, Princeton University, thesis on downsizing, via www.geocities.com.
21. 'Spending Has Failed, So Let's Try Real Public Service Reform', *The Sunday Times*, 31 August 2003.
22. 'The Incredible Shrinking Company', *Director Magazine*, April 1996.
23. *Sunday Telegraph*, 30 March 2003.
24. ICI announcement, 1 May 2003.
25. *The Times*, 28 June 2003.
26. Research by Incomes Data Services (IDS) in May 2003 showed that the average pay package of directors at Britain's top companies rose by 25 per cent in 2002 even though share prices slumped. Chief executive of Telewest, Adam Singer's exit payout was £1.8 million after taking the cable company to the brink of bankruptcy, and Sir Geoff Mulcahy, a 20-year veteran of the retail group Kingfisher, received £502 000 in 2002 after the group's shares fell from a high of 719p in 1999 to 200p at his departure. Handsome pay rises were also given to the directors of the Prudential in 2003 despite a fall in profits and the first cut in the company's dividends since 1914. Over at J. Sainsbury, investors engineered the dismissal of chairman Sir Peter Davis in 2004 after the company's remuneration committee awarded him a £2.4 million bonus after a 8.5 per cent annual profits fall – and just months after the traditional Christmas bonus to other employees was scrapped. In South Africa, Nedcor executives walked off with pay cheques worth R109 million in 2002, having presided over the destruction of a quarter of the bank's capital in the previous 12 months alongside a R1.6 billion loss. In the 2004 New Year's Honours List, Doug Smith, the former boss of the government's Child Support Agency, was awarded a Companion of the Order of the Bath less than two months after leaving the agency over the disastrous introduction of a £456 million computer system to speed up maintenance payments. Richard Bowker, the former head of the Strategic Rail Authority, was awarded a CBE after leaving the SRA shortly before the announcement that it was to be abolished and amid continuing concern over the state of the railways.
27. *Sunday Telegraph*, 16 May 2004.
28. OECD, *Annual Report*, 1992.
29. According to the Employment Policy Institute, London, 1997.
30. Cantos (corporate research and broadcast company), survey, June 2003.
31. According to a pamphlet produced by the Centre for the History of Chemistry (CHOC).
32. *Business History*, 1981.
33. Alan M. Kantrow, 'The Constraints of Corporate Tradition', New York: Harper & Row, 1984.

34. Research into 'design amnesia' by Lance Ealey and Leif Soderberg, *The McKinsey Quarterly*, Spring 1990.

35. Alan Cotterell, acotrel@cnl.com.au, writing on 'Trends in Organizational Learning' , 28 October 2002 at: learning-org-digest-approval@world.std.com.

36. G. Szulanski and S. Winter, 'Getting It Right the Second Time', *Harvard Business Review*, January 2002.

37. C. Argyris, 'Teaching Smart People How to Learn', *Harvard Business Review*, May-June 1991. Harvard Professor Chris Argyris is one of the main exponents of the precepts of the learning organization.

38. Thomas C. Barry, former president and chief executive officer of New York-based Rockefeller & Co. and President of Marlboro, quoted in *Harvard Business Review*, July–August 1991.

39. Stewart Steven, *Evening Standard*, London, 16 June 2003.

40. Deborah Orr, *The Independent*, 1 July 2003.

41. *Sunday Telegraph*, 19 October 2003.

42. *New Zealand Herald*, 31 December 2003.

43. *The Times*, 26 April 2004.

44. Philip Thornton, 'Statistics Watchdog Condemns ONS Data Revisions', *The Daily Telegraph*, 6 July 2004.

45. 'Is Target-itis Breeding a "Culture of Deception"?', Professor Richard Scase, University of Kent, BBC Radio 4 18 August 2003.

46. *The Observer*, 26 January 2003.

47. Y. Malhotra, 'Knowledge Management in Inquiring Organizations', *Proceedings of the Americas Conference in Information Systems*, August 1997, pp. 293–95, available at: www.kmbook.com

48. Ellen Knapp and Peter Keen, *Every Manager's Guide to Business Processes*, Cambridge, MA: Harvard Business School Press, 1995.

49. Karl Wiig, *A Knowledge Model for Situation-Handling*, Knowledge Research Institute Inc. White Paper 2003.

50. C. Lorenz, *Financial Times*, 23 September 1994.

51. Industrial Society survey, 1997.

52. David Garvin, 'Building a Learning Organization', *Harvard Business Review*, July– August 1993, pp. 78–91.

53. Survey by Knowledge Management Consortium International in conjunction with the University of Vermont, 30 September 2003.

54. Employment Policy Institute, London. 1997.

55. Drucker, 'The New Productivity Challenge', op. cit.

56. Ibid.

57. *National Geographic*, January 2003.

58. Alvin Goldman, *Knowledge in a Social World*, Oxford: Clarendon Press, 1999.

59. Bruce Aune, *Knowledge, Mind, and Nature: An Introduction to Theory of Knowledge and the Philosophy of Mind*, New York: Random House, 1967.

60. Verna Allee, *The Future of Knowledge: Increasing Prosperity through Value Networks*, New York: Butterworth-Heinemann, 2002.

61. Wiig, *A Knowledge Model for Situation-Handling*, op. cit.

62. Michael Polanyi, *The Tacit Dimension*, New York: Anchor Books, 1967.

63. Edward de Bono, *Atlas of Management Thinking*, London: Maurice Temple Smith, 1981.

64. Peter Drucker, *Post-Capitalist Society*, New York: Butterworth Heinemann, 1993.

65. Reported by Estelle Sarney, 'Know-how Sure to Rise', *New Zealand News*, 5 November 2003. See 'Judith Meskill's Knowledge Notes – Knowledge Management News', 6 November 2003 at: http://www.meskill.net/archives/00386.html.

66. See 'Story Telling and Tacit Knowledge LO21577', 11 May 1999 at: http://www.learning-org.com/99.15/0120.html.

67. A.M. de Lange, 'Understanding the New Knowledge Management', 6 August 2003 at: http://learning-org.com/03.08/0002.html.

68. Drucker, 'The New Productivity Challenge', op. cit.

69. Ibid.

5 *Where Failure is not Delayed Success*

Everyone complains of their memory, no one of their judgement.

François de La Rochefoucauld, French writer[1]

In February 2003 the local authority in Barnet, one of London's more prosperous outer boroughs, announced that it had decided to increase the year's council tax – the so-named property tax – by a staggering 23 per cent. With national inflation around 3 per cent, the hike generated a rash of protests. The council's literature mechanically advised that 'enquiries' could be made through the mail, e-mail or telephone. Six weeks later, well after the tax increases were automatically triggered, the department nominated to handle the enquiries was still overwhelmed. Many of the written enquiries were still unanswered, with taxpayer's attempts to contact the council in person blocked by telephone queues that continued for months. With the calls paid for at the caller's expense, Britain's telephone companies did very well.

Whilst Barnet Council's example is illustrative of a relatively simple management function – answering queries – its eventual reaction (we've been 'unprecedently busy'[2]) exemplifies the practice of poor decision-making. In truth, a professionally managed administration would have anticipated that the imposition of a near one-quarter increase in taxes in one year was going to herald a particularly busy time. If it was unforeseen, any overload in enquiries should have been rectified within hours. Instructively, the borough's chief executive's salary was raised by 22 per cent to £140 000 per year during this period.[3]

Collecting money efficiently is an equally important management function, yet a similarly inefficient approach is taken by the UK's private-sector electricity provider Powergen in the way in which it deals with 'final' bills, which are issued when clients move home. For some reason, its computers are programmed to issue estimated meter readings, even after the client has telephoned or e-mailed final meter readings, a process which typically generates a successive round of unnecessary enquiries, complaints and correspondence to finalize a business relationship with customers.

Though these instances may be small, but Barnet and Powergen's examples are neither exclusive nor extraordinary. Tune into any of the consumer programmes on TV and radio in the UK or elsewhere and the complaints seem equally endless. Whether to do with utility accounts, salesmen, tradesmen or late deliveries, mismanagement by companies and public services keep on coming, with the apologies seemingly sincere – until the next rash of complaints. The business pages of newspapers are equally full of problems, ranging from announcements of product recalls, mis-selling, safety issues and corporate profit shortfalls. Government business is equally fraught with promises that are rarely met, budgets that repeatedly overrun and other things that constantly go wrong, whether in planning departments, refuse collection or the offices that answer queries. Their collective impact from the boardroom down is illustrative of the wider managerial weakness seen in low productivity.

Management by rote

Where there are injustices, when mistakes become too frequent, start costing too much and/or affect too many people, many managements – often at the behest of government – resort to introducing rules and regulations such as voluntary guidelines or codes of conduct for specific events. When this doesn't work, legislation often follows. Management by rote, which is now widespread, is one of the telltale signs of managerial abdication, leading to the loss of employee imagination, disincentivization, stagnation and higher costs.

In the throes of the conveyer belt of inconvenience, a not unfamiliar chorus by the customer is: 'Why can't they get it right? It's not as though they can't see what's happening. And they've been doing the same thing long enough.' For businesses, the word 'firefighting' is a not unfamiliar term in the corporate lexicon as is the phrase 'It's very easy to be wise with hindsight'.

Although I have not seen any empirical evidence to support it, this absence of hindsight in the corporate world, or at least the consequences of this deficiency, has to be among the largest contributors to personal stress and corporate expense. I know of no one who has not spent huge amounts of time, money and vengeful bile making justifiable complaints against both private companies and public service providers, nor an organization that has not had to indulge in expensive and time-consuming corrective measures to put problems – many of them recurring – right.

The cost of bad decision-making

In reality, we shouldn't be too surprised. Consistent good decision-making is the gold standard of trouble-free business. Unfortunately, its converse is the more common yardstick for all but the most productive and competitive. If one adds up the cost of every unlearned lesson or avoidable mistake, the wastage of resources is astronomical.

However difficult this is to measure accurately and grossly unfair it may seem to some as a way of judging performance ('We can't always be perfect. Humans are, after all, fallible', I hear the plaintive cry) my reply is: Yes, but divide the supposed figure by a thousand, even 10 000, and the potential savings are still big enough to encourage industry and commerce to take better experiential learning processes more seriously. The 70.6 million Internet hits for 'poor management' come to mind.

For just a flavour of an expansive list, I quote two such items that emanate from the UK, which is currently being eclipsed by organizations in ten OECD countries that are doing the same thing up to 26 per cent more effectively.[4] Like me, a columnist for *The Times* did a computer search in *Hansard*, the official record of all legislative utterances in Westminster, for the words 'no stone unturned' which, he decoded, was 'an inflated way to claim energetic action' for something gone wrong. Staggeringly, his computer came up with the number 4933 over the 14-year period to 2002. 'Is it really possible that someone in the House of Lords, the Commons or elsewhere in the political machine has declared their intention to leave no stone unturned, on average, once every single day for the past 14 years?', he asked.[5]

Elsewhere, the boastful estimate of Sir John Bourn, auditor general of the UK's National Audit Office, the independent watchdog over government spending and revenue, is that recent annual savings work out to be £500 million. As a proportion of the £650 billion he oversees, this is a miniscule 0.077 per cent. Using the efficiency levels of any of the more productive nations as the yardstick for what is possible, the potential savings that still lie fallow are, indeed, astronomical. Even more depressing is the fact that, without any experiential learning, many of Sir John's identified problems will inexorably reappear down the line. Instead of showing a continuing improvement, literacy advances in English primary schools for example, have virtually stagnated since 2000,[6] despite decision-makers' well-funded and apparent dedicated earlier efforts. Elsewhere, class sizes in primary schools – the focus of huge spending in the late 1990s and early 2000 to bring in more teachers and one of the platforms on which the Labour government won the 2001 election – have also begun to rise again, with 20 per cent of pupils aged between seven and 11 being taught once again in classes of more than 30.[7]

As these pointers show, calculating the value of poor decision-making is hardly a precise science, but various other statistics confirm its immensity. One other comes from the level of compensation awarded in the courts. Although many detractors will attribute growing totals to a 'compensation culture', compensation is the result of mistakes, including negligence, which – according to Lord Levene, chairman of insurance group Lloyd's of London – is now threatening the entire insurance industry.

He acknowledges that 'the industry is still paying dearly for mistakes of the past' and calculates that the compensation culture in the US has collectively cost industry there more than $400 billion over the past two decades. In the UK it is costing about £10 billion per year – equivalent to more than £400 for every household – and this is rising at 15 per cent per annum, he says. The average cost of an employer's liability claim more than doubled over the five years to 2003. Clinical negligence, which cost the National Health Service £6 million in 1975, totalled almost £500 million by 2002. Compensation and legal costs have soared to £100 million in the Ministry of Defence 'and there is concern now too that this blight is spreading to the rest of Europe, where until recently the practice of suing company directors and officers was unheard of'.[8]

But the grand-daddy of all part-estimates comes from a lobby group that counts John Blundell, director-general of the UK's Institute of Economic Affairs, and Graeme Leach, chief economist at the Institute of Directors, as members of its advisory council. The Taxpayers' Alliance (TPA) calculated in 2004 that 'waste and useless spending' in government alone was costing the equivalent of an average £2000 per family. 'Our research shows that the Government could have cut £50 billion from expenditure in 2003 without closing a single hospital, firing a single teacher or cutting pensions.'[9] Among its recommendations is the scrapping of the Department of Industry and multi-billion savings from eradicating inefficiencies in Network Rail, the welfare system and the civil service. The more costly inefficiencies in the private sector were not mentioned. A year later, the TPA put the government's figure for waste and useless spending at £3330 per family[10] per year, equal to £81 billion and one-sixth of total spending, which has risen from £316 billion in 1996 to a budgeted £580 billion by 2007, the equivalent of £10 000 for every household and 42 per cent of GDP.[10]

Although these figures were initially scorned by government, they were subsequently given some credence by an official department of the Treasury which showed that much of the huge rises in public spending to almost £500 billion per year since 1997 had not always been matched by an adequate improvement in services. For example, leaked figures by the Office for National Statistics (ONS) showed that overall productivity had actually decreased by 10 per cent, with efficiency in the NHS, where spending had doubled since 1997 and will have tripled by 2008, declining by 15–20 per cent.[11] And in education, where spending will have risen from 4.7 per cent of national income to 5.5 per cent in 2005, standards had barely improved,[12] prompting one of the authors of another assessment study into education standards to comment: 'I was absolutely staggered when I saw the figures. They beggar belief for the tiny little impact they have had.'[13] In a classic display of 'massage' learning, which, as I have indicated, is a characteristic of non-learning behaviour, the Labour government had deliberately postponed the scheduled release of the ONS report until after the May 2005 General Election, instructing Len Cook, head of the ONS, to 'help formulate plans to change the way the figures were drawn up'.[14]

Prevention – less costly than cure

Alongside the Barnet, Powergen, House of Commons, NAO and the other examples mentioned, it is not difficult to illustrate how a whole range of private and public companies, industries and countries, fail to learn from experience. As the following examples continue to relate, experiential non-learning is widespread, whether the underlying cause is corporate amnesia emanating from the flexible labour market or for other reasons. My examples are gleaned from a less than exhaustive trawl of the Internet's 70.6 million references to poor management, newspaper cuttings and other readings over a relatively short period and are intended to confirm the extent of managerial dysfunction. An acknowledgement that their performance is less than successful is one of the most difficult admissions to extract from organizations and managers – a characteristic that is, in itself, one of the biggest constraints in their ability to experientially learn. In almost all cases, the overwhelming lesson is that prevention is less costly than the cure, a not untypical example being the pilot scheme by the UK's Department of Work and Pensions into benefits fraud that cost seven times more than it saved.[15] The actual figures showed that administering the mini-project cost £400 000 for a saving of just £52 000. Inexplicably – but perhaps not – ministers refused to rule out extending the scheme nationwide, a clear indicator of management's non-reflective disposition.

The choice of organizations in the US, the UK, New Zealand, South Africa and Israel provides illustrative comparisons of a wide range of modern industry with relevance to most economies, the common theme being the disconnect between experiential learning and quality decision-making.

A country-by-country survey: the US

The US is the world's most productive and competitive country, with a GDP of US$7 824 008 million from its population of 286 million.[16] From a high base, US productivity increased by 22 per cent during the period 1973–1990[17] and a further 20 per cent in the period 1990–2003.[18] The latest competitive rankings puts the US more than 10 per cent ahead of its nearest rival, Singapore, which has risen two places since 2003.

Yet, however efficient the country is, its companies are not free from poor decision-making.

When it comes to non-learning, the Ford motor company illustrates the effects of one of corporate amnesia's causes, the flexible labour market, in the production of its Taurus car.[19] The previous version of the car had been a great success because it met the needs of big-car buyers better than most of its rivals. However, the company experienced a loss of its so-called design memory when it massively cut back on jobs in the recession of the early 1990s. As a result, the new model was largely re-engineered from scratch. Having 'forgotten' what its customers wanted, the result was a model that failed to capture the buyers' imagination.

The price of forgetting – specifically the way in which dominant companies often complacently ignore the effects of mature markets and new technologies – is illustrated at IBM,[20] another of America's more successful companies. In the 1980s a smug Remington yielded dominance of the typewriter market to the electronic age – and IBM. Almost immediately IBM made the same expensive mistake by reacting inappropriately to a technology that threatened its own core business.

On the surface, it simply misjudged one of its product's life cycles but in reality it mishandled the emergence of personal computers, vastly underrating the impact that they would have on its larger mini and mainframe businesses. A memory of how Remington reacted to similar conditions might have encouraged IBM to give its originally independent PC unit a longer life; this way, it might have avoided the US's biggest annual corporate loss of $4.9 billion in 1992.

In fact, a better memory of the slightly more distant past may have helped IBM to avoid the crisis in the first place. Before the computer age really took off, IBM always perceived itself as a service organization that provided information technologies to large companies. Arguably, the company's problems occurred when it began to believe it was a computer company. It returned to profitability when it returned to first principles and finally abandoned barely profitable PC manufacturing in 2004 when it sold out to Lenovo, China's leading PC manufacturer for $1.75 billion, catapulting the Chinese company into third place in the world's PC market.

For a while, Apple, which flourished on a culture that challenged employees to build leading-edge and affordable computers with a distinctive look, also lost its organizational memory when it ran through four chief executive officers in as many years.[21] It subsequently successfully resurrected the past when the company's founder, Steve Jobs, returned to lead the company and produced iMac, reminiscent of the groundbreaking Apple 11 and Macintosh. In effect, Jobs served as the organization's 'memory'.

A persistent mistake is also evident in the way in which Citicorp regularly changes its regional organizational structure.[22] In recent years it has alternated between combining sales and operations and keeping them separate. When the company realizes that sales are not getting the attention they need in the highly competitive financial services industry, they separate them once again. The waste of resources has been colossal.

Elsewhere, a large insurance group represents a similar case of forgetting. Having slimmed down its claims department, it found that it was settling big claims too swiftly and too generously. It then discovered that it had sacked several long-term employees who had created an informal – but highly effective – way of screening claims. It subsequently reinstated them.[23]

A US service company experienced an organizational breakdown after a high level of turnover among front-line employees.[24] Consequently, the potential revenue at a pharmaceuticals company was jeopardized for the next decade by shortfalls in experience departments across the organization's entire drug development cycle.[25] A senior financial consultant who resigned on a Friday night without notice put at risk 1000 client relationships with $175 million of assets under management.[26] And a high-tech company had to offer a $1 million project completion bonus to a key engineer to prevent delay in a new product launch after a high level of departmental departures.[27]

The UK

Lack of productivity has been an endemic problem across British industry for decades, with all attempts to conquer this iceberg-like national demon largely unsuccessful. Historically, the UK's industrial woes have been attributed to labour and the restrictive practices of its trades unions – problems that were addressed head-on by the Thatcher and Major governments of the post-1979 period. From a relatively low base, productivity rose by 113 per cent during the interim (1973–1990)[28], a period that included the downsizing boom. Five years after the Thatcher–Major era's decade-and-a-half of 'curative' measures, labour output retreated once again, indicating that the so-called 'British disease' is more structural.

Recent productivity figures put the UK below the US, Australia, Canada, Denmark, Finland, Ireland, Luxembourg, Belgium, Norway, France, Italy and all Germany.[29] Ranked against 16 European countries, per capita income in the UK is in tenth place, just ahead of Ireland and Italy – little changed in any of the years between 1992 and 1997.[30] The production of machine tools is a bellwether of any highly industrialized country. In the 1960s Britain was among the world's biggest producers. In the year 2000, British companies had the worst performance of 15 large Western European countries, being the only country to record a fall in output. It now ranks sixth behind Germany, Italy, Switzerland, Spain, France, Japan and the US. The latest figures show that the UK ranks twenty-second in world competitiveness,[31] down two places since 2003 and around 27 per cent below the US.

The country's GDP totals $144 786 million from a population of 58.7 million.[32]

Productivity in the public sector is particularly low. For years the criticism has been that public services are generally underfunded, a perception that prompted massive increases in tax expenditure by the latest Labour government. Despite this and the current fashion to impose 'targets' on outputs, the growth in the amount of money pumped into the public services continued to outstrip the resulting increase in performance between 1995 and 2001.[33] In 2003 the Office for National Statistics disclosed that public-sector performance between 1995 and 2001 – almost the Labour government's exact occupancy – fell sharply.[34] Additional figures from the DTI[35] confirmed that public-sector inflation soared 7.8 per cent in the first half of 2003, twice the rate of the wider economy, for an estimated real output improvement of just 3.9 per cent. Uncomfortably, the figures were released on the same day that Mr Blair told his annual party conference that the £66 billion increase in taxpayers' pounds to the public sector since 1997 'was not disappearing down some black hole'. The reality did nothing to fog his infamous ivory smile.

The respected World Economic Forum's annual report on competitiveness[36] puts the UK twenty-second in the list of 104 countries that most squandered taxpayers' cash, below some Middle East countries and nations like Malaysia, Taiwan and even Ghana. Government success at promoting information technology and making the Internet available in schools is ranked a dismal thirty-eighth and twentieth respectively.

In the private sector, productivity is also elusive in many areas. In 2003, for example, research showed that slightly less than 20 per cent of UK manufacturing plants – equal to more than 25 000 units – close each year because they are inefficient.[37]

The UK is ranked thirteenth out of 17 industrial nations in its ability to derive commercial benefit from science and technology.[38] A 1999 PricewaterhouseCoopers global survey of respected companies puts the highest-ranking UK business at twenty-first place.

Low output has served to strip the latent muscle off Great Britain plc. Poorer productivity, for example, has helped to increase taxes and prices to the point where the UK is among the most expensive countries in the world in which to live, a reality that has driven companies like Goldman Sachs, BT, Asda and the insurers Aviva and Prudential to relocate some of their activities to lower-cost countries.[39] It has also kept earnings down to the point where per capita income ranks tenth amongst 16 European countries.[40] This fateful juxtaposition of a low-wage, high-cost economy gives the UK a relatively elevated ranking in terms of GDP – politicians boastfully proclaim that Britain is the fourth largest economy in the world – but, with consequent low levels of disposable income, a disproportionate low position in personal prosperity.

For a recent snapshot of how Britain's output has failed to keep up with its major trading partners, a Cranfield Business School study in 1993 showed that just 2 per cent of British companies were world-class, a finding that was accompanied by the revelation that British managers thought that they were the best in Europe. This lack of correspondence with reality caught the attention of Deputy Prime Minister Michael Heseltine, also Britain's Trade and Industry Secretary and a successful businessman in his own right, who quickly rebuked the nation's managers for overconfidence. In front of the Institute of Directors, he asked his audience for a clear recognition that there was a gap between the UK's industrial perform-ance and the best in the world.

In an attempt to try and find an explanation, *The Financial Times* published an article quoting a senior executive of PA Consulting, one of UK's larger management consultancies, as describing Britain's managers as 'myopic', 'insular', 'self-delusionary' and 'arrogant'. One of his explanations was that managers were reluctant, or unable, to learn from the discomforting experiences of others – shorthand for experiential non-learning.[41]

Four years later, a Royal Society of Arts (RSA) study, which was part-sponsored by the deputy prime minister's Competitiveness Unit in the Cabinet Office, rediscovered the unflattering position in Britain's comparative performance. 'We seem as a nation unable to close the gap between our industrial performance and that of other major manufacturing nations', it concluded.[42] Just months later, after the Conservative government's disastrous defeat at the polls, Mr Heseltine's successor at Trade and Industry, Margaret Beckett, was echoing the same message. A government benchmarking exercise had found that the task faced by UK business in catching up with the best in the world was bigger than the government had expected. The performance of companies throughout the supply chain, even at the top, lagged behind that achieved by companies overseas. More recently, the Skills Task Force has concluded that UK managers are inadequately qualified, trained and developed compared to their international counterparts, and also lack adaptability and entrepeneurial and technicall skill.[43]

Over the last 30 years, government's concern has extended to concerted action to try to improve both productivity and enterprise. OECD and Arthur Andersen studies in 2001 found that the UK had the lowest barriers to entrepreneurship among several major economies and was doing more than most of its European neighbours and the US to stimulate entrepreneurial activity. In addition to the Council for Excellence in Management and Leadership's attempt to identify the inherent problems, a new Entrepreneurship Scholarship was launched to give advice and mentoring support to people in deprived areas with innovative ideas. Also in 2001 a Learning and Skills Council (LSC) replaced the Training and Enterprise Councils and the Further Education Funding Council to promote management education. A Higher Education Reach-Out to Business and the Community Fund was channelling £88 million to UK universities and colleges to foster links with business and the community. In-work training, lifelong learning, a national e-learning network, individual learning, which provide discounts on approved courses, a national network of learning centres, a union learning fund and a network of national training organizations is also in train. Yet – as the nationwide data confirms – productivity improvement and enterprise creation still lags markedly. In the words of The Work Foundation: 'Whatever progress we may be making in research and development, new technology investment, or product innovation is being squandered by the inadequate developments in work organisation across the UK. We're not quite watering the desert, but we're close.'[44]

All this is hardly the expected outcome of the world's oldest industrial economy, where logic would suggest that maturity should give rise to some experiential advantage over competitors.

The macro-figures – and individual commentaries on the UK's decision-making skills – are borne out by the micro-picture.

In a BAA (previously the British Airports Authority) market test[45] to compare building costs in another country where labour and material costs were similar to those in Britain, US contractors were asked to tender for an office block identical to a development already underway at Heathrow for British Airways. Built to US designs and specifications, the American building came out 32 per cent cheaper, thanks to the US architects and engineers spending less time 'reinventing' wheels. Overall in the public sector in 2001, the UK government's National Audit Office found that slightly less than 75 per cent of building projects were either over budget or overdue.

Over budget and overdue were (and are) also characteristics in individual projects such as the Channel Tunnel and its rail link, the British Library, Concorde, the Limehouse Link road tunnel, the Cardiff Bay Barrage, the Luton Airport extension, the Welsh Assembly and the Scottish Parliament, the latter ending up 11 times over budget (at £391 million) and three years overdue. The experience of several of London Transport's projects over the ten-year period to 2000 is particularly striking. Against the background of managers' insistence of long-time underfunding on the London Underground, the National Audit Office's conclusion that much of the £10 billion investment on the Jubilee Line extension, the Docklands light railway and the wider underground system – equivalent to more than 10 per cent of the entire public-sector investment during the period – was wasted because of a failure to integrate systems effectively. Even more sobering is the NAO's conclusion that these performance failures will recur in future investment projects 'because learning from one project was not easily transferred to the next'.

At the turn of the year 2000, ten of the 27 planned millennial landmarks were similarly overdue or over budget, or both.[46] This excluded the national showpiece, the Millennium Dome, which went on to have its own recurring troubles.

An example of poor decision-making exists in the UK government's attempts to reform local councils after 2000. Designed to enable elected mayors or smaller, more powerful executive committees to be more efficient decision-makers, local councils were restructured on a governmental cabinet-style basis. The result? According to a cross-party committee of MPs, the quality and credibility of local authorities did not improve. In fact, councils had become '*more* introverted, looking at their constitutions, rather than thinking about ways to improve services'.[47] Elsewhere, public engagement with local authorities had declined because of confusion about where decisions are made in the new structures and new local strategic partnerships, forged with unelected businesspeople and others, were undermining democratic accountability. Council officers were finding it difficult to give scrutiny committees independent advice. There was just one example where a scrutiny committee's deliberations had changed a council decision. Not only had the workload of executive councillors increased so that it is the equivalent of full-time employment, but non-executive councillors, too, were attending more meetings.

The finance sector is especially rich in examples of experiential non-learning, in particular banking where the record of failures has left a decent trail of evidence that successive generations of bankers continually forget. A graphic instance, which illustrates both the magnitude of the phenomenon and its pervasive nature, can be seen in the banking crisis of the 1980s and 1990s. In the early 1980s the UK banking community was badly mauled by bad debts in South America. Less than ten years later it was again overwhelmed, this time from loan defaults elsewhere in the Third World. Speaking in 1991, the head of one of the UK's largest banks admitted that there were plenty of historical precedents on Latin American lending which 'should have put the red light up for everyone'. He added, 'We have got to ensure that the lessons of the recent past are not forgotten by the rising generation of bankers.'[48] As he was talking the banks were once again making similar errors of judgement – this time at home – with high street lenders having to chalk up further provisions collectively totalling almost £4 billion in their 1992 accounts. 'The biggest worry is that banks do not seem to be capable of learning from their mistakes', a warning that was sounded in 1994 by a banking industry think-tank that analysed the massive write-offs.

There have been continual safety and punctuality issues on the railways under both public and private ownership. Unable to improve its timetable sufficiently, the country's largest railway defaulter, Thameslink, simply moved the goalposts. In 2003, to avoid continued penalties for unpunctuality, it increased the journey times of its trains in peak periods, when the company was liable for the highest fines, which ihad cost the company £2.2 million the previous year.[49]

The litany of repeated problems with computer projects at the Passport Office, the Immigration and Nationality Directorate, Air Traffic Control and the London Ambulance Service. At the time of writing, a project to keep track of, and process, asylum seekers was suddenly axed; even though it was deemed a failure, its private-sector contractors had been awarded huge productivity bonuses. Also in the Home Office, a computerized database of dangerous offenders, which has had seven programme directors in seven years, is 70 per cent over budget, costing £118 million to date. The computer industry is estimating that the computer network currently being installed by the National Health Service could cost over £30 billion – five times the amount originally announced by the government.[50]

Sixteen of 20 weapons systems on order at the Ministry of Defence – among them destroyers, radios, rifles and radar – are overdue by up to five years. Costs are running £2.4 billion ahead of the allocated budget. By 2004 the cost of major defence projects had risen by £3.1 billion over the previous 12 months while delivery times had been delayed by an average of 18 months.[51]

In the agricultural sector the non-learning problem is endemic. BSE, eggs, chickens, vCJD, salmonella, *E.coli* and foot and mouth disease have cost the nation dearly, the latter giving rise to a bill estimated in excess of £9 billion.[52] The BSE debacle is especially notable. Despite the belated and very detailed investigation into cannibalistic recycling, officials from the Ministry of Agriculture admitted in 2000 that feed containing cows' blood products, tallow and gelatine was *still* being fed to cows and other livestock, including newborn calves as a cheap feed to replace their mothers' milk.

The National Health Service's non-learning problems are no less relentless. It now ranks eighteenth in the world performance league behind countries like Italy. Spain, Austria, Norway, Portugal, Greece, Japan and Holland.

In Wakefield, Yorkshire, it took 16 workmen nearly four months and £1000 to change a light bulb in a street lamp and make safe its concrete post, their employer – the local council – saying that the large number of workers was 'normal because electricity was involved'.[53]

When it comes to the bedrock of wealth – the creation of new businesses – the UK also seems not to be learning. Between the mid-1980s and the early 1990s – a period of growth – the UK had the lowest birth rate of new businesses behind countries such as Canada, Sweden and France.[54]

New Zealand

New Zealand's productivity profile is full of contradictions. On the one hand, it is a First World country – GDP US$55 290 million in 2002 – impressively built up by fewer than 2 million taxpayers among a wider population of just 3.8 million.[55] Unlike the UK, enterprising behaviour is not a problem, at least on the surface. It is among the world's top countries at enterprise creation[56] – even higher than the US – and has an unemployment rate, at just 3.6 per cent, that is the lowest among all developed countries.[57] Against this, it comes near the bottom of the world rankings in respect of taking start-ups out of the small business phase. The survival rate of start-ups is also not good; only 40 per cent endure beyond four years.

This apparent paradox is corroborated by the typical corporate profile of a New Zealand company; with an average organizational head-count of just six people, a hefty 84 per cent of enterprises employ five or fewer full-timers, a record endorsed by the New Zealand stock exchange[58] on which is quoted just 132 local companies in 2001, down from just 274 15 years previously (in the same period the number of Australian public companies, for example, totalled 1334, up from 1147). The average market capitalization figures – up from $310 million to just $320 million over the seven-year period to 2001 – also indicates that local companies find it difficult to grow and create wealth. Going back to 1987, just two of the 65 new listings that year are still quoted on the stock exchange; most of the remainder went bankrupt. Standing eighteenth in the international competitiveness league,[59] down two points since 2003, its productivity growth has been in steady decline since the 1960s. Currently, its productivity is about 35 per cent lower than that of the US.[60] It ranks twentieth out of 30 OECD countries in per capita GDP.[61]

Against the background of a long agricultural heritage, New Zealand has only a relatively short industrial history. During the period 1973–1990, the period in which industry started to make its presence felt, productivity increased by 20 per cent[62] but this growth subsequently almost ground to a halt when the economy was absorbing large numbers of unemployed workers. In the 1990s restructuring helped to increase productivity growth slightly but more recently, it has fallen back again,[63] leaving New Zealand even lower in the OECD income rankings (twentieth in terms of per capita income[64]). Whilst the OECD admits to being baffled about why past reforms have not yielded larger productivity gains given New Zealand's 'best practice' in most policies, it clearly overlooks the lack of progress elsewhere in the productivity package. A clue surfaces in an earlier university study[65] that confirmed the country's improvement in capital and total factor productivity but only a slight increase in labour productivity, which is the principal responsibility of front-line managers.

New Zealand managers resemble their counterparts all over the world – they avoid blame, hide when things go wrong and find fault in others,[66] albeit in slightly greater measure than others. A recent study found that New Zealand's culture was not constructive and public-sector cultures were even less so. Shaun McCarthy, the managing director of the organization that undertook the research said: 'The actual culture is basically to avoid blame, don't get involved, don't be the wrong person in the wrong place at the wrong time and protect yourself by finding fault with what other people do.' He concludes that New Zealand is less aggressive and more risk-averse than its Australian neighbour.[67]

The explanation for this lies in New Zealand's egalitarian roots that have resulted in a conservative pay structure. Within a compressed domestic pay scale from top to bottom in most organizations, there is a lack of performance-based incentives for CEOs as part of their remuneration packages. Typically, 4 per cent of a New Zealand CEO's salary package includes long-term performance incentives such as shares or stock options, compared with an average 19 per cent in Australia and 47 per cent in the US.[68] In New Zealand, short- and long-term performance incentives make up only 20 per cent of remuneration packages, whereas Australian companies, where the 'at-risk' element is around 40 per cent of CEOs' pay, follow the US's ratio of up to 75 per cent. This has implications for the ability of New Zealand businesses to grow and compete internationally. According to Ian Taylor, managing director of the Australasian consulting firm that undertook the research, New Zealand's practice of providing a CEO with a high level of fixed remuneration is unlikely to encourage the risk-taking and innovative behaviour inherent in a knowledge-based economy. Nor is it likely to attract global leaders who expect to be rewarded with short- and long-term payments that reflect company results driven by their leadership.[69]

Evidence of incentive-less corporate performance comes in other research by New Zealand's Institute of Management that found that local managers were performing at just two-thirds of their potential, with the architect of the index admitting that there was 'considerable room for improvement'.[70] In fact, the managers themselves ranked their own financial management capabilities highest at 74 per cent and lowest at 63 per cent.

Questionable decision-making is widely evident in the private sector, among them being the decision by Fletcher Forests to consider divesting itself of its forestry interests soon after its ownership deals, first with the Chinese through CITIC and then Rubicon. Over in its sister company, Fletcher Challenge, dubious decision-making in investment policies and management has led to the actual separation of its activities. Safety issues recur year after year at TranzRail and New Zealand Steel.

In the agricultural sector, New Zealand's biggest earner, advice being given by government scientists actually encourages farmers to continue to make old mistakes. Clive Dalton, a government scientist in the 1970s, says that he cannot think of many examples of policies formerly promoted that had been good for farmers. New Zealand's Sheep Council, for example, persists in urging sheep farmers to prematurely turn hoggets (young ewes) into productive animals.[71]

Dalton recalls that their role as public servants was to

save farmers from ruin and the nation from economic disaster by pushing new developments under the belief they've got to be good for you. We really did believe. ... we talked about bonus lambs from hoggets and also about bonus calves from mating yearling heifers.

Commenting after a 2000 Sheep Council Seminar, he said that he was concerned to hear:

... the same old arguments. We boffins didn't like getting too deep into economics and told farmers they would have to decide if the changes we pushed would make money on their individual farms. We believed all our ideas were money makers. We never did any difficult long-term sums on the impact such a new practice would have on a farm system over a decade or more.

He continued: '[B]offins don't like to hear what they don't want to hear.' In keeping up the pressure on production

something has got to give. We could never work out what that was, but it's an urgent priority now before the same mistakes we made are repeated. When you hear the term 'extra bonus lambs' beware – there is no such thing.[72]

Lessons unlearned elsewhere are just as prolific. Frustrated with an inability to grow at home, many companies look overseas. One particular decision-making lapse is New Zealand's penchant for acquisition-growth in geographical areas in which the acquirers have little experience, the increasing number of which has caused the financial press to ask why so many New Zealand companies have made such a hash of their foreign expansion.[73] Air New Zealand's takeover of Australia's Ansett Airlines is just one example of dozens of companies that have put their corporate toes in highly risky overseas deals that have destroyed substantial shareholder wealth. In waiting are the equally risky ventures such as The Warehouse's acquisition of Clints Crazy Bargains and Silly Sollys in Australia in mid-2000, Brierley's takeover of Thistle Hotels, Telecom's purchase of AAPT and Pacific Retail's acquisition of the British electrical retailer Powerhouse. All share the strategy of spurning organic growth alongside an insufficiency of local knowledge. As of 2005, all are hanging on in the hope that their foreign acquisitions may turn positive.

Over in the public sector, where lacklustre performance is even more pronounced, an example of repeated mistakes is evident from several major IT failures; a 2001 study concluded that projects seem destined to stumble and fail with predictable frequency despite expensive enquiries, expert reports and declarations that lessons had been learned.[74] Projects for the police, the Accident Compensation Commission, the National Library and the Justice Department all collapsed at an estimated cost to the taxpayer of more than NZ$130 million. At least three other current projects are classified as high-risk and are being monitored to make sure that anything up to another $300 million is not wasted.

In the health service, an inquiry had to be held to discover why a pathologist at Gisborne hospital's cytopathology laboratory made so many undetected mistakes over a five-year period in what has been described as the country's 'biggest medical disaster'. His recurring mistake was just one of other serious errors that occur at an estimated rate of approximately one in 1000 reportable events in New Zealand's health and disability sector organizations.[75]

The Howard League for Penal Reform, which campaigns for prisoners' rights, claims that 'a lot of fundamental mistakes' are being made in the Corrections Department.[76] Figures released under the Official Information Act show that the department is fighting 18 lawsuits valued at $3.16 million. Inmates and former prisoners are suing the department for breaching the Bill of Rights, breaching their privacy, negligence, unlawful detention and assault. The largest single lawsuit, with several claimants, is looking for $1.35 million from the department for breaching the Bill of Rights.

Successions of similar mistakes have also been admitted in the Child, Youth and Service and well as in the Maori development ministry Puni Kokiri.

South Africa

South Africa's business history has similarities with that of New Zealand. Almost exclusively agricultural until the Second World War, its more recent period includes industrialization on a scale that has put it at the top of Africa's industrial rankings. That is where the similarities end. In modern parlance, it fits into 'Second World' status, with a GDP of US$131 127 million – thanks mainly to its gold and diamond production – from a population of 43.7 million. Per capita income is just $3331.[77]

South Africa's immediate post-war performance was impressive until politics started to interfere. Between 1973 and 1990, the country's productivity declined by about 3 per cent,[78] a function of political machinations and wars in neighbouring countries leading up to the end of apartheid in 1994. Since then, output has further declined as the country has struggled to accommodate its new political realities, with black management largely replacing white management. Unemployment is 4.7 million according to the official definition and 7.8 million according to the expanded definition, which includes people who have given up looking for work.[79] However, a South African labour force survey undertaken in September 2004, reveals that of the country's 15 million 'economically active' South Africans, 11.6 million were employed, putting the unemployment rate at 23 per cent. Debt delinquency is now reckoned to be more than R40 billion, more than R24 billion of which is owed to municipalities for unpaid services such as electricity and refuse removal.[80]

Despite its huge educational investment in the post-apartheid era, South Africa has an altogether different set of non-learning problems. National policy has been to displace its veteran white employees in favour of previously disenfranchised black appointees in the public sector and some areas of the private sector through what is called Affirmative Action, which has coincided with efforts to rationalize activities. Politically desirable though this may be, it has led to the discarding of much of the nation's prior experience. In 1997 South Africa held the uncomfortable distinction of being the most unproductive of 46 developing countries.[81] Out of 60 countries surveyed today, it is ranked forty-ninth in the competitive league table, down two places since 2003. It is approximately 46 per cent less competitive than the US.[82] Indeed, in his 2005 budget, Trevor Manuel, the Minister of Finance since June 1999, expressly acknowledged that frustration over delivery failures in provincial and local government was becoming intense and that he was looking for new tools to enhance central management of crucial programmes.

Due to the nature of its history, South Africa has relatively little business experience to learn from, which accounts for its lack of instinctive enterprising behaviour and a widespread dependency culture, an attribute confirmed by Moeletsi Mbeki, one of South Africa's more outspoken local businessmen. The current model of black economic empowerment that has focused on transferring equity rather than encouraging entrepreneurship has, he says, 'created a culture of entitlement and dependency'.[83]

It is an uncomfortable fact that the best endeavours of government, external investment and the existing private sector can only employ slightly more than half of the country's working population. Between 1994 and 2003, the Human Development Index fell (from 0.73 to 0.67), the poverty line still engulfed 48.5 per cent of the population, income inequality increased (from 0.60 in 1995 to 0.63 in 2001) and the majority of households still had limited access to basic services.[84] The extent of the crisis is illustrated by official estimates that just one in every 100 students who will matriculate will find gainful employment. It is estimated that South Africa needs at least 1 million new small businesses to soak up the unemployment shortfall[85] – a number that will take many generations to achieve without any specific experiential learning programmes (of which there are few). In their absence, the government has resorted to massive public works programmes, one of the latest costing R20 billion over five years, to find work for 1 million people.[86] Whilst welcoming the intervention, many critics have pointed out that much of the work will be short-term.

One expensive example of non-learning is the government's own ongoing attempts at rationalizing and downsizing the civil service, which has been calculated by its own auditors to have wasted R1 billion up to 1995 alone and to have irretrievably damaged the nation's financial management capacity. The government has acknowledged that its best brains have literally walked out of the door, leaving their inexperienced stand-ins to reinvent what had already been learned at great expense. Much the same is happening in the police force and elsewhere in industry as Affirmative Action policies continue to be implemented across the workplace.

In addition to discarding its local experience, South Africa appears determined to also shun overseas experience, especially that considered Eurocentric or colonial in origin. It is a policy that stems from Prime Minister Thabo Mbeki's conception of, and call for, an African renaissance that aspires to the development of local solutions. Again, political motivations aside, the result has been to further widen the productivity gap to the extent that it has produced an outspoken appeal from one of the country's top business leaders not to ignore the benefits of outside experience:

The same basic management tools work across the planet, so there is little point in trying to reinvent the wheel. Executives in countries as diverse as the US, South Korea, Germany and Chile now apply the same techniques, so copying them is smarter than seeking nirvana in some new fad. It is vital to accept and respect the differences in people and their cultures. But companies should beware of falling for ill-defined notions of 'African management' ...[87]

The country's disregard for experience is also confirmed by the United Nations High Commissioner for Refugees and the Japan International Cooperation Agency. A joint study found that it was receiving the cream of African refugees seeking safe new homes but their skills and experience 'go to waste'.[88]

Other examples of poor decision-making involve the acquired South African subsidiary of US food giant Unilever. The company has imposed grand-scale inertia on itself in several of its operations because of management's reluctance to change its traditional way of making top-down decisions. In a vain attempt to introduce a more flexible, coherent and customer-oriented perspective, in the early 2000s, it introduced a complex system of committees covering a range of departments and dozens of people so that their extradisciplinary input could be fed upwards. On successive occasions committees were openly told that decisions had already been taken, so requisite meetings have become inward-looking and perfunctory.

Normally, an outside consultant also accompanies the process with the result that decision-making has become slower and more expensive – and without the benefit of the company's lower-level participation.

In one case, a decision was made to move from a regional to a central call centre. The decision took five months to make and another five months to implement. The original estimated cost saving of R2 million was reduced to under R500 000. A similar decision-making routine is evident in the group's new product launches. Since the new decision-making structure was introduced, fewer new products have been unveiled and more have failed, with launch costs substantially higher than before. The committee structure is also contributing to difficult integration with local acquisitions, where, in one case, departures are three times the rate of the local parent.[89]

At a relatively pedestrian learning level, South Africa's corporate sector has long experience of high stock losses, especially during holiday periods. Up to 40 per cent of all losses suffered by the corporate sector occur during the year-end period,[90] yet many companies continue to neglect to impose any security measures over the Christmas period. They often allow their entire management team to take leave at the same time, leaving the company's stock virtually unsupervised for up to two weeks at a time.

Mistakes are being repeated at a regional level, too. The Southern African Development Community (SADC) , which has been involved in combined peacekeeping efforts in Lesotho and relief operations in Mozambique, doesn't 'practise to correct our mistakes', according to one of the SADC's operational commanders. Major General Tegobo Masire, who is also deputy commander of the Botswana Defence Force, admitted:

… there was a tendency to watch problems develop without making contingency plans to intervene. This leads to last-minute scrambles to hatch up a plan to arrest the situation, resulting in inadequate planning and poor execution. A look at the reports of past missions indicates that the same mistakes are repeated over and over again.[91]

But South Africa, along with many of its African neighbours, holds the dubious distinction of being one of the best and most tragic exemplars of experiential non-learning of all, with regard to the unrelenting advance of AIDS that UNICEF, the UN's children's agency, describes as the worst catastrophe in history.[92] A public health matter with relevant decision-making issues that reflect widely across African countries, its consequences are already having a profound impact on wider questions, including national economies. For whatever reasons – cultural, educational, political, financial – more than two decades of experience has had little effect on most government remedial actions or on individuals' sexual behaviour with the result that, as of the early twenty-first century, it is estimated that AIDS will restrict the life span of at least 40 per cent of the total population of some countries to less than ten more years. In South Africa, the official rate of HIV-positive people in 2004 totalled 15 per cent of the adult population,[93] although the actual figure is almost certainly more than twice this.

Israel

While South Africa appears to want to start from almost scratch, Israel has tended to be more acquisitive in terms of utilizing others' experience. After starting off as an underdeveloped country just 54 years ago, by acquiring skills and experience in large measure – mainly through immigration, a strategy that echoes that of the US over the past 150 years – the country's economic development has been impressive. Its GDP totals US$92 587 million from a population of 6.1 million.[94] It is 35 per cent less competitive than the US, ranking thirty-third.

With regard to learning, however, it has not been all plain sailing. For almost a decade, the emerging hi-tech industry has been running at a pace that has now outstripped the traditional agricultural sector, where marketing skills were always weak, especially in the global arena.[95] This marketing weakness has carried over into high-tech sector, where large numbers of start-ups have been unable to survive the recent high-tech and 'dot.com' crash. A frequent problem for start-up companies, especially in the computer software, computer components and telecommunications industries, is the penchant for launching genuinely innovative products without any serious market penetration strategy, the ritual way of thinking being that 'the market should be listening to us rather than us having to listen to the market'. Surprisingly, this has been going on for at least 15 years with the support of the venture capital industry. Acknowledging this limitation, one of Israel's leading technology investors is on record as saying:

It is painful to see a new generation of entrepreneurs in the Israeli high technology sector repeating the mistakes of their predecessors. These mistakes may lead to either complete failure or the inability to leverage the technology advantage into global leadership.[96]

In the two years to mid-2002, an estimated 15 000 high-tech workers were laid off, most of them in start-ups and small companies.[97]

The failure to learn from experiences also extends to Israel's construction industry. For more than 30 years Israel has continued to employ a low-paid, poorly trained workforce, with the result that local contractors are finding it increasingly difficult to meet the high standards demanded by international developers.[98]

After the Six Day War in 1967 and the capture of the West Bank and Gaza, Israel replaced its own workforce with unskilled and cheap Arab labour. Then, after the 1987 Intifada, it started to replace them with tens of thousands of workers from Eastern Europe, Turkey, Africa, Asia and elsewhere without checking skills or previous experience. By the admission of one of its foremost consultants,[99] building quality is 'horrific', with costs 25 per cent more than in the US and construction times taking three times longer. Israeli training is so backward that young carpenters still learn to make formwork with old 2×4s tied with metal wire. Yet the Israel Ministry of Labour, which is in charge of worker training, prefers to focus on collecting fees by issuing permits to contractors to bring in more foreign workers.

Israel also refuses to accept help from the US, which has offered to bring modern apprenticeship training programmes to Israel and integrate these into government-run craft training schools. The head of a large engineering consultancy to many of the contractors working on the over-budget and overdue $500 million expansion of Ben Gurion International Airport reports that contractors simply accept the labour inefficiencies, telling project owners that slow work and poor quality are 'just the way it is in Israel'. He adds that the situation will probably deteriorate further, 'and Israel's addiction to cheap labour will continue to feed on itself'.[100]

As all these examples show, evidence of learning from experience is less than inspiring despite the constant advice to companies to improve their learning capabilities, which – when it happens – is usually concentrated on networking, on closer contact with customers and suppliers, on more effective ways of marrying advancing technology with emerging consumer patterns and behaviour, and benchmarking. All these are not necessarily the wrong thing to do but they all utilize outside input that overlooks the knowledge that resides inside the front door.

Notes

1. François, Duc de La Rochefoucauld, *Sentences et Maximes Morales*, 1678.
2. Personal correspondence, May 2003.
3. Survey reported in *Sunday Telegraph*, 19 October 2003.
4. Groningen Growth and Development Centre and the Conference Board, *Total Economy Database*, August 2004 at: http://www.ggdc.net.
5. Ben Macintyre, *The Times*, 20 July 2002.
6. Special study commissioned to assess school standards, reported in *Sunday Times*, 1 May 2005.
7. Conference, National Association of Head Teachers, April 2005.
8. Lord Levene, speech, City Forum, 3 February 2004 at: http://www.lloyds.com.
9. The TaxPayers' Alliance, *The Bumper Book of Government Waste and Useless Spending 2004*, 2 February 2004 available at: http://www.taxpayersalliance.com/news/news.php?id=55.
10. The TaxPayers' Alliance, *The Bumper Book of Government Waste and Useless Spending 2005*, 12 January 2005 available at: ttp://www.taxpayersalliance.com/news/news.php?id=55.
11. Leaked report, Office for National Statistics, reported in *Sunday Times*, 1 May 2005.
12. Special study commissioned to assess school standards, reported in *Sunday Times*, 1 May 2005.
13. Peter Tymms, professor of education, Durham University, quoted in *The Times*, 2 May 2005. See http://www.timesonline.co.uk/article/0.2087-1592747.00.html.
14. *Sunday Times*, 1 May 2005.
15. *Daily Mirror*, 19 April 2003.
16. United Nations, *Statistical Yearbook 2002*, New York: UN.
17. United Nations Industrial Development Organization, *Industrial Statistics Database*, New York: UNIDO, 1996.
18. Groningen Growth and Development Centre and the Conference Board, *Total Economy Database*, op. cit.
19. 'Fire and Forget', *The Economist*, 20 April 1996.
20. J. Utterbach, *Mastering the Dynamics of Innovation*, Cambridge, MA: Harvard Business School Press, 1994.
21. E. Abrahamson, 'Change Without Pain', *Harvard Business Review*, July–August 2000, p. 79.
22. Ibid.
23. 'Fire and Forget', op. cit.
24. Corporate Leadership Council, *Employee Retention: New Tools for Managing Workforce Stability and Engagement*, Washington, DC:CLC, 1998.
25. Ibid.
26. Ibid.
27. Ibid.
28. UNIDO, *Industrial Statistics Database*, op. cit.
29. Groningen Growth and Development Centre and the Conference Board, *Total Economy Database*, op. cit.
30. OECD, *Annual Report*, 1998.
31. Institute for Management Development, *World Competitiveness Yearbook 2004*, Lausanne: IMD, 2004.
32. United Nations, *Statistical Yearbook 2002*, op. cit.
33. Office for National Statistics, 4 June 2003. See 'Fall in Public sector Productivity Makes the Case for Reform', *The Daily Telegraph*, 5 June 2003.
34. Ibid.
35. DTI, 30 September 2003.
36. World Economic Forum, *Annual Survey*, October 2004.
37. *The Economic Journal*, July 2003.
38. OECD, *Annual Report*, 2000.
39. As at July 2003.

40. OECD, *Annual Report*, 1998.
41. *Financial Times*, 26 November 1993.
42. The Royal Society of Arts, *Reassessing the Context of Manufacturing Success*, London: RSA, January 1997.
43. Research by the Skills Task Force quoted in 'DTI Launches Investigation of UK Management Skills', 23 October 2002 at: http://www.trainingfoundation.com/news/default.asp?page1D=837.
44. *Working Capital. Intangible Assets and the Productivity Gap*, London: The Work Foundation, 2001.
45. BAA Lynton report, 1993.
46. *Daily Mail* report, January 2000.
47. House of Commons Transport, Local Government and Regions Select Committee, *Fourteenth Report: How the Local Government Act 2000 is Working*, 12 September 2002.
48. Lord Alexander, chairman, NatWest Group plc, speech, Guild Hall, London.
49. *The Times*, 26 April 2003.
50. *Computer Weekly*, October 2004.
51. National Audit Office, January 2004.
52. According to various press reports throughout 2001.
53. *The Sun*, 16 September 2002.
54. OECD, *Annual Report*, 1994.
55. United Nations, *Statistical Yearbook 2002*, op. cit.
56. 'Entrepreneurship in New Zealand's Knowledge Economy', *Global Enterprise Monitor*, 2001.
57. *Statistics New Zealand*, 2005 at: http://www.stats.govt.nz/default.htm.
58. New Zealand Stock Exchange, *Fact Book*, February 2002.
59. IMD, *World Competitiveness Yearbook 2004*, op. cit.
60. Groningen Growth and Development Centre and he Conference Board, *Total Economy Database*, op. cit.
61. *Economic Development Indicators 2005*, Ministry of Economic Development and Treasury, February 2005.
62. UNIDO, *Industrial Statistics Database*, op. cit.
63. Groningen Growth and Development Centre and he Conference Board, *Total Economy Database*, op. cit.
64. OECD, *Annual Report on Competition Policy Developments in New Zealand*, December 2003.
65. Study by Professor Viv Hall, Victoria University, 1996, reported in Roger Kerr, 'Productivity Rises Fatten Pay Packets', *New Zealand Herald*, 4 July 2003.
66. Human Synergistics research, reported I *Business Focus* Newsletter, no. 4, 27 November 2003.
67. Reported in 'Bosses Duck for Cover', *Sydney Morning Herald*, 7 November 2002.
68. Sheffield CEO Compensation Survey, 2001, quoted in *New Zealand Herald*, 12 April 2002.
69. Ian Taylor, managing director, Sheffield Ltd, quoted in 'New Zealand Can Learn From Others' Mistakes on CEO Pay', *New Zealand Herald*, 12 April 2004.
70. New Zealand Institute of Management, *Capability Index*, November 2003.
71. New Zealand Sheep Council booklet, *A Guide to Hogget Lambing*.
72. *New Zealand Herald*, 7 April 2003.
73. *New Zealand Herald*, 5 December 2003.
74. Peter Davis, *Failing To Learn From Failure – IT Failure and the New Zealand Public Service*, Albany, Auckland: Massey University Graduate School of Business, July 2001.
75. *Sentinel Events Workbook*, Standards New Zealand (SNZ).
76. 'The Corrections Department is Being Sued by Prisoners for More Than $3 Million', *The Press*, 9 January 2004.
77. United Nations, *Statistical Yearbook 2002*, op. cit.
78. UNIDO, *Industrial Statistics Database*, op. cit.
79. *Mail and Guardian*, 14 November 2003.
80. *Mail and Guardian*, 11 May 2004.
81. Institute for Management Development, *World Competitiveness Yearbook 1997*, Lausanne: IMD, 1997.
82. IMD, *World Competitiveness Yearbook 2004*, op. cit.
83. *Mail and Guardian*, 29 September 2003.
84. South Africa Human Development Report, *The Challenge of Sustainable Development: Unlocking People's Creativity*, United Nations Development Programme, 2003.
85. Entrepreneurship proposal to the Department of Trade and Industry, 1999.

86. *Medium Term Budget Policy Statement*, November 2003.
87. Tony Manning, chairman of South Africa's Institute of Directors, 'Working Together for a Common Goal', *Business Day*, 12 April 2002.
88. United Nations High Commissioner for Refugees and the Japan International Cooperation Agency, December 2003.
89. Author interview with employee.
90. Survey, GriffithsReid security company, quoted in the *Mail and Guardian*, 30 November 2004.
91. Major General Tegobo Masire, conference on air power at Midrand. September 2000.
92. UNICEF, *The State of the World's Children*, 9 December 2004.
93. *Statistics SA*, Pretoria, 2004 mid-year statistical update, reported in the *Mail and Guardian*, 29 July 2004.
94. United Nations, *Statistical Yearbook 2002*, op. cit.
95. Dr Shlomo Kalish, chairman and founder of Jerusalem Global Ltd., 'Ten Commandments for the Israeli High Technology Entrepreneur', *Jerusalem Post*, 2 February 2000.
96. Ibid.
97. *HaEretz*, 30 July 2002.
98. *Israel High-Tech & Investment Report*, March 2001.
99. Ibid.
100. Ira Braverman, 'Learn from Israel's Mistakes', *Engineering News Record*, 7 May 2001, p. 51.

6 *Going for 20:20 Vision*

Experience. The wisdom that enables us to recognize in an undesirable old acquaintance the folly that we have already embraced.

Ambrose Bierce, US author[1]

Not all is doom and gloom in the business world by any stretch of the imagination. Some organizations do run relatively efficiently and also try to learn from hindsight. As a balance to the last chapter's concentration on how organizations don't learn from their experiences, it is instructive to outline how some organizations do use various experiential learning techniques to reasonably good effect. That said, the numbers of genuine experiential learners are still small and the fact that many of their methodologies are mainly personal innovations highlight the non-formalized approach to the whole discipline – and business teaching's Big Black Hole.

There are two involuntary approaches and several planned learning agendas that have been developed, all of which are discussed below.

Unconscious learning

One involuntary approach to learning is the intuitive approach that is effectively typecast as unconscious learning. A process that is completely unstructured and random, it is the type of learning that is probably the most prevalent of all and is often unrecognized as such. It is almost always self-initiated. In the business world this approach would include the lessons Semco's Ricardo Semler, head of the diversified engineering and consulting group, learned as an 18-year-old in his rock 'n' roll band. 'If the drummer doesn't feel like coming to rehearsals you know something's wrong. You can hassle him as much as you want but the problem remains.' He has applied this to his business life by focusing on how to get people to want to come to work on a grey Monday morning. 'That is really the only parameter we care about, which is 100 per cent a motivation issue.'[2] Some of the methods used at Semco have been picked up by manufacturing companies in the US, schools in Finland, an Australian hospital and the Amsterdam police force, which illustrates the external form of experiential learning called benchmarking. Another example of this external learning format would be the response by some British farmers to the low prices demanded by big chain supermarkets. Among others, Ludlow, Cheshire, farmers have imported the concept of the 'Slow Food Movement' from Italy, where local producers have bypassed supermarkets through direct-sale local markets.

Incidental learning

The second type of involuntary learning is the incidental approach, where the education process occurs through chance circumstances that are out of the ordinary. Like intuitive learning, it is unstructured, informal and usually involves pondering over incidents such as mishaps or frustrations in odd moments. In this case the outcome – the learning – usually, but not always, takes the form of rationalization or justification. Once again, this type of learning is often unrecognized as such and is almost always self-initiated. A business example would be the lesson learned by Gerald Ratner, one-time head of the world's largest jewellery chain, whose remark that one of his product lines was 'crap' led to his eventual dismissal and the group's demise as an independent business.

Planned learning

Almost all of the more formal approaches to learning that fall under the wider category of planned learning revolve around retrospective learning. Involving deliberate reflection of incidents with the clear intention of reaching conclusions it is, like the intuitive and incidental approach, usually initiated by mishaps and mistakes but also includes routine events and accomplishments. Because it involves a conscious intention to learn, the quality of erudition is often more superior to the intuitive and incidental approaches.

Proactive learning

Into this category falls the types of reflective learning that occur both proactively and defensively.

An example of the more proactive type of reflective learning can be seen in Kraft's decision[3] to cut back on the fat and sugar content of its products and reduce the size of its portions. The world's second largest food manufacturer, the maker of Dairylea cheese triangles and Toblerone chocolate, came to this choice because of a range of possible reasons – a social responsibility stimulus because of the global epidemic of obesity and/or the potential hazard of being sued by overweight consumers in the way in which tobacco companies have been litigated by smokers. In Kraft's case, the learning was proactive and personal. When the learning is not proactive and when the issues are, like smoking, matters of wider public interest, the 'learning' is often imposed through, for example, voluntary codes of conduct or legislation.

The use of case studies, internal audits, post-project reviews and/or oral postmortems fall into this category. This type of experiential learning is also relatively rare in industry. Often, they take the form of prosecutional inquiries into disaster-like incidents, the nature of which is designed to detect fault or apportion blame. National Westminster Bank set up one such inquiry in the 1990s after its investment banking arm incurred a £77 million loss by mispricing derivatives. It was an incident that sparked the resignation of the subsidiary's chief executive and the departure of six other senior managers. Governments are devoted to these types of examination, which are usually expensively carried out – but usually without personal sanctions.

Defensive learning

An example of reflective learning in the defensive mode is the erudition that stemmed from the activities of the UK's most prolific serial killer, Dr Harold Shipman, a general practitioner who murdered at least 215 of his patients. It was only after he was caught and convicted – after 23 years – that questions like 'how' and 'why' the system allowed the Midlands doctor to get away with his nefarious activities for so long arose. Several inquiries discovered that the coroner and police services were, literally, fatally flawed. The system, which allowed doctors to sign death certificates without any corroboration, had not been adapted or improved since it had been set up over 100 years ago. It was also discovered that coroners, who were presiding over medical and legal issues, did not receive adequate training. Equally, there were serious shortcomings in the police investigations. While its 'learning' was reflective, it was only initiated after the event – in this case, tragedy. In many cases, such inquiries and their learning are very soon forgotten, the recommendations that emerged from similar enquiries into the UK's 1960s foot and mouth outbreak being one recent example and several rail accident inquiries being another.

Within this reflective category are four general, but not mutually exclusive, schemas that are variously called action learning, cognition learning, reflective learning and experiential learning.[4] In fact all four – like intuitive and incidental learning – are forms of experiential learning that not only recognize the importance of experience as the starting point for erudition but also that its lessons can help improve on both success and failure.

Action learning

Action learning is the approach pioneered in the 1970s by Professor Reg Revans[5] that uses a skilled facilitator to impose a discipline of self-reflection and analysis on team members of individual projects. It conceives learning as rational, linear, deterministic and quantifiable and emphasizes the behavioural changes that take place in managers when solving problems. Behind the concept is the argument that it is difficult to communicate an idea by word and by argument when managers are themselves extremely poor at communication. Project-based, it revolves around the questioning and reflection processes in a process otherwise called single-loop and double-loop learning. The aim is to enable managers to detect and prevent errors, accurately transfer information, or successfully achieve goals.

The cognitive approaches, including so-called 'generative' and 'adaptive' learning, focus on changes in how managers think, specifically the processes of memory, perception, mental models, schemas and representations. As with the action process, problem-solving is important, the goal being to create coherent and orderly representations of complex problems in the minds of managers.

Reflective learning focuses on self-discovery and questioning using historical, social, and cultural implications of management while experiential approaches concentrate on how managers acquire and transform old experiences into new experiences. Knowledge is conceived of as being largely personal and individual.

Prospective learning

Finally there is prospective learning, which I will deal with more fully in my description of Experience-Based Management in Chapter 10. Arguably the most effective at preventing repeated mistakes and building constructively on successes, this kind of learning includes all the elements of retrospective learning along with the more proactive intention of planning to learn *before* an experience takes place and more rigorous processes to capture the more elusive elements of existing data, information and knowledge.

Case studies: company-specific experiential learning

It is instructive how some companies have adapted the traditional 'conscious' approaches[6] to experiential learning, in particular the retrospective approach.

Michael Smurfit, chairman of the Jefferson Smurfit Group paper packaging empire, keeps a personal list of his mistakes to remind him not to repeat them. Believing that mistakes go hand-in-hand with risk, he calculates that his blunders up until 1997 cost the group £120 million.[7]

In a novel twist to the conventional way in which the lessons of experience are passed down from one generation to another, Roger Enrico, the chief executive of American soft drinks giant PepsiCo, spent several months in the 18-month period *before* he joined the company in 1996 with nine corporate executives at his Cayman Islands home. At these meetings he passed on his own experiences. Part of the programme involved the executives working on specific projects, the lessons of which were then passed on to others.[8]

The improvement principle

Benetton, the Italian clothes company, intentionally learns from experience through trial and error, notably by experimenting and retaining what has worked at each stage of the company's development. This is based on its refusal to accept established knowledge as the ultimate truth. Instead, its philosophy is based on the evolutionary principle that today's process can always be improved. The process starts with collecting opinions on a specific issue.[9] These are then used to create a hypothesis about causal relationships. To confirm or disprove the hypothesis, data is then gathered and analysed to make their meaning clear. This is then repeated several times, each time improving the quality of the hypothesis, data, analysis and synthesis until the hypothesis is accepted as meaningful information. Based on this, decisions about the allocation of resources are made and implemented. Then the results are compared with the expectations and the reasons for any deviation are reviewed. The new insights this produces are used to update the existing body of knowledge.

BP in the UK has a completely different approach to experiential learning.[10] The petroleum exploration and refining company has a special post-project appraisal unit to review major investment projects, write up case studies and derive lessons for planners that are then incorporated into revisions of the company's planning guidelines. A five-person unit reports to the board of directors and reviews six projects annually. This type of review is now conducted regularly at the project level.

Selective learning

Yet another approach to experiential learning[11] is taken by the US company Chaparral Steel, a small mill specialist that is especially known for its 1980s innovations in horizontal casting techniques. Founded more than 25 years ago, the company has become one of the largest US steel-makers. Chaparral stands out from other companies in the systematic way in which it selects projects and then applies learning from one project to another. It requires every project to advance the company's capabilities and plans combinations of projects in a logical flow to ensure that they do so. After each project has been completed, Chaparral analyses it to find out what it achieved or failed to, and why.

In their efforts to improve subsequent decision-making, General Motors and Hewlett-Packard have used retrospective historical analysis.[12] General Motors systematically reconstructed the development of its 'X' and 'J' platform cars in 1981 to search for lessons about success and failure. These new cars, which had experienced severe quality, schedule and cost problems, had been rushed through the development process in the late 1970s to give General Motors fuel-efficient models at a time when petrol prices were high and volatile and when small foreign cars were successfully invading the US domestic market. Almost 80 managers were involved in the study to reconstruct the development process. The outside consultants which conducted the study uncovered a range of important deficiencies in General Motors' methods while many participants of the study 'found their attitudes about project management and product quality transformed for the better, and the results are today visible in the high-quality rankings given to several GM models and manufacturing facilities'.

Postmortems

In Hewlett-Packard's case, the company used post-project reviews to internally benchmark its scheduling practices. In 1987, each of its 56 research and development centres was charged with doing postmortems on a number of their recent development projects. Events and processes seen as contributing to project scheduling failures and successes were then shared among all units.

Microsoft, which is among the most successful companies with a good record of learning from both within and without the organization, has an integrated approach to its experiential learning. Part of the process is to deliberately learn from past mistakes and extract lessons for future projects through regular postmortems at the end of each project. Customer feedback is built into the design process through market research, customer support hotlines and usability testing. Input also occurs while the projects are underway in terms of metrics and quantitative measures.[13]

One of the best examples of experiential learning taking place at the prospective level is the approach taken by Boeing when it developed its latest generations of aircraft. Before the company started to evolve its 757 and 767 aircraft, a group of senior employees spent three years on 'Project Homework' comparing the managerial failures and successes of past development processes. They produced hundreds of recommendations. Several members of the team then transferred to the 757 and 767 start-up projects. Guided by this experience, Boeing produced the most problem-free product launches in its history.[14]

The tacit input

To try and share its tacit knowledge management consultants Arthur D. Little complements its employment of expert systems through constant on-the-job coaching and networking on different assignments.

A quite different approach to capturing and applying tacit knowledge was used by Ford and BP in the US,[15] when the companies hired researchers from the Massachusetts Institute of Technology (MIT) to produce a so-called learning history. Using oral debriefing techniques, interviewees recalled their experiences anonymously and in their own words in a way that reflected their collective learning experience. The transcripts were then used to extract insights that become a best practice manual that managers and staff read before starting another project of a similar nature and which personnel specialists are using to design training.

Ford debriefed 1200 employees tracking the progress of teams in the US, Hungary, Ireland and Brazil in a car parts division, at an assembly plant and in product design and development. Vic Leo, a systems dynamics and organizational learning manager at Ford in Detroit, estimates that the assembly plant factory has achieved quality improvements of 25 per cent a year since 1995 compared with less than 10 per cent achieved for two comparable factories: 'The plant was ranked third out of the three when we started. When we stopped our learning history it was number one.' One of the benefits of the learning history, says Leo, was that it helped expose unexpected problems such as culture clashes and knock-on effects on other systems when a new working practice is spread throughout Ford's 380 000-strong workforce. He dismisses traditional consultancy reports – they can put 'too much of their own spin on a story' – as formulaic. 'Often you read reports about teams which are filed away and forgotten. But the learning histories captivate the readers. I also feel they give a much rounder picture.'[16]

At BP, learning histories are calculated to have saved £22.5 million in a three-year trial at just one of its refineries. The approach came to BP when a group of Ohio employees solved a dangerous butane leakage problem that had gone unnoticed by managers for eight years. Since then dozens of other efficiency projects and two learning histories have been launched at the refinery, helping staff to increase productivity, says BP, by 35 per cent in a two-year period. Paul Monus, who launched BP's first learning history at the Lima refinery in Ohio, is now advising other refineries how to introduce the techniques of oral debriefing. Projects have taken between three and nine months to complete and cost from $10 000 to more than $150 000, the larger ones involving up to 100 debriefings and 2000 pages of narrative.

From Benetton's form of trial-and-error learning to Boeing's prospective learning technique and Ford and BP's oral debriefings, such systematic self-analysis is rare in industry. Yet, it is one of the main requirements for any business wanting to be a genuine learning organization. To qualify as such, part of the exercise is to be able to learn effectively from one's own experiences, which necessitates being able to review both successes and failures objectively, assess them methodically and communicate the lessons in a form that employees find open and accessible.

Remember hard copy?

Industry's and commerce's ignorance about how genuine experiential learning works lies primarily in the way in which they now manage the 'capture' aspect of their memory systems. Up until the 1980s, most organizations collected and stored their self-generated or externally acquired data, information and knowledge in voluminous libraries, the fiefdom of scholarly archivists whose corporate knowledge was usually prodigious. Shelving, boxes, folders and envelopes were the outward manifestations and a manual index the *entrée*. In-house social networks added to the store of knowledge available to organizations, providing the underpinning to their experiential learning.

Came the computer revolution and the opportunity arrived for a new approach to preserving and using OM through huge investments in sophisticated IT systems such as intranets and electronic bulletin boards. The intranet was the institution-wide communications network and database that could store and provide access to codified knowledge ranging from business proposals, project descriptions and client communications while electronic bulletin boards, originally set up by Lotus Notes, was a forum through which individuals could post questions, share resources or solutions to problems, or engage in discussions about specific topics. The former allowed hard copy to be replaced by digital reproductions that could be accessed in seconds rather than hours or days, while the latter enabled individuals to request help from people who were beyond the reach of their social networks.

Socializing: the other knowledge-sharing medium

Social networks were also supposed to continue their valuable role as a conduit of tacit knowledge alongside a new innovation called knowledge centres comprising formal groups of experts who collected and provided documentation generated by projects, best practice and solutions to specific problems. They gathered the knowledge from the personal experience of its members and from contributions from individuals throughout the firm. The information was usually accessed through directories of experts and background information or through indexed systems on electronic bulletin boards and knowledge centres. It is a concept that has also spread beyond the organization in a collaborative movement called communities of practice comprising groups of people who share their collective learning.

Social networking covered three other approaches to allow the cross-fertilization of knowledge. One was job rotation, the policy that was supposed to give employees wide disciplinary exposure across an organization. In some companies a two- to three-year tenure was considered optimum; anything more was a signal that the individual's career was going nowhere. A sign that organizations are falling out of love with this approach comes in Shell's decision at the end of 2004 to scrap its controversial 'gifted amateur' management promotion scheme under which top executives switched jobs every three years. The company decided to extend the policy to five years or more in one role following project handover problems and assignment delays in transition. Although it was not specifically given as a reason, the flexible labour market must also have had a hand in the decision, circumstances that are also affecting the second and third aproaches to modern 'social networking' – cross-functioning teams and mentoring.

Mentoring is perhaps the most effective of all the socializing approaches, mainly because the close nature of the professional relationship between mentor and protégé allows the successful transfer of tacit knowledge. The practice is different from the role of the teacher, who is a paid servant, or a coach, which has a shorter, sometimes time-bound relationship with the mentee and usually focuses on more immediate results to help achieve goals, solve problems, learn and develop. A mentor, whilst also a coach, is a benevolent master who shares advice, accomplishments and experience by trying to help a learner articulate some of his or her tacit knowledge. In fact, mentoring is not a modern practice. It was practised commonly in ancient Greek, Roman, Chinese, Indian and even African civilizations. In medieval times it was the cornerstone of many a university's educational programme. There are also references to mentoring in Greek mythology some 2500 years ago. In Homer's

Odyssey, for example, Mentor was the name of the teacher of Telemachus, the son of Odysseus. He was described by Homer as a 'wise and trusted counsellor'. When Odysseus went on long voyages, Mentor also had to look after Odysseus's household and act as father to Telemachus.

The use of these social networking approaches was an acknowledgement of the advantages of being able to retrieve and refer to past documentation, records and experiences. Yet, although they provided organizations with what appeared to be a more efficient way of learning from experience, wider productivity is not being fully matched by the availability of all this potential knowledge.

Why modern systems are not working well

Clues to the reasons for this anomaly can be found in an academic study[17] of the memory systems in six offices of a large multinational consulting firm, three of which were located in the US, one in Canada and two in Europe. The company was considered to be a relevant case study because of its knowledge-intensive character. More than 40 per cent of users rated the intranet and electronic bulletin boards as less than effective whilst just over 30 per cent felt the same way about knowledge centres. In addition to specific system-specific shortcomings (for example, available information was too generalized and incomplete, with slow updating, poor search engines, indexing and filtering systems), the paper's author then flagged up the issue of high staff turnover. Confirming that social networks have continued their role as (potentially) the most effective means for storing and accessing organizational memory, he observed:

> … it is interesting to note that, in the case of social networks, turnover affects the accessibility of experiential knowledge. Some respondents described instances where they were looking for project-related experience but the people involved had already left the organization.[18]

What he was referring to was, of course, the departure of tacit and other related OM that generations prior to the onset of the flexible labour market did not have to contend with. The tacit component of OM is the cornerstone of any process of experiential learning, which raises its head in another aspect of modern information systems. Apart from outside input such as independent research, the content of the intranet comprises the contributions of the organization's own employees, the initiation for which usually comes from a group that manages the database or from an individual or project team. There is usually a formal process whereby the individual is required to provide a detailed description of the project and nature of the contribution which is then evaluated and, if deemed valuable, added to the database. In the past, with a less flexible labour market in tow, this type of contribution was largely unnecessary. Its requirement today calls for managers to be good communicators on paper (which they're generally not), candid (almost impossible) and have an awareness of what is tacit (rare).

Modern information systems may well boast great learning potential but the reality is very different or – better said – still largely unutilized to anything like their full potential. In any event, the 'capture' component of OM is still only part of the experiential learning process, with the main element being the actual cognitive process of applying the evidence.

For the purposes of this book, I will not get involved with the possible pedagogic issues of this part of the cycle; I prefer to leave this to constituencies with far more resources. Rather, I will deal with solutions to a whole array of more practical problems of how best to apply existing experiential learning techniques to industry and commerce's special environment. They are issues that neither academics nor anyone else for that matter have yet addressed and would exist whether or not new pedagogic slants were incorporated into conventional theory and practice. Whilst accepting that improvements are possible, even necessary (they can only be integrated when business teaching, industry and commerce allow the methodology to be used more widely) the underlying doctrine nevertheless remains sound.

Addressing the innate problems

The raft of inherent problems with traditional experiential learning – however it's done – starts with its design. Most of the work on the subject is focused on pre-school, primary and secondary schools and universities for applications on training programmes for professions such as social work or classroom teaching. Whilst useful because it embraces an understanding of all the formative stages of individual development, the specific attention that practitioners have given to the world of business is negligible. Consequently, I have specifically adapted their basic methodology for corporates, using decision-making – the single most important skill of any manager – as the core focus.

Second, the experiential learning that *is* practised is individual-centred. Because the power base of knowledge has moved away from organizations to transient employees, I have refocused the methodology to also provide benefit to organizations through a schema that I've called the 'Lessons Audit'.

The third problem I have addressed is the retrospective aspect of all experiential learning. At first sight this statement might appear to be transparently obvious. To learn from experience, the experience must first happen. Yes, but the fact that the necessary reflection for any experiential learning to take place happens *after* the fact brings with it an important constraint. The required contemplative aspect means that accurate recall is a prerequisite. On its own an *accurate* memory is unattainable, so with inaccurate or incomplete data/ information/ knowledge, the learning potential of existing methodologies is necessarily limited. For good experiential learning to take place, then, experience has to be 'captured' in some way. This is where the inherent chinks in the corporate armoury start to complicate the picture. The very flexible labour market ensures continuous job disruption, the organization's knowledge base goes walkabout on a regular basis and individuals' short and selective memory recall further trims the organization's evidential base from which good experiential learning might derive.

Alongside these in-built constraints there is the accepted difficulty of capturing experiences. Whether the data/information/knowledge is transferred to an IT application or left on paper, the recall is generally the responsibility of individual managers who provide the input in their own written hand. Alternatively, their accounts are rewritten by third parties as in the case of Booz Allen & Hamilton's knowledge managers. The problem with these approaches is that most managers, burdened with short, selective and defensive memories anyway, are, as already suggested, notoriously bad communicators, especially on paper. The other drawback, as knowledge managers have acknowledged, is the common difficulty of communicating one of the most important elements of any core capability – tacit knowledge, a feature of learning that few managers would even know how to define, let alone relate in any useful form.

To anticipate these problems, I have introduced, remodelled and upgraded two 'capture' mediums that are both cost-effective and suitable for learning, one to secure short- and medium-term organizational memory and the other to preserve long-term OM. For those organizations that find managerial defensiveness a dominant constraint to any form of knowledge capture, I have also innovated an approach designed to short-circuit any self-protective behaviour.

Finally, I have accepted that experiential learning can never be all-encompassing. Otherwise, individuals and organizations would be spending more of their time learning than doing. To accommodate this, I have built into the learning cycle a provision for organizations to preselect important events that are considered prime learning prospects. This is done through four separate but interrelated exercises that I've called the 'Knowledge Chart', the 'Project Map', the 'Employee Transit Audit' and the 'Knowledge Retrieval Plan'.

As already indicated, I've called the model experience-based management (EBM) to give the whole process an identifiable name.

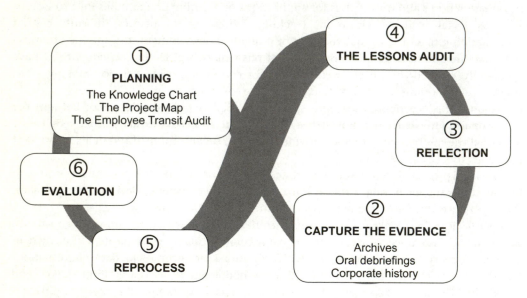

Figure 6.1   The continuous six-stage EBM learning spiral

As shown in Figure 6.1, its six-stage learning cycle incorporates:

- a *planning stage* to prune the potential learning opportunities down to a manageable size that harmonizes with the organization's perceived requirements
- a *knowledge 'capture' stage* to ensure that experiences don't walk out of the front door and that organizational memory, when it is recalled, is not imprecise
- a *'reflection' module* to make sense of information, extract meaning and relate this to everyday organizational and wider business life
- a *Lessons Audit* to allow for institution-wide fertilization across the organization and down the generations so that learning becomes more corporately-based
- A linked, two-part *'reprocess/evaluation'* stage to ensure continuous learning.

Although large improvements are not ruled out, its running objective is to make many small, incremental improvements. If every manager identified just one lesson per month that was translated into a better decision, the collective impact across an organization over a relatively short period would be considerable. It's the trumpet call of all education, training and coaching.

Notes

1. Ambrose Bierce, *The Devil's Dictionary*, 1881–1906.
2. Management Page, *Financial Times*, 15 May 1997.
3. Kraft announcement, 1 July 2003.
4. D. Christopher Kayes, 'Experiential Learning and its Critics: Preserving the Role of Experience in Management Learning and Education', *Academy of Management Learning and Education*, vol. 1, no. 2, 2002, pp. 137–49.
5. W. Revans, *Action Learning: New Techniques for Management*, London: Blond & Briggs, 1980.
6. A. Mumford, 'Four Approaches to Learning from Experience', *The Learning Organization*, vol. 1, no. 1, 1994.
7. *Sunday Telegraph*, 14 September 1997.
8. N.M. Tichy with E. Cohen, *The Leadership Engine*, New York: HarperBusiness, 1997.
9. Mastering Management series, *Financial Times*, 22 March 1996.
10. D. Garvin, 'Building a Learning Organization', *Harvard Business Review*, July–August 1993, pp. 78–91.
11. 1992 research study at Harvard University, the Massachusetts Institute of Technology, Purdue and Stanford universities. Findings published in Kim B. Clark, H. Kent Bowen and Charles A. Holloway, *The Perpetual Enterprise Machine: Seven Keys to Corporate Renewal Through Successful Product and Process Development*, New York: Oxford University Press, 1994.
12. A. Leucke, *Scuttle Your Ships before Advancing: And Other Lessons from History on Leadership and Change for Today's Managers*, New York: Oxford University Press, 1994.
13. M. Cusumano and R. Selby, *Microsoft Secrets*, New York: Free Press, 1995/ New York: HarperCollins, 1996.
14. Garvin, 'Building a Learning Organization', op. cit.
15. *Personnel Today*, July 1997.
16. Fernando Olivera, 'Memory Systems in Organizations: An Empirical Investigation of Mechanisms for Knowledge Collection, Storage and Access', *Journal of Management Studies*, September 2000.
17. Arnold Kransdorff and Russell Williams, 'Swing Doors and Musical Chairs' *Business Horizons*, May–June 1999.
18. H.A. Simon, 'Bounded Rationality and Organizational Learning', *Organizational Science*, 1991.

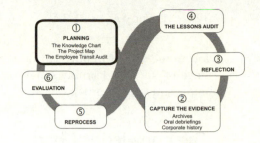

CHAPTER

7 *Cutting the Workload*

In preparing for battle I have always found that plans are useless, but planning is indispensable.

Dwight D. Eisenhower, US general and republican president[1]

One big impediment to any experiential learning plan is the perceived amount of time that employers think employees might have to devote to the exercise. For most organizations, regular in-house training already occupies enough of the clock so the thought that employees, and especially managers, should spend even more time off the job usually provokes an extra wince. Another barrier is, of course, the cost.

But the reality is disarming. As the wider national output figures show, existing skills training is not generating much in the way of productivity gains in developed countries; in many cases, progress is achingly slow, even retrogressive, with many organizations finding that the added value of increasing the skills base on its own is marginal, especially when the flexible labour market constantly disperses much of the training investment. This observation flags up an important bit of understanding about the nature of *traditional* skills training and the tactical side of getting things done.

The former is about the essential trappings of expertise, which is usually confined to raising vocational skills, while the latter concerns how the skills wheel is greased. To revert to one of my aeronautical analogies, it is all well and good aiming to put the equivalent of rocket scientists on the payroll, but this is only half the answer. Getting to Mars and back efficiently involves not constantly repeating mistakes, not reinventing wheels time and time again and not having an indiscriminate learning process, all of which falls into the orbit of good management decision-making. As the record shows, not all rocket scientists are automatically good decision-makers.

The big question is why higher proportions of more 'skilled' workers are less efficient in today's modern workplace. I suggest that when the shopfloor doesn't learn, the results can be costly but when managers don't learn, the results can be extremely costly, as Capgemini's research – to which I referred in Chapter 1[2] – confirms. Given this, learning should be deliberately geared towards managers in both low-skill and higher-skill economies. After all, and to requote Peter Drucker, it is managers that make resources productive.[3] All of which means that there's more mileage in getting managers to make more good and better decisions than depending *only* on raising the skills base of operatives.

Assuming that the arguments in favour of experiential learning have found fertile ground, how best, then, to manage such a programme without overwhelming the organization and individual managers? Given that lessons are, technically, buried in *anything* that a business or other type of organization does, where does one start? Obviously, an organization cannot learn from *everything* it does, otherwise it would spend little time on the job. Some sort of priority-setting is essential, if only for budgetary reasons. The planning stage of the EBM learning spiral (see Figure 6.1, p. 124) is designed to preselect the most important opportunities.

The Knowledge Chart

The first step is to decide where in an organization its knowledge lies. I call this investigatory exercise the Knowledge Chart, which, in essence, is an informal ranking of occupational positions. This approach is comparable with the conventional methodology known as knowledge mapping with one important difference.

Traditional knowledge mapping's objective is to discover the location of existing explicit knowledge within an organization, usually in knowledge storage technologies such as databases or physical archives. This would include its intellectual property such as patents, copyrights, trademarks, brands, registered design, trade secrets and processes whose ownership is granted to the company by law, licensing and partnering agreements, and rules and procedures contained in process manuals. It would also include important documents, files, systems, policies, directories, competencies, relationships and authorities.

Although all these are important to decision-making in their own right, the EBM Knowledge Chart approach is to identify the living, breathing and *occupant* holders of specific knowledge, those who are still accessible in the organization. This should include both managers and their key operatives. The reason for this is to identify the main decision-making points where the organization can access its important tacit knowledge and experience rather than just whatever explicit knowledge is lodged within the organization's archive.

Who, then, are the most important job-holders in dispatch, in research and development, in production, in inventory control, in sales, in head office and so on? I recall doing one such exercise where the chairman's secretary was considered among the most important knowledge-owners in head office, even the organization. In a manufacturing company running old machinery, it was an indispensable elderly maintenance engineer and in a computerized service company, a computer wizard in his mid-20s. The objective is to arrive at a list of positions whose incumbents would, if they fell under the proverbial bus, have a serious impact on the business.

Who does the grading and how it is done depends entirely on the organization. There is no specific methodology. In some companies it is done by a senior executive, in others by a long-standing employee or, in larger organizations, it is delegated to departmental heads. There is also no defined way of scoring the relative importance of jobs although most companies use salary as their yardstick along with a generous dosage of common sense. Names of serving incumbents are added to the jobs classification.

In companies of up to 100 employees, numbers might add up to 15; in larger organizations they might total 100 or more. Given the rate of staff turnover, the Knowledge Chart should be updated annually.

The Project Map

With this information in hand, the next stage is to identify a list of main activities or 'events/experiences' that are considered key to the organization's business.

I call this stage the Project Map which, like the Knowledge Chart's graded-list of important job-holders, is intended to identify the organization's main 'experiences'.

Depending on the institution, these might include anything that the organization considers could be improved upon – where, for example, quality could be enhanced and/or the cost reduced. This could apply to everything: from a group rationalization, a new product launch, the way in which capital is raised from the bank or a new investor, an employee strike, how a new manufacturing outsource company is selected or the employment of university graduates. These 'experiences' should be selected on the basis of an audited result (for example, the latest product launch was twice as expensive as last year's product launch) or should be important in their own right (how, for example, a marketing campaign was managed or a salesman managed to persuade a previously reluctant potential client to switch allegiances). The choice should also include repeatable events where the timescale of recurrence is more than the average tenure of the main decision-makers and/or from work areas that have a particularly high rate of non-managerial turnover.

Additionally, the organization should select both successes and failures although it should be kept in mind that more can usually be learned from the latter than the former. This observation is backed up by the experience of researchers at Xerox who, after studying the record of three of its troubled products, concluded that 'the knowledge gained from failures (is) often instrumental in achieving subsequent success. In the simplest terms, failure is the ultimate teacher',[4] a sentiment also articulated by a recent book on high-flyers, in which the author says: 'Learning from failures can prove essential for a successful career. The real leaders are those who learn from experience and who remain open to continuous learning.'[5]

The 'experiences' can also be delineated into any number of categories, such as responses to internal issues (for example, an increase in sexual or racial harassment), responses to external issues (implementation of new government legislation for example), defensive measures (price reductions, for instance), assertive measures (when the availability of labour exceeds demand), non-profit issues (sponsorship/corporate social responsibility) and key appointments such as graduate recruitment.

Development projects such as new product design, outsourcing enquiries and investigations into new institutional practices are a particularly good source of learning because they are a microcosm of the whole organization. Since project teams are usually made up of people from many parts of the organization, development projects test the strengths and weaknesses of systems, structure and values. Project auditing, especially when done only to ensure compliance with formal procedures rather than to analyse its positive and negative aspects, is invariably a lost opportunity.

To each of these activities or 'events/experiences' is then added the name or names of the main decision-makers. Choices should not be confined only to management as lessons learned can often be just as valuable to an organization when they emanate from the shopfloor. In any event, managers themselves should have an intimate awareness of both strategic and operational issues before any decision-making exercise. As with the Knowledge Chart, the judgements involved are the organization's. Given the way in which most organizations change, the Project Map should, like the Knowledge Chart, be updated on an annual basis.

The Employee Transit Audit

The final roll call of individuals and projects to be targeted for knowledge capture is then determined after an analysis to plot the organization's actual staff turnover, with the aim of being able to choose judiciously between what is considered important and where the greatest level of job turnover resides. If choices have to be made, it is logical to gravitate towards those whose decision-makers are more peripatetic.

I call this the Employee Transit Audit, which can be undertaken relatively easily by an organization's HR/personnel department. Designed to plot the level of job discontinuity across an organization at regional, functional and departmental levels, it is an analysis of an organization's employee turnover and, particularly, its occupational positions. Depending on the type of organization, job turnover can be computed on a six-monthly basis for seasonal firms or annually for others.

In many cases, leisure companies that are dependent on weather and voluntary organizations can have turnovers of around 80 per cent in their annual operational periods. For companies employing continuous part-time labour, the job-change can often be just as high, but in many industrialized countries the norm for non-seasonal organizations that employ full-time staff – the majority of organizations – ranges from about 15 per cent to 30 per cent a year depending on individual industry sector (see Figure 2.1, p. 40). In times of corporate distress, the figures can be much higher. I've recounted a number of examples in Chapter 3 and will refer to several more in Chapter 8.

Not all the lost occupational appointments will be jobs where the knowledge loss is critical but this exercise will provide a first-level gauge of the scale of the underlying problem. The Audit should be updated annually.

The Knowledge Retrieval Plan

Having identified the potential size and location of the knowledge leaks, the next task is to compare all three analyses, a job best undertaken by a senior manager in consultation with the person(s) who will eventually manage the knowledge capture process. Any replication of posts and names will help to pinpoint priorities. From there it becomes a process of matching perceived importance with a budget to arrive at a definitive Knowledge Retrieval Plan that identifies events/activities and candidates for knowledge capture.

For a medium-sized organization, this list might include a dozen posts that have a particularly high level of turnover. Alongside this might be another dozen 'events/activities', each of which identifies three or four main decision-makers and key operatives. In addition, the organization might identify the chairman, chief executive and finance director. Space in the budget could be left for several additional unexpected events and departures.

Budget is always a thorny issue. How much is it worth spending to stockpile and learn from organization-specific knowledge? Maybe 10, 15 or 20 per cent of an individual manager's annual salary? Perhaps a percentage of the value of a project/event? Or the estimated cost of a continually repeated mistake of repeatedly reinvented wheels and of change that takes an inordinate amount of time to realize? Or the cost and time of fire-fighting? For me, the value that organizations put on this esoteric commodity invariably provides a nuclear indicator whether or not they are genuine learning organizations. For many, knowledge is just an all-purpose article of trade that can be acquired *when* required, simply by hiring. For them, their organization-specific experiences and knowledge are of little value. For others, it represents the potential added value of not having to relearn their own experiences or repeat past mistakes. For both, it is a conscious determination like any other decision.

The Knowledge Retrieval Plan will consist of a list of individuals and events and a schedule of when the 'capture' exercise might or should take place. For specified jobs, for example, the knowledge-owners who leave at short notice should be scheduled for knowledge capture in the last month of their employment. For the specified 'events', the date and duration of the event will be specified along with the names of the relevant knowledge-owners, with a related timetable for knowledge retrieval, whether it be before its conclusion or after its end. For key appointments such as the chairman or chief executive, knowledge acquisition might be scheduled in a specified non-busy period before the New Year.

Like the Project Map, the Knowledge Chart and the Employee Transit Audit and the Knowledge Retrieval Plan should be repeated annually. A low-cost exercise, it is an essential part of the overall cycle that can better target many of the organization's learning opportunities.

Once planning is completed, EMB can then move into its next phase – collection of short- and medium-term OM.

Notes

1. A favourite maxim of President Dwight D. Eisenhower, quoted by Richard Nixon in his 'Khrushchev', *Six Crises*, New York: Doubleday, 1962.
2. Emma Giles, *Business Decisiveness Report*, Capgemini UK, August 2004 available at: http://www.sinoia.biz/download/Capgemini_BDI_survey%20(2).pdf.
3. P.F. Drucker, 'The New Productivity Challenge', *Harvard Business Review*, vol. 69, no. 6, November–December 1991.
4. M.A. Maidique and B.J. Zirger, 'The New Product Learning Cycle', *Research Policy*, vol 14, no 6.
5. M. McCall, *High Flyers: Developing the Next Generation of Leaders*, Cambridge, MA: Harvard Business School Press. 1997.

CHAPTER

④ THE LESSONS AUDIT

① PLANNING
The Knowledge Chart
The Project Map
The Employee Transit Audit

③ REFLECTION

⑥ EVALUATION

② CAPTURE THE EVIDENCE
Archives
Oral debriefings
Corporate history

⑤ REPROCESS

8 *Talk Talk*

> *"We learn through experience and experiencing, and no one teaches anyone anything. This is as true for the infant moving from kicking to crawling to walking as it is for the scientist with his equations. If the environment permits it, anyone can learn whatever he chooses to learn; and if the individual permits it, the environment will teach him everything it has to teach.*
>
> Eric Hoffer, US philosopher[1]

Relatively new the term 'organizational memory' may be but most institutions will invariably understand it to mean all the data, information and knowledge stacked up in their archive. Covering everything from managerial position papers, correspondence with clients, memos between employees, the research undertaken to investigate the demand for a new product, newspaper cuttings and photographs of the installation of a new piece of machinery, it usually resides in a dingy outhouse in an isolated part of head office or on a very big hard drive of a relatively new computer system.

Organizations will mostly also understand it to be its body of prior knowledge – not perfect, perhaps, because there was the 'Great Flood of 1990' that destroyed 50 boxes of paperwork going back to the early 1980s. Wrong. Whatever remains is just the explicit part of OM – and very dead. Valuable in its own right (and usually adeptly captured), it is only the skeleton of institutional knowledge and OM. To possess a complete body of an organization's knowledge base and to get the cadaver to breathe again – in other words, experientially learn – requires as much as possible of that functional life force known as tacit know-how that used to be around when the flexible labour market wasn't so flexible. Even if flexible working is not an issue, it is this building block of knowledge that is the missing link in most organizational understanding of how experiential learning works, and it is the subject of this and the next few chapters.

From cave drawings to DVDs

In all of history, there have been a number of time-applicable mediums used to capture 'experience' in a permanent format. In pre-history, it was cave drawings, a technique that evolved into the more disciplined forms of painting and other 'art' that developed into pamphlets, books and the other printed documentation and which, today, encompasses the audio mediums of the tape recorder/DVD, the visual equivalent of the still camera and its moving counterpart, the movie camera. The artist and photographer might insist that their pictures are the equivalent of a thousand words but there is no prize for knowing the most comprehensive and portable repositories of them all.

Of all the ways in which experience can be captured, the most efficient, cost-effective and portable formats are books, the humble tape recorder and, in its more sophisticated visual format, the video cassette recorder and DVD. They are truly the modern world's experiential tongue. Books – in particular, the institutional-specific repository of experience, the corporate history – are an exceptionally efficient storehouse of long-term OM while the tape recorder and video cassette recorder/DVD are even more effective at securing the short- and medium-term form of OM.

I will discuss books later; meanwhile its oral equivalent has, in one form or another, long been an accepted form of passing down experiences from one generation to the next. The Greek historian Thucydides wrote in *The History of the Peloponnesian War*:

> *And with regard to my factual reporting of the events of the war I have made it a principle not to write down the first story that came my way, and not even to be guided by my own general impressions; either I was present myself at the events which I have described or else I heard of them from eyewitnesses whose reports I have checked with as much thoroughness as possible.*[2]

Thus, Thucydides set a precedent for the judicious use of oral witness. Down the years many societies without a written tradition – Pacific Islanders and Kalahari Bushmen for example – perpetuated their folklore through spoken narrative while, today, the most celebrated example is perhaps the use of personal testimony of many thousands of the Second World War holocaust survivors organized by film producer/director Steven Spielberg's charitable Shoah Foundation. South Africa also used the oral debrief as part of its national healing process ahead of the Truth Commission's activities. For historians, it is a primary source technique to help interpret the past and, until very recently, practitioners have seen its employment as mainly benefiting the interviewee; hence its widespread use in areas such as grief therapy. Tailored differently, its application in industry, in fact, is much wider.

As a discipline in the modern age, oral debriefing is the systematic process of collecting an individual's spoken memories, of people known, and the events witnessed or participated in at first hand, importantly while they are still able to do so effectively – that is, with sufficient powers of recall. Another version of the technique is 'storytelling',[3] where individuals are encouraged to relate their experiences through narrative witness, usually in some theatrical way, or through the use of the linguistic framework of metaphor. Although there are similarities in both approaches, storytelling is a time-sensitive activity. Because it is impulsive and usually not recorded, it is only available to organizations while individuals remain *in situ*; once they join the flexible labour market their experiences become 'lost' to the organization, as does the dynamic between individuals. Oral debriefing is a capture medium for organizations to secure the knowledge and experiences of both present and past employees from which both their colleagues and their successors can benefit. Its methodology is also more rigorous and deliberate than storytelling, and this makes it an efficient way of securing elusive tacit knowledge.

My own picturesque description of tacit knowledge is the pea under the mattress and pile of soft quilts on which slept the princess in the classic fairy tale by Hans Christian Andersen. By which I mean that its character is iceberg-like. Not only is it very difficult for individuals to articulate on their own, but the inherent competitiveness between colleagues discourages them from sharing it. Accessing tacit knowlege requires a skill that strips away the layers of quilts and mattress and effectively teases out the hidden and complex knowledge buried in the recesses of individuals' skills and experiences. Oral debriefing involves skilful questioning that starts with a generalized enquiry about an identified area of an individual's knowledge and is followed up by probing questions such as 'What do you mean by that?', 'I'm not sure I understand?' to

'Why?',' 'When?' and 'How?'. Like the tears that come from peeling a raw onion, the tacit knowledge can pour out. The tool is powerful and the medium friendly in the right hands.

But while the tape recorder and now ubiquitous VCR/DVD remains a popular tool for historians, psychotherapists, in sports coaching and, to a growing extent, as a decision-making tool in the military, it is still rarely used and applied in industry and commerce. For its use to increase organizations must first realize that their hard-won intellectual capital, in the form of their OM, *is* a valuable resource. At the same time, oral debriefing practitioners have to learn to reposition the technique to focus specifically on industry and commerce – a competence that also requires an astute knowledge of management and business. Also, the interviewing techniques need to be directed more intensely on uncovering the metaphorical pea beneath the quilts if oral debriefing is to be any use as a decision-making tool.

The history of oral debriefing

In their contemporary formulation, the techniques of oral debriefing were first explored in the US in the 1940s in New Deal projects to preserve the reminiscences of former slaves and unlettered rural folk, and then were used in Europe.

Its first major proponent and practitioner was the American social commentator and writer Studs Terkel. Born in 1912 and trained as a lawyer before becoming a journalist and writer, his fascination with the medium came soon after the tape recorder's commercial exploitation when he started interviewing a whole cross-section of American society in order to piece together a jigsaw of experiences. From taxi drivers and teachers, the poor and the rich, young and old, his books on subjects ranging from race relations to war have provided a rich range of social opinion and attitudes of a nation undergoing rapid social change.

Terkel's pioneering work was concurrent with the efforts of the US academic Professor Allan Nevins who, after successfully persuading educationalists to introduce oral history as a tool for serious scholarship in the 1940s, founded the Oral History Collection at Columbia University. Since then other universities, including Harvard, Princeton and the University of California, Berkeley, have also developed extensive collections of oral history. In the early 1950s Nevins brought oral history to industry when he organized the interviews of more than 400 people for a history of the Ford Motor Company. Since then, a handful of companies have supported similar programmes, among them ARCO, Beckman Instruments, Bristol-Myers, Eli Lilley, Kaiser Aluminum and Chemical, Monsanto, Proctor & Gamble, Rohm and Haas and Standard Oil Company.

Oral debriefing in the US military

While industry broadly continued to ignore oral history's employment as a capture 'vehicle' or even decision-making tool, the main thrust of the discipline then transferred to the US military, where it was seen as an essential means of preserving the experiences of past battles and of imparting those experiences to younger soldiers. Since the Second World War, oral history has become an increasingly critical adjunct to the more traditional sources of historical documentation. Army historians, in preparing the official histories of the Second World War, the Korean War and the Vietnam War, conducted extensive interviews to uncover the personal insights often lacking in written documentary sources.

During the Second World War, for example, the army decided to play a more significant role in telling its own story. A former journalist, Lt Colonel (later Brigadier-General) S.L.A. Marshall, was assigned to pioneer the army's oral history effort, which subsequently involved several hundred soldier-historians. Moving freely about the battle lines to gather interviews, the soldier-historians began their collection process either while units were still in action or up to ten days or more after the action. As an example of the scale of the oral history effort, historians assigned to the European theatre alone collected over 2000 interviews by the end of the war. A special collection of interviews provided a 'view from the other side' when captured German and Japanese general officers were debriefed in order to provide intelligence information on successful combat tactics as well as useful historical material.

Similar, improved techniques were employed in the Korean War and, later, in the Vietnam War, as well as the US's military deployments to Grenada, Panama, South-west Asia, and, more recently, Afghanistan and the Gulf. The growing importance of oral history in the army was highlighted in 1970 when Chief of Staff General William C. Westmoreland directed the US Army War College and the US Army Military History Institute to sponsor jointly what has become known as the Senior Officer Oral History Program. The programme, designed to allow most retired officers to convey to younger officers the qualities and experiences that had made their careers successful, has produced more than 100 000 transcribed pages. The idea was adopted by the US navy in 1969, and there exists in the US Naval Institute's oral history programme alone more than 200 bound volumes, and interviews have been done to produce dozens more.

In 1977 the US Army Corps of Engineers expanded the range of army oral history activities by establishing an active biographical and subject interview programme. This was extended in the early 1980s at most of the US Army Training and Doctrine Command's centres and schools. Today, in each army major command (MACOM), interviewers collect data for preparing monographs or to teach lessons learned to young soldiers. In 1986 the Department of the Army directed that exit interviews – also called end of tour (EoT) interviews – also be conducted with departing school commandants as well as division, corps, and MACOM commanders so that they could be made available to incoming commanders in order to increase their understanding of the issues faced by their predecessors.

In the late 1980s the Center of Military History went even further by creating an Oral History Activity to coordinate issues concerning all the army's oral history programmes. The Center's oral history office establishes interview guidelines for army historians, conducts interviews with members of the Army Staff, advises the army staff on the uses of oral history and biannually reports the status of the programme to the Army leadership. The office also assists historians in using proper oral history techniques and aids researchers searching for oral history resources.

Oral debriefing in industry

In Europe and the UK, most of the efforts in oral history have been confined to non-business activities such as sociological and straight historical research, where its use is relatively widespread. In a rare business-type project called *City Lives*, the National Life Story Collection attached to the British Library National Sound Archive has been conducting interviews with about 100 top men and women from financial institutions who have lived through the changes since the Second World War. Aside from that, only a small number of British companies have undertaken projects to record the memories and experiences of their employees, among them London Transport, which has made a special effort with their West Indian workforce, the brewers Bass, the telecommunications company Cable & Wireless and, until the project was aborted in 1991 as a cost-saving exercise, Ford UK. The uses to which they have put the information have generally been for museum exhibits or public relations, despite the range of views worldwide championing the genre as an efficient way of capturing and using one of the most valuable assets of any institution.

One such champion is Jochen Kraske, head of the World Bank Group Historical Office, whose account of his staff's activities is instructive. Through his office, the World Bank maintains a continuous historical record with a well-defined set of corporate objectives that goes beyond its value to future economic historians. In this, oral debriefing is key.

Kraske admits that, even though most company work processes are largely designed around documentation, much remains unrecorded. Decisions taken, especially those regarding policies, are not always reflected in the files:

The voluminous paper record may provide no more than bare facts, and even that record often reflects the desire to gloss over disagreements and serious questions, or the desire to sell or excuse. An additional vital source of information is the views and perceptions of those who participated in the decision-making processes. We can learn much about what happened and why by asking those involved when a loan was identified and appraised, a crucial policy decision taken, a particular contract awarded.

An effective oral history programme, he says,

... can address the problem of this gap by recording, before time dilutes or erases them, the memories of executive directors, borrowers, managers and staff, who participate in key events and developments in the bank's evolution. Catching and questioning key participants in important decisions before time takes its toll will do much to fill in the record.

The Bank's experience, he adds:

... is also of interest to policy-makers, development practitioners and academic communities in both developing and advanced countries, who look to it to throw light on what was done, and whether it worked, thus helping – they hope – to avoid the errors of the past. With the passage of time, and older staff retire, there has been a loss of institutional memory. It is easy today to be unaware of what happened yesterday on important issues. Staff often learn of the past, if they learn it at all, accidentally or incidentally, in a fragmentised fashion. Without the history, new staff in particular may be missing an important component of institutional culture – of understanding what the bank is and how it got there.[4]

Over in industry proper, Joseph Marchese, writing in a *Resource Guide for The Centre for History of Chemistry (CHOC)*, a joint endeavour of the American Chemical Society, the American Institute of Chemical Engineers and the University of Pennsylvania, says that important repositories of a company's folklore and traditions are often overlooked in attempting to gain control of the corporate past. 'Oral history, the systematic collection of historically important recollections through the use of recorded interviews, provides a useful methodology to tap this resource.'[5]

And in the UK comes the conclusions of a study by Robert Rosenfeld, a senior research fellow at the Centre for Corporate Strategy and Change at the School of Industrial and Business Studies, University of Warwick, who examined the evolving competitiveness of nine firms over a period of 30 years. In a clear indictment of the way in which many corporate histories were researched and written, his researchers found that the historic accounts were generally disappointing. Although they provided interesting portrayals of the events that organizations had been through, they were not seen as having any relevance to what organizations were presently facing:

One of the most fruitful ways of collecting relevant data is by asking senior or retiring employees to provide an 'oral' history of their recollections. This can be particularly important when trying to understand some of the forces for inertia and change which characterise every organisation. While written accounts may provide a more accurate representation of chronological events, the processes of managing change will frequently be unrecorded. Oral recollections provide much which more formal written material does not.[6]

For another good example of a company that understands the potential of formally embedding a resource for experiential learning, it is necessary, ironically, to turn to a relatively young company. The leading American computer company, Digital Equipment Corporation (DEC), is just over 40 years old, yet finds that its 'history' is of constant relevance.

As part of a broader exercise to exhibit its past products to 'make encounters with history possible', it runs an oral history programme to record the memories and experiences of its employees. Since the programme's initiation in 1989, more than 300 individuals have been interviewed. Each interview is audiotaped and transcribed, with a copy of the transcription provided to the interviewees for comment and/or correction. The interviewee is then asked to sign a release form which allows the material to be made available through the company's archives. In addition to key individuals, the company debriefs selected employees who are either retiring and leaving to join other companies. Transcripts are filed on diskette and hard copy, and indexed by topic and individual.

In addition to providing valuable anecdotal information for later use, the programme can extract from departing employees their understanding of past situations and how they responded to them. Although staff may have left, the company has ensured that it still derives benefit from the years they were employed.

The resource has its visual embodiment in a central collection covering 2500 sq. ft at a company site in Marlborough, Massachusetts, and at five subsidiary locations, where exhibits focus on specific aspects of DEC's history such as the design and production of microchips or the development of memory technology.

Since 1960, when the company started out with a venture capital loan of $70 000, DEC has grown to the point where it now has more than 121 000 employees in 1200 locations in 82 countries and earns annual revenues in excess of $12.9 billion.

The purpose of DEC's historical collection is to record and share a sense of the creativity of working in the company.

In fact, the company, which is at the leading edge of computer technology, believes that the internal creative process owes much to its sense of history. Examples of this are evident throughout the history of the company, from the PDP-1 (the world's first 'personal' interactive computer) building on the values developed in DEC's Whirlwind Project and to the design on new-generation VAX systems using design simulations that run on earlier VAX generations.

Elsewhere, oral debriefing techniques have been used by Ford and BP in the US, details of which I related in Chapter 6 as examples of companies engaged in serious experiential learning.

As these applications show, oral history need not just be the contents of an exit interview. In today's workplace, where the dissipation of corporate knowledge is now so widespread as to impact on institutional productivity, it is one of the few mediums available with which this corporate asset can be captured professionally and economically.

Embarking on an oral debriefing programme

In the world of evidence-gathering where rigorous substantiation is a prerequisite for all experiential learning, my own experience is that the oral route is often more valuable than anything extracted from written sources simply because managers are generally better speakers than they are writers. Also, their spoken word is invariably a more efficient way of conveying the abstract and complex nature of such elements as the nuances of corporate culture, management style and the often obscure issues surrounding decision-making within groups. Importantly, it is effective at capturing the tacit 'humanware' elements of OM. It is this that makes oral history different from capturing data/information/knowledge within conventional information technology (IT) applications. Professionally structured, the methodology, in fact, goes to the heart of good decision-making, experiential learning and the principle of the learning organization.

Knowledge is mine. Why should I share it?

To embark on an oral debriefing programme organizations must first persuade their employees to participate in knowledge-sharing. This is a contentious issue and is one of the main stumbling blocks for employers vacillating about such projects. After all, so-called 'knowledge' is an individual's most important personal asset. Without it, their bargaining power as an employee is reduced. Why should they give it away?

However, this issue contains a subtle but important misunderstanding on the part of many employees that is unchallenged by employers and which needs to be clarified – namely that workers, whether management or otherwise, are not *giving* knowledge away. It is, or has been, already paid for under the contract of employment for which employees are already remunerated – and, in the case of managers, quite highly. All an employer is asking is that the knowledge within their corporate context be documented. To overcome this widespread misunderstanding and encourage a general acceptance of the discipline at all levels, the company needs to make this clear at the time each employee is taken on, preferably in a non-aggressive way that emphasizes that, to optimize its investment in the individual, the organization needs to have a detailed understanding of individual employees' experiences. In fact, an employee's contract of employment can specifically include the company's right to document an employee's knowledge, even that annual performance reviews depend on employees' cooperation in this matter and, where employment is not terminated by dismissal, a necessary part of individuals securing their exit packages.

Other ways of encouraging employee participation in the learning process would be to remunerate or provide some other incentive to individuals but, however people are brought on board, the organization will need a management touch as sensitive as a surgeon's knife on an unanaesthetized patient and an unwavering resolve to justify high reward with much higher performance. In my experience the exercise rarely becomes an issue if handled sensitively and couched in language that professes a genuine desire by the organization to learn from an individual's experience.

There is another aspect of 'testimony' that frequently has a powerfully beneficial spin-off.

The apparent fickleness of employers since the onset of the flexible labour market has led many employees to develop a mindset that encourages a less than enthusiastic performance. Why should workers care too much when, at the drop of a hat, they can be made redundant? This attitude persists in many areas of business even though most staff turnover in today's workplace – around 80 per cent of it – is now unrelated to the economic cycle.[7] For most individuals, being told that their work is potentially valuable to others is flattering, giving them an enhanced dignity in their work; moreover, if they know that their footprints are going to be tracked, they will try to ensure that the decisions they make are better considered than they might otherwise be. Sharing knowledge can be a source of pride – and, for the employer, a subtle but potent way of implanting an attitudinal change advantageous to corporate performance.

The four types of debriefing

In practice, there are generally four types of oral debriefing applied in the business world: biographical, subject, critical incident and exit.

The *biographical debrief* focuses on an individual's life or career. Conducted at stages during or at the end of an individual's career, it is usually directed at very senior officers, often founders or people with decisive effects on organizational development. It has a significant educational value to the organization because it can provide industry- and organization-specific insights into such aspects as culture, values and the way in which strategy has altered over time alongside a changing marketplace. In addition, it doubles as a motivator to successive generations.

In this type of debrief, it is better to conduct the project *before* the individual leaves the company, while work disciplines are still in place. Once they have left their job many people let their concentration slip – along with their memory.

The second type, the *subject debrief*, concentrates on obtaining knowledge about a single event or topic, such as a product launch or new building development, and may require interviews with several people to obtain complete coverage. It is a valuable tool when projects are frequently over budget or overdue.

It is important to conduct subject debriefs as soon after the event as possible while the experience is still fresh in people's minds. It is even better to conduct it before anyone can put a value judgement on the outcome, since this will automatically defuse any defensiveness on the part of the individual decision-makers. If the organization's culture is considered excessively defensive debriefings should take place *during* the experience. In this way, events can be assessed in real time as opposed in hindsight. This gives the company something like a Black Box flight recorder that is installed in all modern aircraft; if something goes amiss, the 'real-time' data is stored can be used to find out what went wrong. At a stroke, it improves the qualitative character of the evidential input and the learning potential of the subsequent analysis.

Third, there is the *critical incident debrief*, which, as the name suggests, takes place when there is an unexpected event, usually something damaging.[8] Examples might include a product recall or an unfavourable item of publicity. In this case, debriefs should be carried out as soon after the episode as possible and include as many of the people involved, even non-managers.

Finally, there is the *exit debrief*, commonly known as the exit interview. Similar to the biographical debrief, it is more often directed at lower-hierarchy individuals but its application at higher echelons can be just as valuable. Typically not an interview at all, it is more often the output of a formulaic, 20-questions means of trying to uncover reasons why employees leave. Because of their prescriptive nature, many exit interviews are limited in the quality of knowledge capture. When done well in non-questionnaire format, however, the debrief usually centres on the issues and decisions unique to the exiting individual's job and can be especially instructive as a decision-making tool. With senior decision-makers the most common candidates, such debriefings are always conducted near the end of the individual's tenure. Although they are also related to subject interviews, they are often categorized separately because they may cover many topics.

British merchant banker N.M. Rothschild used the exit debrief technique when its director of corporate affairs, John Antcliffe, decided to leave the company before a successor could be appointed. The merchant bank was conscious of the need for job continuity and the fact that a key employee was leaving with a wealth of experience that – if not captured in some way – would be lost forever. The debriefing was carried out by an independent practitioner two weeks before Mr Antcliffe's departure, after which Mr Antcliffe said:

It fleshed out areas I would not have thought of mentioning to my successor, even had I the opportunity. As a succession planning tool, it has considerable value for the new entrant and the company. It is an extremely effective way to quickly familiarise one's successor with all the subtle aspects of both a new job and their new employer.

Rodney Lonsdale, Rothschild's Personnel Director who commissioned the project, said:

The project went far beyond any of our expectations. Unless a new employee reads the culture here right, then they're going to find it extremely difficult, if not impossible, to be productive. It is a very insightful and efficient way of reflecting the reality of the job and the company, and a well-balanced way of crystallising all the issues that someone coming into this organisation cold needs to know. It will give the new entrant a very good understanding of how this business ticks.[9]

Video equipment is currently too expensive for most oral debriefing programmes. But for those organizations that can afford it, videotaping interviews can add another dimension to oral debriefing by recording visual associations and movement such as body language and time-susceptible speech such as hesitations, all of which can give added meaning to interpretations. The video can also record an object or setting that is the subject of the interview, such as the installation of a new machine, and/or visual enhancements, such as photographs and maps. It is not always possible to carry out video debriefings, however, as they require locations with suitable lighting as well as a small back-up team. It is normally impractical for the debriefer to also manage the camera and sound equipment.

Whatever the vehicle, oral debriefing is designed to supplement written records, complement secondary sources, and provide data, information and knowledge that would exist in no other form.

Dealing with false memory

On the wider subject of memory, there are two aspects of recall that should always be given house room in any discussion of experiential learning. They are false memory and lying, both of which – by definition – affect the quality of all testimony and thus the potential value of any reflective thinking. The former is a recollection that is a distortion of an actual experience, often the result of a traumatic event in the donor's life. Lying, on the other hand, involves deliberate falsification. Depending on definitions, however, a lie can be a genuine fabrication or a selective truth, a lie by omission, or even the truth if the intention is to deceive or to cause an action not in the listener's interests. Although accuracy is important to the evidential collection process, such limitations are typically far less crucial than the primary absence of OM. Also, a skilled knowledge practitioner should, through third-party corroboration, be able to accommodate such occasions, which are, anyway, usually a small fraction of any overall OM collection. In any event, I have built into EBM a provision to help overcome this deficiency.

As with all the debriefing techniques, a skilled interviewer is essential. Whether the debriefer comes from in-house or is recruited externally, he or she needs to be commanding enough not to be intimidated by the interviewee and perceptive enough to identify and pursue pertinent questions. The skill of oral debriefing is the art of asking relevant questions and, when the answers are unclear or fudged, asking even more probing questions. In many respects, the questioner is the more important component for, when left to their own devices, the subject's contribution is typically bland and lacking both incisiveness and rigour.

Capturing the evidence

For industry and commercial applications, there are several indispensable steps in the EBM 'capture the evidence' stage. Having identified the individual/project in the cycle's initial planning stage, the debriefer's first job is establish the objective of the debriefing. Whether the actual debrief is biographical, project-related or of the exit kind, a clearly identified purpose – induction, management development/decision-making or both – will dictate the type of questions to be asked. The next job is for the debriefer to request interview(s), which is also one of the most important steps in the whole process, not least because a poorly made approach could discourage a potential interviewee from being fully cooperative. An uneasy subject always furnishes an unsatisfactory debriefing.

The introduction letter

A letter or e-mail should introduce the debriefer, the purpose of the interview, the potential product, the probable number and length of sessions, the key topics to be covered, the procedure in terms of editing the transcript and the necessary authority that allows an organization to use the subsequent typescript, which will be discussed later in this chapter. Some debriefers even provide subjects with the questionnaire but, in my experience, this is less productive than just advising interviewees about the general subject areas because prior warning normally encourages 'preparation' that results in a formality that affects the quality of the recall. As a rule, it is best to allow the interviewee to 'wing it'.

In the case of exit-type debriefings, the debriefer's initial introduction should also explain that the organization considers it important that there should be as much continuity as possible with the individual's successor and that the new appointee should also have the benefit of their predecessor's past experience. With other types of debriefing, it should be emphasized that disregarding the interviewee's example, however it turned out, restrains natural managerial evolution – and that the organization doesn't want successive generations to have to reinvent the wheel. Categories of specific questions can be listed – for example, the organization's corporate culture, management, communications and decision-making style, the special internal and external relationships necessary for prime performance, job content, advice to colleagues and unfinished business. In some cases, it can be suggested that this type of information can best be divulged by using anecdotes, so individuals should feel free to recall incidents and the detail of particular events. Also necessary are the procedures that follow, including how the transcript will be edited and who will see it.

Serious research

With the interviewee on board comes the next stage of the process – thorough research. The debriefer needs to be familiar with the subject and, in the case of individuals, their career and their job, their employer, its industry; even more important, he or she must have a keen appreciation of management and business processes. With projects, the debriefer has to have an equally keen awareness of process and procedure and the dynamics of group interaction.

Research can originate in the organization's archives and also in discussions with individuals who work with the interviewee, all with the objective of the next stage of the process – preparing a list of pertinent questions. I call it the Interview Plan.

Depending on objectives, biographical and exit debriefs will tend to require broader questions that will illuminate the important facets of the interviewee's life. Project debriefs require more focused questions centred on the detail of practice.

The debrief – and follow-up questions

It is essential that the debriefer maintain control of the whole process whilst allowing the interviewee to be as expansive as possible. To this end, it is useful to categorize questions in broad topical areas, in order to encourage developmental themes and a logical momentum.

But it is in the actual questioning and the techniques surrounding the asking of the questions – the next stage of the process – that the debriefer's individual skill becomes paramount. The debriefer needs to use appropriate body language, deliberate silences and, specifically, eye contact, and the questions need to be couched in ways that elicit tacit knowledge around relevant data and information in the context of personal experience.

In addition to being a good questioner, the debriefer needs to be an even better listener, for a large part of the debrief lies in the asking of supplementary questions when the interviewee's responses are unclear, imprecise or evasive. Also, a well-prepared debriefer will be aware of gaps and inconsistencies in the available source materials and will ask questions to clarify or, in some instances, confirm the record. Such responses might shed new light on an issue or serve as yardsticks to judge the accuracy of other information provided by the interviewee. It is here that most tacit knowledge resides.

The debriefer should also get interviewees to explain the meaning of acronyms and jargon, as well as provide additional information on any unfamiliar subjects or individuals mentioned during the interview. Requests for accurate spellings are also appropriate.

One of the closing interview questions should provide the interviewee with the opportunity to discuss relevant matters that may not have occurred to the debriefer.

It should be taken into account that the process is extremely tiring for both the debriefer and the interviewee. As a general rule of thumb, no debrief should last more than three hours separated by a refreshment break – convenient because modern tape cassettes are 90 minutes in length. Subsequent interview sessions should take place on different days.

For corporate applications, it is invariably more productive for debriefings to take place individually rather than in groups. In groups, individuals tend to be supportive of each other's memory recall and less inclined to be incisive. It is also an invitation to argument.

Transcripts and editing

Once the debriefs are completed, the interviews must be transcribed and edited. Depending on clarity and interviewee's diction, a good transcriber can copy a three-hour tape in around 18 hours but it often takes longer. Once transcribed, the transcript will require careful editing to cover language, spelling and – usually extremely difficult – sense. It is customary to allow the interviewee to check and, if necessary, amend the text, after which the transcript is given a final edit, prefaced by an explanatory overview and indexed with key words. With modern word processors, this can be done electronically. As a courtesy, the interviewee normally receives a hard copy along with a copy of the original audiotape. When memorabilia such as diaries, letters, photographs or other historical materials are provided to support the interview, it is standard practice to return them after copying.

Depending on the corporate policy, transcriptions can be kept private for limited and/or selected distribution, or even placed on the organization's intranet.

Ethics and legal issues

Given the relative recent emergence of oral debriefing, it is useful to be aware of relevant practical steps that have been accepted as norms of practice for the technique.

When constructing any of these types of debriefing, there are several ethical and legal issues that should be considered, the first being copyright. In corporate context, such as education, this should not present any problems if the recordings are not 'published'. Although copyright law differs throughout the world – and up-to-date national legislation would need to be checked anyway – the convention is that, while oral debriefs are like other forms of 'publishing' and are subject to certain copyright laws, there is usually nothing in law to prevent sound recordings being played or even transcribed. Copyright law only comes into play when copying takes place in an activity concerned with publishing, performing, broadcasting or electronic transmission such as over the internet. In these cases, copyright owners are entitled to sue those who make unauthorized use of their words and seize 'infringing copies' of their copyright works. That said, it is considered unethical, and in many cases illegal, to use interviews without the informed consent of the interviewee, in which the nature of the use or uses is not clear and explicit. However, many of the legal constraints can

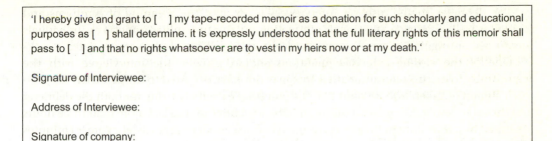

'I hereby give and grant to [   ] my tape-recorded memoir as a donation for such scholarly and educational purposes as [   ] shall determine. it is expressly understood that the full literary rights of this memoir shall pass to [   ] and that no rights whatsoever are to vest in my heirs now or at my death.'

Signature of Interviewee:

Address of Interviewee:

Signature of company:

Date of agreement:

Figure 8.1 Example copyright release form

be very simply avoided if such consent is obtained. This is usually done through a simple release form, an example of which is shown in Figure 8.1.

In the event that companies elect to undertake oral debriefings in group situations, it should be borne in mind that copyright can also be jointly owned. To get round this, employers can get employees to sign either a release form separately or a common release, provided that all agree to the wording.

Confidentiality

Another issue to be seriously considered is confidentially. In this there are two separate matters – the possible confidentiality of the debrief itself and the requirement for confidentiality if an outside practitioner is used to do the oral debrief. For the former, it is instructive to understand the nature of 'confidential information', which occurs when there is a restriction on its disclosure, normally placed by the person or organization which provides it.

The company needs to ensure that, exactly like other sensitive internal issues that are the handled by outside consultants, the content of debriefs is kept private. Like the release form giving informed consent to the company or other organization to use an oral debrief, this can done through a standard confidentiality agreement. Restrictions can be formal (for example, a contract of employment may forbid the disclosure of business information to unauthorized persons) or even implicit. In practice, if an oral history interviewee states that information is confidential, then it must be treated as such by interviewers and its custodians. A person or organization obtaining confidential information has a duty not to disclose any of it unless authorized by the informant. Informants can sue interviewers for unauthorized disclosure and obtain restraining orders and damages.

The issue becomes a little complicated because a 'duty of confidentiality' can arise without the supplier of information explicitly stating that it is to be treated as confidential. If the information is of a confidential nature or is supplied under circumstances that indicate that the supplier wishes it to be treated as such, then a duty will arise. If any form of agreement is made to keep information confidential, breaking it will amount to breach of contract, which is also actionable. In practice, much of the content of debriefings could be defined as confidential but to avoid possible legal action, clearance forms should state the uses to which debriefings will be put, and no other use should be made of them without the consent of the interviewee or their successors. Ownership of the physical recordings, transcripts or copyright is immaterial. Thereafter, interviewees should not pass on confidential information, which could include information about current employment and work content, or information covered by the Official Secrets Act, without permission. Also debriefings and transcripts should be kept in secure conditions.

Defamation and freedom of information

There are two other issues.

The first is defamation. The law allows people to take action if untrue or harmful statements are made about them. In the event that an interviewee should say something possibly libellous or slanderous, it is wise to have legal advice available. As a general rule, though, the procedure is that where statements are believed to be untrue and potentially damaging to a third party, the relevant portion of the debriefing should be removed.

The second issue is the Freedom of Information obligation – worth checking for the different national slants it might present. Ordinarily, its obligations are only applicable to certain public authorities – that is, publicly funded organizations where information held by has to be made available to anyone who requests it in writing. Some public bodies – for example, national security services – are exempt, as are many types of information, often because access is prevented by other laws such as the personal information covered by data protection legislation or that protected by the law of confidence. Such organizations are obliged to prepare a guide to the types of information, including oral history collections that will be made easily available without a formal written request. Once material is included in the guide, it has to be made available. Access to oral history material may be restricted through agreement with the donor or informant to maintain confidentiality. These regulations do not apply to private organizations.

Copyright differences

Curiously, there is a difference in the duration of copyright for recorded speech and sound/video recordings, at least in the UK. Broadly, copyright in speech recorded since 1 August 1989, remains in force for 70 years after the end of the year in which the speaker died or dies. If recorded before 1 August 1989, copyright remains in force for 50 years from the end of 1989 if this is longer than 70 years after the death of the speaker. Put another way, if the speaker died before 1 January 1969, copyright expires on 31 December 2039. If not, copyright expires 70 years after the death of the speaker.

In contrast, copyright in sound recordings expires 50 years after the end of the year in which the recordings were made, unless the recordings are published (including web publication) or broadcast, in which case copyright expires 50 years from the end of the year of publication or first broadcast. Thus if a recording was made in 1993, copyright in it would expire on 31 December 2043, unless it is, say, published in 2010, in which case copyright would expire on 31 December 2060.

Copyright in unpublished sound recordings made during the currency of the 1956 Copyright Act (1957–89) expires at the end of 2039 – 50 years after 1988 Act came into force.

If such recordings are published within this period, copyright expires at the end of 50 years following the date of publication.

Recorded speech and recordings which are 'in copyright' may not be copied, 'issued to the public' (for example, in a publication, exhibition or website), performed or played in public, adapted or broadcast without the copyright owner's permission. Where the recorded content of oral history interviews is 'in copyright', some 'non-commercial' activities are still permitted, such as copying for private study, research, criticism or review, the use of short extracts as illustrative matter in publications, copying by libraries and archives for preservation purposes or copying for instructional purposes by educational establishments, subject to various limitations.

A new provision of the 1988 Copyright Act gave oral history interviewees the right to be named as the 'authors' of their recorded words if they are published or broadcast; and publishers and broadcasters are obliged not to subject their words to 'derogatory treatment' by, for example, editing, adapting or making alterations which create a false impression. These rights are retained by interviewees whoever owns the copyright. The right to be named needs to be stated formally, preferably in writing, by the interviewee in order to have legal force. However, except in cases where interviewees have asked not to be identified, it is recommended that interviewers and custodians should ensure that informants are credited whenever their words are made public.

To pay or not to pay?

An additional item of background intelligence to the medium is that publishing and/or broadcasting aside, it is established practice that individual interviewees do not normally expect payment if their words or recordings are copied or distributed. Partly for this reason, most are willing to transfer recordings and assign their rights to custodians such as their employer or previous employer, sound archives, museums, or local history collections in libraries, which can prevent the abuse and unauthorized copying of interview material and provide suitable facilities for proper use.

In their construction, it should be noted that oral testimonies are not substantially different from any other historical sources such as diaries, correspondence, official documents, newspapers and photographs and so on and, as such, pose equally relevant problems in its collection. Interviewees are human. They can forget things. Their memories often play tricks on them and their recall is subject to all the biases and vagaries inherent in human recall. Because of this, they must be subjected to the same tests of evidence as other sources, and examined along with other contemporary sources for corroboration and authentication. That said, these biases may themselves constitute important data for the debriefer's consideration. Unlike other resources, however, they are not subject to the constraints of written report, with their primary value coming from oral delivery's enhanced communicability.

Telephone interviews

It is legal in the UK to record one's own telephone conversations for personal use, and there is no legal obligation to inform the other person or persons that their words are being recorded.

UK laws and codes of practice, such as the Regulation of Investigatory Powers Act (2000), and the Telecommunications Regulations (2000), are mainly concerned with recordings made for security surveillance ('telephone tapping') or various monitoring and market research activities, where the recordists are not being recorded themselves. However it is unethical and legally risky to make telephone interview recordings available to anyone else without the permission of the speakers. If telephone interviews are to be deposited in a public collection or made available for research or for any other purpose, all this should be explained in detail by the interviewer before the interview starts. Arrangements should be made for interviewees to sign clearance forms (perhaps by post or e-mail) or, at the very least, the interviewee should state clearly in the recording that he or she agrees to the uses described by the interviewer.

Summary

As a tool, oral debriefing has high value in that it allows organizations to gain control of their short- and medium-term knowledge in a permanent format. It also allows a formalized methodology to 'tease out' the complex tacit knowledge that otherwise never gets recorded.

Doing a good oral debrief is a skilful job requiring exhaustive preparation. As a rule of thumb, the better the pre-interview research, the better the output. This invariably applies even when the interviewee is articulate. An inelegant way of describing the exercise is: 'crap in, crap out' – which is exactly what also needs to be avoided with the other medium that is perfect for capturing even longer-term OM described in the next chapter.

Notes

1. Eric Hoffer, *Reflections on the Human Condition*, New York: Harper & Row, 1973.
2. Thucydides, *The History of the Peloponnesian War*, 431 BCE, trans. Richard Crawley, London, 1874.
3. G. Klein, *Sources of Power: How People Make Decisions*, Boston, MA: MIT Press, 1998; and Stephen Denning, *Squirrel Inc. A Fable of Leadership Through Story Telling*, San Francisco: Jossey-Bass, 2004.
4. Jochen Kraske, William H. Becker, William Diamond and Louis Galambos, *Bankers with a Mission: The Presidents of the World Bank 1946–95*, New York: Oxford University Press/World Bank, 1997.
5. Joseph Marchese, *Resource Guide for the Centre for History of Chemistry (CHOC)*, n.d.
6. Report to a conference run by the British Archives Council, 1988.
7. OECD, *Annual Report*, 1994.
8. R.E. Boyatzis, S.S. Cowen and David Kolb (eds), *Innovation in Professional Education: Steps in a Journey from Teaching to Learning*, San Francisco: Jossey-Bass, 1995.
9 . Author project through Pencorp, January 1994.

9 *From Hagiography to a Powerful Management Tool*

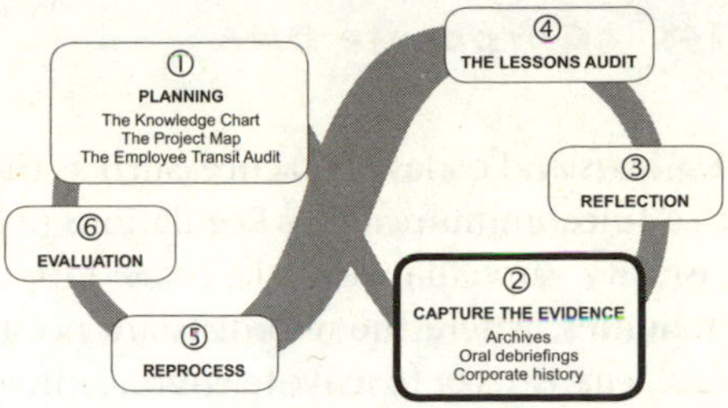

The diagram at top shows a cyclical process:
① PLANNING — The Knowledge Chart, The Project Map, The Employee Transit Audit
② CAPTURE THE EVIDENCE — Archives, Oral debriefings, Corporate history
③ REFLECTION
④ THE LESSONS AUDIT
⑤ REPROCESS
⑥ EVALUATION

The palest ink is better than the best memory.

Chinese proverb

Corporate histories, product histories and biographies of business leaders are the most comprehensive and portable repositories of long-term organizational memory (OM). As a modern medium, they are around twice as old as their oral equivalent and around four times the age of their visual counterpart, the VCR and DVD.

Externally funded corporate histories

Corporate histories come in a variety of forms, all of which typically generate their own uncertainties and production difficulties for the subject organization. Some get external funding such as the autobiographies of well-known businessmen and women, several examples being Margery Hurst's 1967 *No Glass Slipper,* an account of how she formed the Brook Street Bureau chain of employment agencies, the 1968 account by Percy Hunting entitled *The Group and I*, the story of the transportation group bearing his name, the 1970 'memoirs' of Marks & Spencer's Israel Moses Seiff and, in 1991, Anita Roddick's *Body and Soul*, the story of how she created the Body Shop. Top managers are invariably better at making money than trying to explain how they did it, so many of them use professional writers – so-called ghostwriters – to write the books which appear under their names. Lee Iacocca, for example, the plain-speaking boss of Chrysler, used the services of novelist William Novak to write the bestseller *Iacocca*. Victor Kiam's *Going for It!* was written by Richard Lally, a former sports journalist who had previously written an autobiography of a famous baseball player, while, in his *Off The Rails*, British Rail's Sir Richard Marsh collaborated with the biographer and historian who also provided professional assistance to Lord Forte in his *Forte*.

Independent corporate histories

Then there are those wholly written by independent authors that are funded by publishers without the help of the subject company, just like commercial books. Sometimes the company cooperates with the author, a category in which would fit, for example, books on the Rothschild banking family company, Ford, Jaguar and foundations like Lloyd's of London. *The Rothschilds – A Family of Fortune*, for example, was written in 1973 by the popular historian and journalist Virginia Cowles while the 1986 novel-like account of Henry Ford and his Michigan empire was written by the journalist Robert Lacey.

In this category of book, it was, curiously enough, one of the first attempts at writing serious corporate history that has managed to be the most impressive and subsequently influential. In 1899 Ida Tarbell, a young woman journalist, somehow persuaded a senior director of Standard Oil Company to talk freely and openly about the rapidly developing oil industry and the company in particular. The company, which was run by the legendary businessman John D. Rockefeller, dominated US business in the last quarter of the nineteenth century. Out of two years' work with a research assistant, her objective was to produce a chronological history of the Standard Oil Company rather than anything controversial. In the event she produced a conspicuously influential book.

In serialization form, the story ran for two years from November 1902 in *McClure's*, one of America's leading periodicals at the time with a circulation of several hundred thousand. She literally captured the imagination of the American public with her account of buccaneering entrepreneurs, often working on the fringes of the law. Published in book form in 1904 as *The History of Standard Oil Company*, the company, which *was* encountering considerable criticism for some of its competitive practices, was more dissatisfied with the public reaction to the company's image portrayed in the book rather than to the book itself. Contemporaries viewed it then as one of the most remarkable books ever written in America and the company later came to view the book as probably the most widely bought and disseminated work on American economic and business history.

The book contained a wealth of management lessons, the most important of which the company, unfortunately, chose to ignore. Despite the warnings sounded in the book about corporate ethics and public accountability, Standard – along with many of its competitors – continued to operate in an unbridled freewheeling business fashion. The company, by this time America's largest corporate enterprise, refined more than three-quarters of all US crude oil and marketed four-fifths of all domestic kerosene. It also maintained its pre-eminence through tough competitive tactics and even developed a particularly efficient network of industrial spies. In conducting business in this fashion, Standard totally misjudged the mood of the times, which was moving against the big conglomerates, or trusts, and in November 1906 the Roosevelt administration charged Standard Oil with violating with conspiracy the Sherman Antitrust Act of 1890 to restrain trade. By ignoring the public response to its corporate activities, the main case against the oil company was proven in court in 1909, and Standard appealed to the Supreme Court – unsuccessfully. Standard was given just six months to dissolve itself. The break-up meant the creation of seven new competing parts, the largest of which was the former holding company, Standard Oil of New Jersey (later Exxon).

Given the dissolution of the company, the book – the only detailed, comprehensive and surviving record of the company during its heyday – has assumed an even greater importance to posterity. Arguably it actually triggered the Rockefeller legend. And 84 years later, one of the new generation of business historians, Harvard's Professor Alfred Chandler, was using Standard Oil's competitive example to illustrate how – through a logic he christened 'managerial enterprise' – Germany became the most powerful industrial nation in Europe before the Second World War, the US became the most productive country of the world for 40 years until the 1960s and Japan their most successful competitor since. In 1977 Chandler won a Pulitzer Prize for his 1977 book, *The Visible Hand*, the study of managerial capitalism based on the history of US, British and German businesses in modern times.

Unauthorized corporate histories

When the books do not have the cooperation of the subject company, they are sometimes called 'unauthorized' or 'investigative' works. These are often quick-off-the-press books on subjects like the Guinness and BCCI scandals in the late 1980s and early 1990s, but they also include attempts at full-blown corporate histories. One example was Lonrho's, the multinational trading company run by Roland 'Tiny' Rowland who ran foul of Prime Minister Edward Heath in the 1970s. Before starting their research, the authors approached members of the board with requests for information but were unable to arrange a meeting on terms that Lonrho found acceptable. On completion of the manuscript the authors presented the company with a draft for comment. It was only at this stage that some information was provided. When *Lonrho. A Portrait of a Multinational* was published in 1976, the publisher described it as 'a sustained piece of investigative journalism'. An example where the subject provided no cooperation whatsoever is the 1992 'biography' of Ireland's most famous businessman, Tony O'Reilly, president of the Pittsburg-based H.J. Heinz food company. In this case the author relied almost exclusively on public archives, newspaper cuttings, various editors and journalists and the hearsay evidence of unidentified people in Europe, the US, Africa, Australia, New Zealand and Ireland. Legal proceedings were instituted to try and prevent publication of *Oh Really O'Reilly* – without success. The author, whose acquaintance with the subject was limited to a mutual interest in sport, used his own resources to publish the book. Any pretension towards publishing professionalism was discharged by a loose insert to the book which regretted any grammatical and typographical errors, adding: '… we trust you will understand these shortcomings in the light of the legal efforts made to prevent the printing, publishing and distribution of this work'.

Independent corporate histories with company cooperation

Companies sometimes give independent books their cooperation but the project can still run roughly. In the case of the book about the giant Japanese securities houses, *The House of Nomura*, the dispute ended up in the courts, costing both the author and the company an estimated £1 million in costs. The author, who researched the book in his spare time while working as a stock salesman in Tokyo, maintained that he obtained permission from the Nomura family for access to archives and to interview 100 company executives. The author also claimed that the Nomura family read the proofs before publication. Upon publication, the company immediately started legal proceedings against the author, Al Alletzhauser, and his British publisher, for libel. In its action Nomura claimed there were 'many false stories in the book', that it suggested the Japanese securities house had had dealings with gangsters and that it wanted a retraction, payment of damages and a promise that alleged libels would not be repeated. Preparations for a trial were still underway in July 1991 when the company's chairman and vice-chairman resigned after taking responsibility for a series of scandals. The chairman, Setsuya Tabuchi, said that his resignation would show that the company genuinely regretted its improper behaviour, which also included compensating favoured clients for trading losses and lending to a gangster group. Nomura dropped its libel action in July 1992 under a so-called 'drop hands settlement' under which both sides covered their own costs.

A more successful independent and 'authorized' example was a book produced on International Telephone and Telegraph Corporation (ITT). In the late 1970s, Robert Sobel, Professor of Business History at New College of Hofstra and a financial columnist for *Newsday*, was approached by the company's public relations department to write the group's history. The company, with interests ranging from seeds and hotels to creating the electronics-based technologies of the future, was approaching its fiftieth anniversary and the directors had decided to make a record of the past. Told that ITT was prepared to sponsor a full-scale work, Sobel replied that he believed subsidized histories to be of limited and questionable worth since the payment of funds established a dubious nexus between the writer and the subject. However, intrigued by the opportunity to do a major work, he bravely offered to find an independent publisher and entered into a contract that did not require or involve any direct or indirect ITT subsidy. In return, he suggested, ITT would have to assure him complete access to records, files and individuals except for matters in litigation. ITT would have the right to see the finished manuscript and to comment on questions of style or content but could not demand changes or alterations of any kind. The company agreed. Four years later, in 1982, Truman Talley Books/Times Books published *I.T.T. The Management of Opportunity*, a 'warts-and-all' look at the world's largest conglomerate. Notable for its candour, it laid to rest long-held allegations that founder Sosthenes Behn aided the Axis powers during the Second World War; it also revealed unpublicized aspects of ITT's damning behaviour in Chile during the Nixon era. Above all, it gave a valuable insight into the workings of a major American institution. Despite the controversial aspects of some of its top personalities and the fact that there was no editorial control over the manuscript by the company, ITT executives were delighted with the result. Significantly, the group's UK subsidiary, Standard Telephones and Cables, was taking a different route in its centenary history, which was published a year later. It chose a former company employee as author and preferred to vest copyright in the book in itself. The book, perhaps predictably, had less of an impact than its US counterpart.

Another example of an independently written corporate history with a difficult conception and gestation was the story of the US law firm Sullivan & Cromwell. The book had its genesis when a young sociologist, Nancy Lisagor, took an interest in the organization's secretive activities. It caught her eye because its client list was unmatched in Wall Street, among them a large percentage of banks, a number of oil giants and top Japanese companies. With a secretary of state, director of the Central Intelligence Agency, Supreme Court justice and test-ban negotiator among its distinguished alumni, the firm ranked high among unexplored subjects in the law. She started her research at Princeton University, which houses the archives of John Foster Dulles and his brother Allen Welsh Dulles. The former had been senior partner in Sullivan & Cromwell for 20 years before becoming secretary of state while the latter also spent 20 years at the company prior to his move to the CIA. Supplementing her researches with National Archives material she eventually decided to approach the firm to see whether they would allow her to talk to employees and pensioners. After trying to arrange a meeting with a pensioner whose great uncle might have introduced Sullivan and Cromwell, the two founders, she discovered that the firm disapproved of the book. Even though lawyers were, by now, allowed to 'advertise' and take a more public profile, it seemed that the main reason was their tradition of secrecy and that they distrusted an outside company assessment over which they would have no control; there was also no doubt an element of embarrassment over revelations unearthed by Lisagor in the public archives that the company cooperated with Adolf Hitler until the US entered the Second World War.

It was at this stage that Lisagor brought on board her husband, Frank Lipsius, a journalist with *The Financial Times* and *The Economist*. Together, they tried once again to elicit the help of the company, emphasizing that the firm's input would, if nothing else, make the book more accurate. Insisting that it was a firm tradition to avoid the modern practice of soliciting press coverage, the company again refused to cooperate, although it did advise all former employees who telephoned in to enquire about company policy towards the project that they could talk to Lisagor and Lipsius if they were so inclined. Once again, research stalled.

A year later things suddenly changed when the firm switched its chairman. The change coincided with four embarrassing incidents in which the firm's lawyers, three of them important partners, had become the object of headline-making lawsuits, prosecutions or investigations. More interested in the need to present the firm's side of the case than retain its constricting traditions, the new chairman agreed to cooperate with no conditions attached to the interviews. In 1988, four years after starting the research, *A Law Unto Itself* was published. It was the first social history of a US law firm, showing how the firm's partners had had a crucial impact on American business, government and international relations for more than a century. Although it recorded the firm's assistance to the Nazi regime in Germany, it registered the fact that this cooperation occurred pre-war; it also chronicled the firm's influence on the building of the Panama Canal, the Great Depression, the post-Second World War recovery (especially in Japan) and the mergers and acquisition boom of the 1980s which reorganized much of America's business.

In their preface, authors Lisagor and Lipsius wrote:

Afterward we speculated on how the book might have turned out had we had the firm's co-operation at the beginning of the project nearly five years before. We realized the result would have been quite different, relying much more on the firm's persuasive opinion of its own accomplishments and less on the public record. We thank the partners for their interviews and assure them that the process of writing the book has enhanced our respect for their intelligence and devotion to their clients and work. If we raise the wider issues of those loyalties, we do so in part because of the very effectiveness of their professional achievements.[1]

PR: the main motivation

I relate these examples to give just a taste of the experiences of some companies undergoing such projects. They are not extraordinary, and illustrate how difficult the process is for both subject and author. Nor are they many in number, signifying that the volume of recorded OM through these types of project is nominal across industry and commerce. Furthermore, they are all of large organizations, no doubt because of the management perception that they are, quite rightly, important and that size tenders some obligation to be recorded. And not forgetting, of course, that the publishers see an opportunity to sell more than few copies. But, significantly, in not one case is the motivation of the subject organization a genuine attempt to preserve the past for the benefit of the organization's future.

The examples I have related are of independent or semi-independent conduits of OM, the construction of which, whilst professionally put together, still falls far short of the content possible for optimal experiential learning. They are classically designed to be 'interesting' for an external audience and although excellent for purposes such as induction, often lack the necessary management perspectives for decision-making purposes. It is a structural flaw that offsets their 'credible' character and which is either overlooked in the project's conception or is a limitation of the individual author.

The sponsored corporate history

But there is another format, by far the larger category of book, that would allow such perspectives to be deliberately included. It is the sponsored corporate history, where researching, writing and, when the organization doesn't object to public exposure, publication is exclusively funded by the subject company. Despite being the largest category of corporate history, however, very few such books exist across industry and commerce. And despite the genre's relative maturity – more than 100 years – the medium is still widely unprofessionalized in the business world.

With comparatively few exceptions, the genre is generally poorly researched, badly written by ill-chosen authors, inexpertly edited, glossily printed by the subject company under its own copyright, ill-used and, when sold commercially, expensively priced. Few are reviewed, even fewer authoritatively. And of the better ones, the numbers that are used as learning tools in business schools are trifling. Much like their cousins, the independent or semi-independent books, the motivation for their existence is almost never a conscious effort to provide a vehicle with which future generations can benefit from hindsight. In the wider world of history books, they have the undistinguished qualification of being among the least read. They are very lowly ranked, almost as low as books that have been self-published – and for one simple reason. In almost every instance, they are the creature of its subject and almost always funded and managed by the subject organizations themselves. Sadly, their content typically provides little specific erudition useful for decision-making, despite the opportunity that full funding presents.

The fact that they require subject-company funding and subject-company cooperation typically dictates how they are produced. Simply, when the company acts as paymaster, manager, editor and/or publisher, the unavoidable – and often justifiable perception – is that the work is a partisan, company production. Effectively, the direct relationship between author and the subject company establishes a conflict with author independence. In the classic description of no-win, they are, in many respects, products caught between a rock and a hard place.

Although there are examples of fine corporate histories produced within these constraints, they are routinely denigrated and any application they otherwise might have is lost. Notably, this attitude persists despite business sponsorship being an accepted element in other academic endeavours – for example, collaborative ventures abound in other important areas of research and commercial endeavour. Successful sponsorship is even evident elsewhere in the book world. Famous names like General Foods and Maxwell sponsor cookery books, Safeway, the supermarket chain, used to pay for books on dieting before its takeover by Morrisons, the chemist chain Boots funds books on skincare, make-up and haircare and nappy manufacturer Peaudouce pay for books on pregnancy. Elsewhere, the sponsorship of books on sports, health, money management, childcare and travel has become big business – except when it comes to companies backing books about themselves.

In this chapter I am not going to deal specifically with the books that are funded or part-funded by publishing companies. Neither am I going to deal with the 'unauthorized' versions, which have to depend entirely on outside sources. Whether or not they become private or public documents, my attention is focused on those – the vast majority – that would not otherwise exist without the funding of the subject company. In the absence of such backing, the institution's OM would be lost forever.

Oddly, few companies do them as private documents destined only for a confidential readership such as the chairman's or chief executive's exclusive eye. More commonly they are embarked upon *with* the intention of public exposure for public relations reasons. However, if the final document is deemed unsuitable, it gets locked away in a safe forever more. As a general rule they are disasters waiting to happen – boardroom indulgences that portend literary fiascos and corporate white elephants. In print, I often equate them with the fable of the emperor's new clothes because the subject companies invariably think they have produced something edifying.

It is easy to explain why they are done so defectively. Some of the reasons I have already mentioned. There are a host of others.

Without a full appreciation of the genre's powerful applications, the subject company's instinctive motivation almost always defers to an anniversary or similar 'tribute' occasion such as the retirement of a founder or high-profile executive, the editorial approach for which always requires a completely different mindset to any other, more serious, application. Also, the funding organization always finds it extremely difficult not to interfere with facts, figures and judgements that might reflect (however accurately) on their own performance. The temptation to 'control' content is irresistible and rarely passed up – a clear gauge of managerial arrogance, ego, insecurity and defensiveness, which manifests itself in classic censorship.

In addition, most organizations use in-house employees to write their histories, usually individuals with long tenure because companies believe they will receive a more 'sympathetic' treatment and/or that an outsider will know less about the organization than someone not steeped in its culture and tradition. Their output is often less than book-like – or incisive – in character, even with outside editing help. Some use professional researchers or writers whose work, although more readable, is characteristically deemed insufficiently authoritative for serious application in industry or education, often with good reason. All this might suggest that the academic treatment might be more acceptable. Unfortunately not. The output by university-based academics, who produce just a handful of the total number of corporate histories – mainly of the larger companies – is invariably heavy-handed and lifeless, often written in what is known in non-academic circles as 'PhD-speak'. In the main, their efforts are invariably written for the approbation of colleagues, supporting a core scholarly belief that equates ease of comprehension with lack of rigour. Whether produced by academics or non-academics, most writers also generally insist on recording the past for its own sake without any functional application other than PR. In their printing, publishers – including those attached to the main universities – traditionally receive healthy stipends from subject companies. With minimal editing and marketing, they rarely give them the attention they might give to more commercial books. Only a handful goes on public sale, with their cover price typically twice or three times the cost of conventional business books. Readership levels of both, typically small, are sustained by giveaways to family, employees and corporate 'friends'. It often surprises me when employers even restrict circulation among their own employees and, despite having surpluses stored in a warehouse, refuse to give them to new employees. It is the model recipe for hagiography, whether produced by professional writers or academics, and a product with a very low stature. And for knowledge management/education purposes, the product is largely wasted as a repository of corporate experience and knowledge. This is a characteristic that knows no geographical boundaries, at least in the more developed countries where higher levels of education provide more critical awareness of lack of transparency.

The UK illustrates this attribute in both the academic and professional author categories. With the notable exception of Charles Wilson's 1954 history of Unilever, no corporate history of a British company written by an academic has achieved bestseller status – unlike many examples of academics writing about other types of history. A bestseller is a book that sells at least 10 000 hardback copies. And in the non-academic grouping, there is just one modern example – Sir Richard Branson's *Losing My Virginity* (ghosted, self-published and sold at £9.99), which was top of the Bestselling Business Books chart for at least a year. It is instructive that neither appears on any academic reading list of any British business school, despite the fact that they are prime examples of British business enterprise. Nor, in fact, do the reading lists include any of the commercially produced books of other famous British companies.

Some corporate history disasters

For just a taste of some corporate debacles, a relatively modern example of a sponsored book that went wrong belongs to Staveley Industries, one of the UK's oldest publicly quoted companies. The relationship between the chosen author and the subject company actually broke down. Having decided against using a professional project manager and publisher, the company commissioned the author directly, choosing a freelance writer, Patrick Beaver, who had previously written around ten 'PR'-style histories of companies such as the Initial Group, Empire Stores and Bryant & May. However, the company subsequently employed an outside journalist to reduce the text from 70 000 words to about 25 000 without consulting Beaver who consequently refused to allow his name to appear anywhere in the publication. Staveley admits to having changed the text 'rather a lot'. The final document, entitled *Survival Against the Odds*, was published anonymously in booklet form by the company in 1988 with a foreword by the chairman, who wrote, unashamedly: 'We have tried to give only a "flavour" of Staveley's somewhat tortuous progress through this century of industrial revolution and change. In doing so, we may be guilty of some omissions.'

The 1985 history of the 128-year-old Britannia Building Society was produced to coincide with the retirement of its chairman, Sir Hubert Newton, after 51 years' service. The building society had previously published soft-cover narratives to celebrate its fiftieth anniversary and, in 1958, its centenary. On the first page its author, who came by way of recommendation, illustrates Sir Hubert's 'kindliness and good humour' by recalling that the 80-year-old took him to see a match played by 'his beloved Stoke City F.C. on the dreadful day in the 1984–85 season that they first plunged to bottom place in the First Division'. In recording that Sir Hubert was appointed president of Stoke City Football Club in 1982, the narrative, which was edited in-house, did not make clear the relationship between the Britannia's business activities and the chairman's interest in football.

In the 1976 history of Fyffes, produced to celebrate the shipping and banana importer's seventy-fifth anniversary, the company admitted that, in terms of objectivity, the document 'looked on the bright side'. Entitled *Yes? We Have Some*, any pretensions towards seriousness was discharged by reference to 'sleeping' as one of the author's spare-time occupations.

Illustrating a lost opportunity, even in PR terms, was the corporate history of Addis, the brush and housewares company, which published a 55-page biography to celebrate its bicentennary in 1980. The company decided to do its history because of the Addis family's early involvement in toothbrush manufacture. It said that it also hoped to gain some unusual publicity from the book. Through a brief chronological narrative and a series of short sketches of major acquisitions and overseas activities, it outlined the story of the company, which has been led by one family through seven generations. Typically for a 'PR' history, the company retained copyright in the book and it did not go on public sale. An unusual stylistic problem for the author resulted from the fondness by the family down the years of calling their sons by the same first name. Four of the early leaders of the company were named William while three of the more recent heads – including the then current chairman – were named Robert. To overcome confusion the author inexpertly referred to each individual by numbers – for example William (2) or Robert (1).

In other examples, 160 years of the 1991 history of Scotch whisky distillers, George Ballantine, part of the Allied Distillers Group, were covered in 61 heavily illustrated pages. The history of the group's Teacher's Whiskey subsidiary, whose origins go back to 1830, was even shorter, with the author tactlessly concluding the 47-page illustrated narrative with the words 'The End'.

In this category, one of the more guileless PR histories in recent years was Lonrho's, which used a 1988 book about itself as a lobby tool against the interest of the Egyptian al-Fayed brothers. At the time, the company was enmeshed in its long-running tussle with the brothers who, in 1985, had acquired House of Fraser and its flagship, Harrods. Department of Trade investigators were investigating the takeover. As part of its campaign, Lonrho published its own account of the saga to put pressure on the government to publish the DTI Inspectors' report. Differing radically from the investigative history written 12 years before, the 185-page product, entitled *A Hero from Zero*, was written anonymously in flowery prose and contained chapters entitled Pharaonic Fantasies, Eastern Folly and Hapless Harrods. A group subsidiary printing company printed, it is thought, about 15 000 copies for distribution to merchant bankers, lawyers, MPs and the media.

Even the 'academic' route taken by some larger companies is never straightforward. In Glaxo's 1982 sponsored history, the pharmaceutical giant decided to use the recently formed Business History Unit at the London School of Economics. In the event, the Unit appointed as author one of its part-time staff, Dr Richard Davenport-Hines, who had just written *Dudley Docker: The Life and Times of a Trade Warrior*, which had won the Wolfson Literary Prize in 1985 and the Wadsworth Prize for business history in 1986. Docker was a highly influential, right-wing Midlands industrialist and international financier who founded, in 1916, the Federation of British Industries, the forerunner of the Confederation of British Industry.

The university had another reason for appointing Davenport-Hines – it wanted to employ him on a more permanent basis. Using an arm's length arrangement Glaxo engaged the university as project manager; the university, in turn, commissioned Davenport-Hines through a separate contract which gave the university copyright of the manuscript and Glaxo copyright of all the quoted material in the manuscript. Davenport-Hines spent four years working on the commission, with Glaxo's full cooperation. When it was handed in in 1986, it was rejected.

The author admits that the manuscript was unsatisfactory. He explains the circumstances:

I was originally hired to write the company's history to 1963. I was later asked to bring the book up to date to the 1980s, which I started to do. That decision was referred to the board that became upset at the idea. That instruction was then withdrawn. When the manuscript was handed in, it was shown to a former chairman who, I was told, strongly disliked it. He apparently thought the historical method entirely inappropriate because the book was initially conceived as a management textbook on marketing, the company being particularly proud of its marketing of products like Zantac and their global strategy plan based on Italy. The former chairman was apparently against the project on grounds of principle. Over the research period the nature and purpose of the project changed three times. As a result I had to chop and change the manuscript. There were clear errors in liaison between the university and the company. It was dogged by misfortunes and was badly handled – both by myself and the university.

Davenport-Hines attaches no blame to the way in which Glaxo handled the project.

We were under no obligation to accept the company's suggestions for changing the goalposts. We were incautious. With hindsight we should have said 'no' but we were awed, anxious to please a benefactor and agreed to the idea unreflectingly.

Davenport-Hines also admits that he was a bad choice as author:

I think I was ill-suited to write the book on temperamental grounds. Also, my writing style is quite unsuitable for that type of book. In the meantime I had had various disagreements with people at the university, which had been building up for some time. In addition I had no faith in what was being proposed to resuscitate the project.[2]

In the event, the only way of reviving the project was to bring in another author. In 1987 Judy Slinn, who had just completed the histories of May & Baker and Freshfields, was commissioned to recast the manuscript. The book was eventually published under the joint authorship of Davenport-Hines and Slinn in 1992 – ten years after it was first conceived. Like most other company biographies in the UK, it was given no explicit corporate application despite the fact that the timing of publication provided a propitious opportunity to use it as an induction tool for the soon-to-be Wellcome merger.

The roll call of such examples is long. The first volume of Phoenix Assurance's history, for example, which took eight years to produce and cost more than £350 000,[3] received a company order of just 750 copies. Elsewhere, the definitive account of Royal Insurance's history, produced to coincide with its 150th anniversary in 1995, cost a total of £360 000. It took a Cambridge history graduate two years to research and write. Although it was given to all employees, it did not go on public sale. In a two-inch review of the 287-page book, the copyright of which had been sequestered from the author, *The Financial Times* said: 'Unfortunately its attempts to pep up the history of insurance by linking developments to contemporary events leave a bit to be desired.' Four years after its printing, more than 7000 of a 10 000 print run of Blue Circle's corporate history were still lodged in a company warehouse. In the case of Bradford & Bingley's 1989 corporate history, the building society still had almost two-thirds of its 13 000 print run in hand years after publication. The average outside sale for all the company histories published by the Cambridge University Press during the 1980s – among them Bowater's, BP's, Phoenix Assurance's and British Rail's – was just 700 copies per title, a print run that *included* the books given to the captive 'give-away' audiences of the subject companies.[4]

Then there are the attempts that do not see the light of day. Although hard statistics are difficult to come by, it is not unreasonable to speculate that fewer corporate histories are published than those that that get hidden away in a corporate safe, among them the history of the Institute of Chartered Secretaries & Administrators, one of Britain's oldest professional associations, which was planned to coincide with an important anniversary in 1991. It was shelved because of what the association's own chief executive admitted was 'less than constructive co-operation by the committee set up to manage the project'.[5] The author, an award-winning business writer, eventually gave up in despair having spent 18 months trying to accommodate hundreds of comments, many of them contradictory, from individual committee members. Elsewhere, the Association of British Chemical Manufacturers, the Federation of British Industries, Guinness, Kleinwort Benson, Carr's Milling Industries, William Heaton & Sons and J & J Colman, the foods company, have all kept accounts of their history firmly under wraps.

However trying it is for the subject company to do their corporate history, many of the authors who research and write the documents also find the work extremely difficult. The internal author, for example, usually flattered by the invitation from his peers, invariably finds the job more onerous than it was ever believed at the outset. Archibald Richards, a former chairman of the board of partners at chartered accountants Touche Ross & Co. recalled:

When the board asked me to write a history of the firm, I readily agreed – believing in my innocence that I already knew a great deal about the firm. Had I known then the enormity of the task and the great amount of research it would entail I am sure I would have respectfully declined.[6]

About his efforts to write his autobiography, which was done with the help of a professional writer, Lord Forte, chairman of Trusthouse Forte, said: '... writing a book is a damned sight harder than cutting sandwiches',[7] while S.T. Roberts, the employee author of *The History of Pitney Bowes*, admitted that the task was 'formidable'. For external authors, the difficulties are no less forbidding. Academic David Kynaston, who wrote the *The Financial Times: A Centenary History* (1988), said of his two-and-a-half-year project:

Researching and writing a company history is rather like playing a game of Chinese whispers. Rumours which turned into anecdotes pass down from one generation to another and become accepted facts, and reasonably well-adjusted personalities achieve legendary status for one or two exaggerated traits. The living have highly contradictory accounts of past events and the dead of course can only bear witness through fading documents and board minutes.[8]

A successful example

But not all achieve such testing heights. Bankers Coutts, which, unusually, decided on a serious approach to its biography, had a largely problem-free experience with their corporate history, although it *did* miss its original publication deadline by a year and the company's distribution policy was affected by a remarkably high printing cost imposed by the publisher. It was notable for the amount of pre-project planning, in particular their efforts to give the author clear editorial guidelines.

The history was commissioned in 1984 for planned publication in 1991, a year ahead of the 1992 tercentenary. In the event, the manuscript was completed in June 1991 and publication took place in February 1992. In their prepublication conceptualization, the company accepted that the book was not intended to be a definitive, complete history. According to the brief:

While an accurate and sound historical basis is required it should be impressionistic rather than precisely photographic. ... It should be more a history of people and their influence on the bank and of the bank's influence on people and events than a financial business history. The business history must not, however, be totally neglected. The relationships between partners may well lead to the influence of certain families or personalities giving a theme to the book but the part played by staff will hopefully come in.

No doubt referring to the Royal Family in particular, the brief added:

The trap should not be fallen into of writing about interesting customers apart from their influence on the development of the bank or the bank's influence on their careers.[9]

The company's brief to the author also covered more general editorial aspirations:

It should be a book that would (and hopefully will) sell as well as being given away. If it can give rise later to television productions so much the better, provided it is not, as a book, too episodic. It should be almost an historical novel or saga rather than a history – a biography of the bank rather than a history of it.[10]

The company chose an author who was both a well-known 'name' and an Oxford English graduate to write the 300-year history. Edna Healey, wife of the Labour politician Denis Healey, was selected because of her association with the bank through another book, *Lady Unknown*, a biography of the philanthropist Angela Burdett-Coutts, the granddaughter of one of the family members who gave the bank its name.

However, although the company employed the resources of an outside writer with a high profile, it chose not to assign copyright to the author. When the manuscript was handed in, there were two 'editing' processes – a team of in-house editors undertook what the company describes as 'fairly intensive' factual corrections and elaborations while more stylistic editing was done by the publisher.

Although the company commissioned and managed the author directly, it used the resources of the author's literary agent to select an outside publisher and negotiate a printing fee. In deciding how many copies it needed, the bank first considered its possible applications. Among these were to use it as a corporate marketing device and for 'inculcating the culture' with new younger staff and mature recruits. At first, Coutts thought it might be given to the bank's entire customer base of 50 000 on the basis that selective distribution would cause rancour. However, on the advice of the author's literary agent that the retail cover price of the intended hardback edition should be in the region of about £20 and that the company could anticipate a discount of up to 50 per cent on bulk purchase, the publisher's projected cost – at an opportunistic £500 000 – was, unsurprisingly, considered exorbitant. In the event, the company decided on a more limited print run of almost 14 000, with the publisher printing an additional 2500 for outside sales at a cover price of £25. Distribution was restricted to long-standing customers amounting to 10 per cent of the customer base. In addition, copies were given to all staff and pensioners, so-called 'influencers' or introducers of business, journalists and 'dignitaries', including Royal households. It represented another lost opportunity.

The history of corporate history

Corporate histories were originally undertaken by Victorian businessmen, either company founders, members of the surviving family owners or long-serving employees. Rather than being chronological histories in the modern manner, many of them were diary-type personal recollections or short, superficial public relations exercises – characteristics that would persist down the years.

Since its pioneering days more than a century ago, the corporate history has developed in fits and starts. Thousands of companies across the industrialized world have put their stories to paper, albeit in their own unique way – from relatively benign, albeit colourful chronicles, usually written for the private archives of founding families, to titles with well-defined corporate applications. The US has been particularly prolific, with the UK always a hesitant patron even though one of its earliest corporate histories, that of a publishing company called the Catnach Press, predates the 1902 Standard Oil biography by 16 years. In fact, an inspection of bibliographic references[11] reveals that more histories of British companies were being produced in the last year of the nineteenth century than were published in the last year of the twentieth century. The first wider history of British business by an acknowledged academic business historian saw the light of day only in 1995[12] and there is *still* no twentieth-century history of British management on the shelves.

Between the world wars, the majority of business histories in the UK were house histories, consisting mainly of reminiscences and anecdotes. Only a tiny handful of serious work existed using business records which had found their way into museums, county record offices or the private possession of collectors.

The first academic involvement was probably in 1924 when Professor George Unwin and co-author George Taylor wrote a detailed history of *Samuel Oldknow and the Arkwrights: The Industrial Revolution at Stockport and Marple*, published by the Manchester University Press. Then, in 1938, the Bank of England commissioned a two-volume 250-year anniversary history. Written by J.H. (later Sir John) Clapham, professor of economic history at Cambridge, it took six years to produce. It was a transparently celebratory vehicle for a famous British institution.

The reason for the existence of corporate histories was usually accidental. The records were often discovered by chance and deemed interesting enough to turn into historical narratives which were funded either by the family descendants of the long-dead businessmen in question or, less frequently, the author in association with a publisher. They all had one thing in common: they were generally records of companies that had died or otherwise dropped out of sight.

Nothing happened during the Second World War and for several years thereafter, but then modern corporate history took its first big conceptual step when, by chance, a hitherto unknown young academic was given the chance of becoming the corporate historian of one of the world's largest manufacturing companies based in the UK. Typically, the opportunity resulted from the personal patronage of a company director who had a casual interest in the value of company history. It was in 1947 that the then chairman of Unilever, Geoffrey Heyworth (later Lord Heyworth), approached G.N. Clark, who had led the national campaign against the destruction of business records, for his advice on writing the history of the Anglo-Dutch manufacturing company. Clark, who had just become a professor of modern history at Oxford, suggested as author a younger colleague, Charles Wilson. The result was a classic, two-volume work that transformed the writing of business history in the UK from a public relations exercise into a reputable branch of scholarship. His authorship of this trail-blazing account of one of Western Europe's most important companies confirmed him as the father of modern corporate histories in the UK.

Despite these and a handful of other large-company models, the majority of books that continue to be written are still PR projects expressly designed to celebrate important anniversaries. A loosely-based percentage estimate would probably expose a 95:5 bias that would probably be not too dissimilar to equivalent projects in the US and Germany, with the main difference being their utility and the extent of their distribution. Many more corporate histories in the US, for example, are used in the education system.

The acknowledged limitations of corporate history

Many of the genre's shortcomings, at least in the UK, have been recognized (and even acknowledged publicly) by business history's main academic campaigners over the years. Perhaps the most voluble domestic critic is former Reading University's Professor Geoffrey Jones, who, in frustration at trying to manage the decline in the British university system joined Harvard Business School in the early 2000s, admitted that the output of Britain's corporate historians made no impact on anybody. Although he was referring to academia, his view would similarly apply to the non-academic variety. Turning to business history, the more general historical study of the subject that may or may not include the investigation of numbers of company histories and their records, he acknowledges that the 'nature of our product' must take much of the blame. He holds up Professor Chandler's work in the US – and the fact that the MIT/Harvard academic is the only business historian regularly quoted in British books on management – as an example of what can be achieved: 'I believe that British business can learn from the past, and that one – but not the only – function of business history is to help educate British management to perform more effectively than their predecessors.'[13]

Another articulate critic is Dr Richard Davenport-Hines, who co-authored Glaxo's 1982 history. In his capacity as a former editor of the journal *Business History*, the 'voice' of UK academic business historians, he notes that almost every major commissioned project contains some phrase in the preface to the effect that the author has been free to publish conclusions without any strings, and adds:

This is often a straightforward lie. The pressure may be overt, or it may be subtle, but the pressure for changes is always exerted. Some of the most distinguished academics engaged in commissioned histories deal with this problem by omitting objectionable or potentially controversial bits even from their drafts submitted to their company.[14]

Disagreeing with the popular view encouraged by the academic establishment that the mortar board was an exclusive licence for literary respectability, he says that his experience through *Business History* over several years revealed censorship in every sort of book of this kind.

With the vast majority of all corporate histories and many of the more serious examples falling on deaf ears, it is clear that the story of business is not being efficiently passed to successive generations of workers. What is also clear is that the treatments are also restraining the educational application of corporate and business history.

How to improve corporate histories

So, how can lead balloons be made to fly?

What is needed is a fundamental reappraisal of the genre's utility as a corporate and educational tool. Both industry and education must acknowledge that experience has a value and that the failure to recall it accurately allows little business inheritance across the community and within organizations, disempowering the opportunity to learn experientially. Without the knowledge of prior experience, values such as enterprise and wider economic development have to be continually relearned, as does operational efficiency.

If both constituencies accede, the shoe needs to fit both populations, by which I mean that some accommodation has to be found for industry 'models' to also suit academia and vice versa. That way, both versions of the medium would have wider functional applications.

Any solution must also necessarily include business and management history, which is the preserve of mainly academics whose output and application in business schools is also low in almost every country except the US. Without a good base of corporate history, business/management history is inevitably narrowly sourced and the wider subject less rigorous than it might otherwise be. Business history academics could even justifiably argue that its dearth even affects the quality of wider economic history.

Once the principle is recognized, and against the backdrop of humankind's short, selective and defensive memory processes and the very flexible labour market, it becomes – or should become – a process of deciding how best to capture it and apply it efficiently. On the basis that corporate history is the most efficient repository of an institution's long-term memory, how, then, to turn company biography from a corporate indulgence into the powerful learning tool it portends?

Enter business historians, who must then listen carefully to the requirements of their two main constituencies. Part of this may be well be the provision of advice by pointing out the genre's wider potential applications like induction, management development, shareholder relations and marketing (as well as public relations) for the subject company and/or teaching applications in the wider educational system. It is a role that practitioners in other disciplines routinely assume as part of their professional role.

Thereafter, the genre has to become more professionalized.

Formulate a code of conduct

To help overcome the specific problem of product credibility, it is suggested that the genre's main professional associations help formulate a code of conduct for authors, publishers and subject companies, in exactly the same way as many companies, media bodies and some universities, which also accept outside funding for projects such as research, have originated such codes. As a way of promoting self-regulation, such a convention would help ensure that all corporate histories are not tarred with the same brush. It would also demonstrate the determination of business historians to have their work taken seriously, marginalize the PR product and enhance the received worth of the genre in industry and academia.

In the business history world, the institutions that could facilitate this are the national business history associations, among them the Business History Conference in the US, the Association of Business Historians (ABH) in the UK, the Associazione di Storia e Studi sull'Impresa (ASSI) in Italy, Nederlandsch Economisch-Historisch Archief (NEHA) in Holland, Gesellschaft für Unternehmensgeschichte (GUG) in Germany and the European Business History Association (EBHA) for Europe generally. They would specifically have to liaise with sectoral history associations in industries from agriculture, mining, building and banking associations, as well as national business/management organizations.

Historically, membership of the business history associations has been largely academic. Given that writers not in full-time academia dominate the genre's output, it is suggested that they make a special effort to recruit non-academic authors with a view to influencing wider standards in a positive way. This will require them to change their focus from representing only academic interests to wider author and industry-wide interests, in particular finding a more cooperative accommodation between academic and non-academic operatives, between themselves and management educators and – just as important – industry, which is the ultimate beneficiary.

Given this and the traditional difficulties of getting academic bodies to front-run new initiatives, it is further suggested that such a project be managed by industry itself, possibly through individual national business organizations. In the US, business history is considered important enough to be a separate functional division of the Academy of Management, which is one body that comes to mind.

A number of academics and corporate historians in the US, the UK, Germany and Japan, where client patronage similarly undermines the genre, have already indicated to me they would welcome a formal code of conduct to combat the genre's automatic lack of perceived credibility. This proposition, which I first made in 1997,[15] stimulated a round-table discussion between senior US business academics at Ohio State University, the University of Houston, the University of Maryland and the Winthrop Group, the main US private-sector producer of corporate histories, with a view to professionalizing the profession and expanding economic and business historian's influence in the academic and corporate worlds. The participants noted that sociologists, archaeologists and anthropologists had had some success in professionalizing themselves, with the latter being hired as corporate consultants to advise, for example, on whether or not proposed mergers would work. 'Surely business historians have something to offer here?' they asked. Nothing has since transpired – a reason, perhaps, for someone else to run with the idea?

Change departments

Elsewhere on the academic patch, business history has generally subsisted within already established Economic Departments of most universities (and on the back of economic history), which have been enduring their own financial strictures over the past decade or so. With the record showing that the genre has not developed much in this location, it is recommended that the subject transfers into Business Departments proper where its application would, arguably, be more relevant.

The agreed accommodation between industry and academia must also be reflected in the attitudes of the subject organizations that commission their own corporate histories and the authors that write them. In addition to agreeing clear corporate applications for their work before research starts, business historians need to establish a formalized approach that suits both their respective business education systems and their subjects. If the work is intended as a teaching/learning tool, it must, for example, incorporate historical insights into organizational decision-making processes and a concentration on the use of tacit knowledge. Business historians must also learn to speak to a wider audience. In addition to communicating to their main readership – industry – both academic and non-academic authors have to be able to communicate in a mutually accepted format, an approach that requires completely different editorial and publishing styles. This will involve also devising their own clear methodology for doing both corporate and wider-based business history in common with their US counterparts, who have taken the genre through at least two evolutionary phases since Alfred Chandler's pioneering contributions after the Second World War.

Then, in the UK, where the powerful ESRC and the Research Assessment Exercise dominate business history's academic output, some way has to be found to shift their conservatively ordered, unambiguous theoretical bias that does not suit industry's more practical application.

Develop a new mindset

Thereafter, the solution is in the hands of companies themselves in the way they produce their corporate histories. For the subject company, it is essential to confront the choice between making a faithful record and presenting a good PR profile. Even though companies may believe these treatments to be contradictory, they are, in fact, complementary, as several of my examples have illustrated.

To help ensure editorial objectivity, some companies form special committees to oversee the project. The 600-year-old history of The Haberdashers' Company – one of the oldest livery companies in the City of London – was supervised by a so-called 'historiographical committee', which appointed the author and managed the production. In the case of the 1987 history of Toyota, supervising and reviewing various sections of the book were the responsibility of two full professors at Hosei and Meiji universities, who were backed up by two special editorial committees, a 21-member body headed by the group's vice-chairman and the other comprising 50 general managers throughout the group.

Others use academics as supervisers. In BP's case, the company's chairman formed a special editorial advisory board to help choose the author and assist in consultation during the compilation. The committee, formed to safeguard the independence of the history, the integrity of the historian and the company, consisted of himself, a former chairman, three outside academics, a past president of the British Academy and two successive company secretaries. For their history, accountants Ernst & Whinney (now merged into Ernst & Young) formed a history committee to 'correct misconceptions' and provide other assistance. An outside academic historian was brought in to supervise the author, who was given full access to all surviving documents. In the case of Butterworth's *History of a Publishing House*, the company hired an outsider to act as final editor, his 'skilled diplomatic help' helping to ameliorate defects in structure and sequence.

As a general rule, authors find this an extremely inefficient and exasperating way in which to conclude the writing of a document as detailed, creative and – because of the sensitivities involved – difficult as a corporate history, the case of the Institute of Chartered Secretaries and Administrators being just one example. In another case, the regional history of a major British financial services group was so altered by the committee set up to oversee its production that the academic author – who had several corporate histories to his credit – refused to allow his name to appear on the dustjacket. Today the manuscript lies unused in the company's safe.

Construct an arm's-length approach

With only a few examples where this 'collaborative' route has worked efficiently, my own counsel to companies is to construct a unique arm's-length process where both the author and client are managed by an independent project manager and/or publisher. In essence, the author is commissioned by a project manager, who has a separate contract with the subject company. The subject company agrees to give its full cooperation, with safeguards built in to accommodate any client concerns about confidentiality and so on. After the research, writing and editing is complete, the subject company is given the opportunity to comment and, if they think it necessary, amend the manuscript. Should the author disagree with any revisions suggested by the subject company, the author has the right to disclaim authorship and the project manager/publisher would relinquish any further involvement in the project. The subject company can then assign authorship elsewhere; it can become a ghosted book, for example, or be published under another name. In effect, the subject company still gets something for which it has paid, only not with the endorsement of the independent author or the publishing company.

Should no changes be required or the suggested changes have the agreement of the author, the manuscript's copyright is assigned to the author, thus enhancing its integrity further. The manuscript is then printed under the publisher's imprint, giving it an additional credibility boost. Depending on the arrangements between the subject company and the project manager/publisher, the publisher then undertakes marketing, sales and distribution.

The choice of author is critical. As a rule, the author should be an individual whose business knowledge and insight is at least matched by an ability to research and write. This may seem obvious, real life examples have demonstrated that the message is invariably lost without the ability to convey it. A good author will also endow the project with authority. Subject to the actual subject company and their book's specified application, I usually advise that projects are managed using an academic or professional researcher as the researcher and a professional writer as the author, the former to contribute rigour and credence to the project and the latter to add the necessary element of readability.

A good project manager should be able to bring to the project a number of distinctive skills, including:

- advising on the best editorial structure and build this into a working set of objectives
- headhunting a suitable author and researcher
- constructing the contractual arrangements between the author/researcher and the project manager/publisher, and the subject company and the project manager/publisher
- managing on a day-to-day basis, the author, researcher and subject company to ensure that momentum is maintained and deadlines achieved, and providing monthly reports to the subject company
- editing the manuscript
- brokering any changes that need to be made to the manuscript

- publishing according to the subject company's requirements
- depending on the arrangements between the project manager/publisher and the subject company, marketing, selling and distributing the book.

Distancing the author and subject company from each other in this way should ensure that a subject company's biography can be professionally produced as a 'real' book, giving it the necessary authority for powerful applications beyond mere public relations.

Wider applications

I've already mentioned the uses to which corporate history can be put by the subject companies themselves – for the induction of their highly transient workforce and as a repository of their long-term OM for management development, shareholder relations, marketing, and even good PR. But an equally powerful function also resides in the educational sector. Like inspirational teachers, the anecdotal evidence suggesting that biographies/ autobiographies are key career motivators is vast, a notion that was, coincidentally, the precise stimulus for Sir Arthur Knight, a future chairman of the international textiles company Courtaulds and a key figure behind the creation of the Manchester Business School in the 1960s, when he arranged the commissioning of the Donald Coleman history of Courtaulds in the late 1960s.[16] Corporate history, he believed, was as important to the education and training of businesspeople as was the study of political history to future statesmen or military history to future generals.[17] Because of the way in which the book was subsequently envisioned, commissioned, written and published, it was a role that never materialized, even though Sir Arthur was chairman when it was eventually published.

The model is even acknowledged by the powers that be, albeit in other forms. In the UK, for example, where enterprising behaviour is notably undistinguished when compared with many of its international competitors (about one-third the rate in the US[18]), the government has gone to the trouble of arranging a series of roadshows at schools and colleges, where so-called business 'heroes' – the likes of Amstrad's Alan Sugar, Virgin's Sir Richard Branson, inventor James Dyson of vacuum cleaner fame, Reuben Singh, the UK's youngest self-made millionaire, and lastminute.com's Martha Lane Fox – recount their experiences as a way of helping to motivate the next generation of entrepreneurs. Further acknowledgement of experiential learning's value came in early 2001 with the government's unsuccessful call to recruit more than 100 000 over-50s to act as unpaid 'mentors' to pass on their skills to younger people in the public services. Although unrecognized as such, what these individuals are, or would be doing, is recounting their own organizations' corporate/business history. It takes no imagination to conclude that their individual contributions are an inefficient way of passing on their models of corporate enterprise. Surely the introduction to the curriculum of corporate, management and business history – in exactly the same way as other categories of history – would be a more enduring and systematic way of passing on the difficult-to-teach culture of business and enterprise?

When they enter the workforce, most students start from scratch. To facilitate the maximum business 'inheritance', schools and universities should, at the very least, be able to provide them with a selection of local biographies of companies in whose industries they intend to work. As part of their coursework, students could intellectually apply the companies' experiences in ways that would illustrate how previous mistakes and successes could be improved upon, an approach that would counterbalance the pervasive theoretical teaching style of business generally, establish the overlooked concept of experiential learning more firmly and give the genre a learning application that educational policy-makers and management educators can identify with.

Why corporate and business history?

The importance of corporate history can be corroborated in some unusual research in the UK. On the basis of the notion that people pick up their ideas about business from sources like radio, television and literature, the Institute for Economic Affairs, the free-market think tank, found that, almost without exception, the great English novelists from Jonathan Swift in 1710 to Martin Amis almost 300 years later projected commerce and industry as oppressive, humiliating and dangerous, and businesspeople as venal, corrupt, self-seeking and unimaginative.[19] If, as this work suggests, fiction can be instrumental in shaping public attitudes so unhelpfully in the vital wealth-creation process, non-fiction in the shape of corporate history should be just as effective at helping to redress any attitudinal shortfall.

The dearth of corporate and business history in the educational system is even acknowledged by such luminaries as Sir Peter Parker, a former chairman of British Rail, who has said: '… business history is a missing dimension throughout the educational system. We need to build back into the business school approach the significance of a historical perspective.'[20] Alex Fletcher, a former secretary of state for corporate and consumer affairs, has also said:

There is a great deal of material in our schools and elsewhere about how babies are born but there is a tremendous shortage of publications about how businesses are born. Only a tiny number of people know there really was a Mr Barclay, a Mr Beecham, a Mr Cadbury, a Mr Rolls and a Mr Royce, and the marvellous stories of how they created these now world-famous companies. Generations can only understand these examples if they learn and understand the process, innovation and the leadership that made it possible.[21]

The business world doesn't even have to look far for history's wider endorsement:

The further backward you can look, the further forward you can see.

Winston Churchill

We cannot escape history.

Abraham Lincoln

Histories makes men wise.

Francis Bacon

History decides the future.

Mikhail Gorbachev

Yet the genre is still widely overlooked as a legitimate teaching tool.

The exception is the more imaginative US, where corporate and business history is better used than anywhere else. Whilst the main criticism in the US is that it is confined to a relatively small number of specialist universities, the concept is at least accepted and up-and-running in ways that help their businesspeople to become the best experiential learners and the most productive and wealthiest business operatives in the world. The US is even experimenting with old films as a teaching tool. Some educators, for example, are using a documentary produced by Forbes Inc., publisher of Forbes Magazine, called *Some Call it Greed*, an overview of capitalism in the early twentieth century while the Columbia College in Missouri, a liberal arts college, uses film biographies of Andrew Carnegie, John D. Rockefeller and Henry Ford as well as documentaries on the Sears and Roebuck catalogue and various US railroads produced by the Public Broadcasting Service and the Arts and Entertainment Network; it even uses an independent film called *Roger and Me*, a documentary released in the late 1980s that humorously explores the relationship between General Motors and Flint, Michigan, at a time of corporate downsizing and restructuring. Elsewhere, the Brookings Institute has used several commercial movies, among them the 1940s *The Grapes of Wrath* and the Second World War era movie, *The More the Merrier* as depictions of businessmen as 'robber barons' and to demonstrate the interaction of business and Government. One university – Ohio State – is even using the Internet. In 1997 it used a World Wide Web exercise to teach a course that included business history. Of the books assigned in the course, the most popular with students was Harold Livesay's *Andrew Carnegie and the Rise of Big Business*. The tutor, Austin Kerr, advises that he used the Internet:

… to have the students explore aspects of that subject, and of industrialism more generally, on the lives of Americans during 'the gilded age and progressive era'. Although my web exercises are a crude first effort on my part, the students responded favorably. As time and energy allow, I hope to refine these exercises and develop new ones that present some key business history concepts in an interesting and (possibly) interactive way.[22]

History is knowledge

For those who subscribe to the premise of a relationship between education and national prosperity, the widespread absence of corporate, management and business history as curricula subjects is a glaring omission. In the new information age, the genre is as much knowledge as anything else and, as such, should not be treated as a narrow-interest scholarly pursuit. Without it, the unsighted end up leading the unsighted.

To quote Professor Leslie Hannah, the UK's first professor of business history, history provides experience cheaply. My own take on the subject is that experience, whether successful or otherwise, is our single most valuable resource bar none. Through archive preservation, good research, its assembly into comprehensible commentary (oral, written and visual) and – essentially – applied teaching, it is the *precise* vehicle through which industry and education can provide a constantly changing employee base with the knowledge necessary for a practised workforce to benefit from hindsight and improve enterprise, productivity and competitiveness. It is not a cure-all, because it provides – along with shorter-term OM – just the evidence. To be relevant for today, tomorrow and the day after, it still has to be *applied*.

Notes

1. N. Lisagor and F. Lipsius, *A Law Unto Itself: The Untold Story of Law Firm Sullivan and Cromwell*, New York: Paragon House, 1989.
2. All cited quotes from interview with the author, October 1997.
3. Phoenix Assurance assessment given to the author on the book's launch.
4. Author research, 1992.
5. Interview with author, October 1997.
6. Quoted from 'Acknowledgements' in Archibald Richards, *Touche Ross & Co. 1899–1981 – The Origins and Growth of the UK Firm*, London: Touche Ross & Co., 1981.
7. Quoted from 'Acknowledgments' in Charles Forte, *Forte: The Autobiography of Charles Forte*, London: Sidgwick & Jackson, 1986.
8. Quoted from 'Acknowledgements' in David Kynaston, *The Financial Times: A Centenary History*, London: Viking, 1988.
9. Coutts archives.
10. Ibid.
11. Author research, 2001.
12. J. Wilson, *British Business History 1720–1994*, Manchester: Manchester University Press, 1995.
13. *Business History Newsletter*, October 1986.
14. Interview with author, October 1997.
15. *Essays in Economic & Business History*, vol. XV, 1997 – the journal of the Economic and Business Historical Society.
16. *Business History Newsletter*, no. 8, March 1984.
17. Ibid.
18. Scottish Enterprise research, 1991.
19. The Institute for Economic Affairs, 2000.
20. Correspondence with author, 1992.
21. Speech, 1988.
22. See http://www.history.ohio-state.edu/courses/hist563/default.htm.

10 *Lighting the Lamp*

The diagram shows a cyclical process:
① PLANNING — The Knowledge Chart, The Project Map, The Employee Transit Audit
④ THE LESSONS AUDIT
③ REFLECTION
② CAPTURE THE EVIDENCE — Archives, Oral debriefings, Corporate history
⑤ REPROCESS
⑥ EVALUATION

Experience is not a matter of having actually swum the Hellespont, or danced with the dervishes, or slept in a doss-house. It is a matter of sensibility and intuition, of seeing and hearing the significant things, of paying attention at the right moments, of understanding and coordinating. Experience is not what happens to a man; it is what a man does with what happens to him.

Aldous Huxley, British author[1]

We covered stage 2 of the EBM learning spiral in Chapters 8 and 9 and we now move on to learning from it. This is the most demanding of all the components of experiential learning, and is something that most organizations leave entirely to their managers.

Those companies which think that they are true experiential learners expect their decision-makers to first extract appropriate documentation from their archive, which probably houses a not untypical collection of bulk deposits of old ledgers and other records taken in on acquisitions, papers deposited by central management departments, minutes and related working papers of various councils and committees and miscellaneous items such as photographs, publicity material, newspaper cuttings and posters.

Usually, these resources – much of which has doubtlessly been digitized – would be used ahead of decisions related to matters such as trading policy or to the function and structure of the company's institutions. The archive, for example, would be consulted over a decision whether or not to move its weekly pay-day, where – hopefully – information about the historical pattern of payments in recent decades could be extracted as well as details of when the matter had previously been discussed and what reasoning, if any, lay behind earlier decisions on the subject. Using this 'evidence', the belief is that their decision-makers will then talk to as many people as possible, do their sums and, using their prior experience and any in-house management training provided, arrive at the right determination through their own judgement.

In reality, few decisions are made this way. Many managers only use their employer's archives sparingly, often complaining that source material is inadequate.[2] Furthermore, the chances are very high that the people who may know something about the subject in question have left the organization, leaving prior experience, education and judgement as the only available resources. Prior experience is then subject to the individual manager's innately short, selective and defensive memory of, most likely, some other employer's experience if they're a recent entrant, while his or her education is probably mainly theoretical. That leaves personal judgement alone, which is reliant on all the above factors, and is not the most helpful basis for steering the fortunes of individuals, companies and/or other organizations, or, indeed, the nation.

The make-up of survival

In this book I have endorsed the accepted wisdom about the importance of historical perspective. In my business life I have researched and edited enough business biographies to make an intriguing observation about corporate survival that has some relevance to modern-day decision-making.

All businesses, without exception. start off in exactly the same way. An individual group of individuals realize that he, she or they have a product or service for which someone else is prepared to pay. Thereafter, decision-making takes over. It is the single most important factor in the life of any business or organization, whether profit-making or not for profit, and the subsequent development of all institutions is entirely person-specific, time-related and geographically special. No two examples would have developed in the same way had different people been in the driving seat. Equally, every one would have evolved in another way in other times and other localities. Without exception, every organization has also changed in a way where every institution-initiated event was closely interconnected, interrelated and interdependent.

Given that this is the nature of organizational management, why has decision-making apparently become less successful? My historical eye has picked up several contributory causes.

First, managers have been largely trained to administer fixed assets. Over recent years the activity base of companies has changed from manufacturing to employee-rich service industries, where people are now the predominant corporate asset. Because of its inanimate quality, machinery is much less difficult to manage but the flexible labour market has introduced the additional complication of continuous job disruption and corporate amnesia. The huge increase in skills training has also fragmented and 'professionalized' occupational jobs to the extent that previously single activities have split into many speciality tasks that require more convoluted management skills, including the ability to understand a plethora of newborn 'management-speak' that has also been extended by the semantic language differences offered up by globalized trade.

This has manifested itself in an accelerated tendency towards more bloated management. By this I mean that, in today's workplace, many more managers are required to supervise fewer workers. In the UK, for example, managerial mass is legendary in most public-sector activity, but this even now extends to the private sector. Overall, managers and senior officials total almost 15 per cent of the workforce, compared with 11.9 per cent in 1981.[3] In the City of London the management tally is more than one in four. With falling productivity figures, the conclusion this brings is anything but ambiguous.

Chains and weak links

The longer the organization survives and the bigger it gets, the more complicated its inter-related factors become. Disregard any of the interconnected links and the corporate chain becomes increasingly vulnerable. Thanks to a variety of additional extra-mural factors – among them the more intimate involvement by government in both the micro- and macro-factors of business – companies today are also much more multifaceted and complicated, requiring a greater level of cognitive skills for the decision-making process. Management, which is completely mesmerized by technology, has come to believe that the ubiquitous computer can help it through this miasma. It can and has: managers are now often better able to identify what to do, but not *how* to do it – mainly because they can't carry out, and haven't been taught to do, joined-up management.

And although, over time, the technology and language of management has changed, the practice of management, and particularly the process of decision-making, is unerringly analogous to what it has always been, whatever the product or service, whatever the geographical location and whatever the situation. Whether the manager uses a quill pen, a manual typewriter or a word processor in downtown Timbuktu or New York, the determinations are made in exactly the same old way. It's an analytical action that is, or should be, investigative, diagnostic, methodical and logical – a three-part process of first deciding what best to do, how best to do it and, then, when to do it.

It is against this background that industry, whilst apparently happy with the ability to hire'n'fire at will, has not adequately addressed the 'disconnect' factor, which some academics estimate could be responsible for regressing output levels by up to 52 per cent. Except in isolated patches, it is something that has also not been accommodated in the educational sector along with other defects, not least the experiential component of learning and the specific inclusion of institutional experience to the decision-making process of the host organization.

For individuals, learning is essentially a personal process but, for managers, it necessarily has to be closely associated with the employing organization. It makes sense, then, that the individual's host organization should provide the structure and the agenda.

Experiential learning explained

Enter experiential learning proper. According to its main proponents, it is not just about looking into the archives, talking to colleagues, remembering how one did it last time round and then fitting it into the process of a two-day seminar explaining the latest management fad. Rather, it integrates four management learning processes into a single framework, some of them overlapping, through a distinctive process using memory and critical reflection of prior experience to make sense of information from which meaning can be extracted and erstwhile knowledge reinterpreted. Action-driven approaches, explored by the likes of academics Reg Revans, Chris Argyris, Donald Schön and Etienne Wenger, emphasize the behavioural changes that take place when managers solve organizational problems. It is designed to detect and prevent errors, transfer information and achieve goal-directed outcomes. The cognitive approaches of people such as Robert Kegan, Stephen Klein, Etienne Wenger, Daniel Goleman and Peter Senge focus on ways in which managers think – specifically on individual and group thinking processes such as memory and perception – with a view to creating coherent, orderly representations of complex problems. The reflective approaches of individuals like Russ Vince, Michael Reynolds, Jack Mezirow, Gordon Dehler, Ann Welsh and Marianne Lewis focus on the process of critical reflection using historical, social and cultural evidence while the experiential approaches of the likes of William Torbert, David Kolb, Judy Le Heron, Ikujiro Nonaka and Peter Reason focus on how managers acquire and transform old knowledge into new knowledge.

Kolb's unique contribution

Kolb's specific approach occupies a unique place in the study of management learning because it integrates multiple epistemologies into a formal theory of learning, notably John Dewey's pragmatism, Kurt Lewin's social psychology, Jean Piaget's cognitive development, Carl Rogers' client-centred therapy, Abraham Maslow's humanism, and Fritz Perls' Gestalt therapy. In its own way, Kolb's approach is a good illustration of experiential learning's own precept.

The wider concept, as well as Kolb's approach, is a process that has wholly reshaped educators' thinking into how people learn, the traditional model being that the learner ingests information that the teacher dispenses. In the rarefied world of learning systems, it has even been described as 'the greatest single event' in the twentieth century, yet the methodology – more than 25 years old in its latest evolutionary phase – is still scarcely used in industry or management training, let alone taught in most business schools. Less than a third of the top-ranked business schools in the US, where experiential learning is most evident, offer the subject as a teaching method to their students.[4] Within this, an average of just 15 per cent of their students take up this option. Most education, including that offered by business schools, ignores learner experience as the educational medium, with tutors still inclined to be more concerned with the more passive approach of imparting information. This exclusion is endorsed by Stephen Brookfield's observation that teachers tend to be so concerned with presenting information that they overlook student needs to reflect upon it. His view is that students need 'interplay between action and reflection', and he proposes that curricula should not be studied in some kind of artificial isolation, but that ideas, skills, and insights learned in a classroom should be tested and experienced in real life. Formal study is 'thus reinforced by some appreciation of reality'.[5] Although his remarks refer to the classroom, the same sentiments apply to experiential learning in the corporate environment, where the emphasis on 'information' is reminiscent of British novelist E.M Forster's view that '[s]poon feeding in the long run teaches us nothing but the shape of the spoon'.[6]

The origins of modern experiential learning

The concept has its origins in the field of psychology, not education or industry. In the first half of the twentieth century, so-called behaviourialism – a Pavlovian view of human behaviour – dominated the field. Without knowledge of what was going on in the brain, scientists limited their theories to aspects of stimulus and response, a view that spilled over into other disciplines such as education, sociology and even linguistics.

First on the scene was Jean Piaget, the Swiss philosopher and psychologist, who spent much of his professional life listening to children growing up in the fast-moving days of the early twentieth century.[7] In the course of his work with Alfred Binet, the creator of the first intelligence test, he became interested in the reasoning process used by those performing intelligence tests rather than whether or not their answers were correct. He found that there were age-related regularities in the reasoning processes, as well as differences in the way in which children thought about things. These insights led him to undertake a study of experience and human knowledge. Over a near 70-year working life his pioneering researches in developmental psychology and genetic epistemology gave him an insight into how knowledge grows, a discovery that Albert Einstein described as 'so simple that only a genius could have thought of it'. What Piaget realized was that children were not empty vessels to be filled with knowledge – as traditional educational theory held – but active builders of knowledge through the continuous creation and testing of their own perceived theories of the world. It was an understanding that others, among them Maria Montessori[8] in Italy, would later develop as individualistic teaching approaches in their own right.

Enter John Dewey, an overlapping contemporary on the other side of the world. American-born Dewey is acknowledged as the foremost US philosopher of democracy in the twentieth century. Like Piaget, he believed that education must engage with, and enlarge, experience through interaction and reflection. He observed that traditional teaching was teacher-driven, and that the chief business of a school was to transmit to the new generation 'bodies of information and of skills that had been worked out in the past'.[9] From this he reconceptualized vocational teaching to be learner-centred, with knowledge and skills being commodities to be delivered by the teacher to the student. Dewey rejected knowledge of the past as the goal of education; rather, he said, it is a means. For educators, the challenge was how to use experience to educate.

Lewin's group dynamics

The issue was then taken by up Kurt Lewin,[10] a seminal theorist in philosophy and psychology who was educated in Germany, where he encountered Gestalt therapy. He moved to the US in 1930 where he became involved in various applied research initiatives at the University of Iowa that were linked to the Second World War. These included exploring the morale of fighting troops, psychological warfare and reorienting food consumption away from foods in short supply. For Lewin, who had a profound impact on researchers and thinkers concerned with group dynamics, the realization was that learning is best facilitated in an environment where there is dialectic tension and conflict between concrete experience and analytic detachment. Bringing together the immediate experiences of learners and the conceptual models of teachers in an open atmosphere where inputs from each perspective could challenge and stimulate the other, he created a learning environment of remarkable vitality and creativity.

Lewin also refined what he called 'action research',[11] a problem-based process of making changes through a self-reflective cycle where the research is either self-validated or validated by another who examines the evidence behind the claim of the action researcher. His approach, based on feedback processes that he borrowed from electrical engineering, was first applied to education in the US in 1953, in the UK in 1975 and in Australia in 1982 as a way of promoting school-based innovation and change. The principal concern for Lewin was the integration of theory and practice.

Lewin's experiential learning model consists of a concrete experience, from which observations and reflections are made that lead to the formation of abstract concepts and generalizations. From this, the implications of these concepts are tested in new situations.

Upending Pavlov

But what of the Pavlovian view of personal growth? Classical conditioning alone did not explain Piaget's observation that children go through stages of development that have no relation to external stimuli. Somehow, he proposed, the brain itself was actively involved in the learning process. Like Dewey, Lewin became convinced that the way to understand anything was to understand experience's evolution.

As a result, the traditional reductionist view experienced a paradigm shift towards new interpretations known as cognitive and humanist theories, which later spawned Benjamin Bloom's work with the hierarchical nature of knowledge and Maslow's ideas on how learners attempt to take control of their own life processes, Robert Gagne's identification of the main categories of learning and the Argyris[12]–Schön[13] collaboration that innovated the ground-breaking methodology known as double-loop learning.

For the American duo, the most usual starting point for many learners is in the detection and correction of errors within governing variables such as given or chosen goals, values, plans and rules – what is recognized as incremental, or single-loop, learning. Learning is usually limited to new skills and capabilities, with applications in quality problems. Usually based on negative feedback, it involves doing something better without necessarily examining or challenging underlying beliefs and assumptions. Double-loop, or reframing, learning, on the other hand, is the process of questioning governing variables with a view to changing the organization's underlying norms, policies and objectives and is oriented towards professional education, especially leadership in organizations. It often embraces single-loop learning but takes the process a stage further by fundamentally reshaping the underlying patterns of thinking and behaviour through reflection and self-analysis. Through this process, routines, thinking and behaviour outside an individual's level of conscious awareness are exposed, enabling individual and organizational change.

Life experiences = learning = knowledge

Although the importance of experience had now been acknowledged, there was still no adequate theory as to experience's precise function in learning. Experience was still seen as a source of stimuli – until Saljo observed that the more life experience students had, the more likely they were to view learning as an internal, experience-based process.[14] His hierarchy of student views of learning concluded that learning increased knowledge, that it involved storing information for easy recall, that it was about developing skills and methods, acquiring facts that could be used as necessary, making sense of information, extracting meaning and relating information to everyday life. In summary, it was about understanding the world through reinterpreting knowledge, confirming the earlier models of learning and cognitive development that said that intelligence was shaped by experience, and recognizing that intelligence was not an innate internal characteristic but rather a product of the interaction between individuals and their environment.

Nonetheless, although the concept was recognized and up-and-running, the theory of experiential learning did not gain prominence until the work of Jack Mezirow, Paulo Freire, Anthony Gregorc and Carl Rogers in the 1980s who all stressed that the heart of all learning lies in the way in which experience is processed, particularly in its critical reflection. They spoke of learning as a cycle that begins with experience, continues with reflection and later leads to action, which itself becomes a concrete experience available for the next round of reflection.

Mezirow, for example, introduced the powerful concept of transformative learning in a groundbreaking study of women who returned to community college to continue their education while Freire's main work concerned popular and informal education through conversational rather than a curricula form, where educational activity was situated in the actual experience of participants. Others have come, or have been taken, to the learning party, among them Etienne Wenger,[15] a pioneer of 'community of practice' groups, the older Fritz Perls,[16] one of the originators of Gestalt therapy and the even older Australian-born psychologist George Elton Mayo,[17] who became an early leader in the field of industrial sociology in the US, emphasizing the dependence of productivity on small-group unity. Peter Senge also punched heavy by introducing the learning organization and systems thinking to the world in 1990.[18] Whilst advocating reflectiveness as part of the learning process, his focus is on decentralizing the role of leadership to enhance the capacity of employees to work more productively. There is even a newer model called triple-loop learning, sometimes called multiple-loop learning or transformational learning,[19] which introduces an additional learning phase in order to manage organizational diversity by helping individuals create a shift in personal perceptions through the questioning of inconsistencies and incongruencies in organizations.

But it has been David Kolb,[20] Professor of Organizational Behavior at Weatherhead School of Management at Case Western Reserve University, and his associate Roger Fry, who have taken the concept to its most developed stage.

For Kolb, learning is the process 'whereby knowledge is created through the transformation of experience'.[21] The experiential way of learning, he says, involves the application of the information received from the educator to the experiences of learners. It does not consist of activity generated in the classroom alone, and learners do not acquire their knowledge exclusively from the educator. Rather, they learn through the process of taking the new information derived in the classroom and testing it against their familiar real-life experiences. The learner thus transforms both the information and the experience into knowledge of some new or familiar subject or phenomenon. In Kolb's model, the educator is a *facilitator* of a person's learning cycle.

Endorsing Piaget's original model of learning and cognitive development, Kolb's belief is that learning is not conceived in terms of outcomes; that it is a continuous process grounded in experience; that it requires the resolution of conflicts between dialectically opposed modes of adaptation to the world; and that it is a holistic process that involves transactions between individuals and their environment. From this, new knowledge is created.

With this under his belt, Kolb went on to develop what he called a learning style inventory to help learners understand their strengths and weaknesses. The inventory measures whether individuals are activists, reflectors, pragmatists and/or theorizers, where partiality to one or more modes indicates a preferred learning style. The theory is that understanding their preferred learning styles helps individuals realize their strengths and weaknesses and allows them to make relevant accommodations to become better learners. By providing crucial information about learners, it also allows the educator to better direct the learning process even though, as Kolb himself admits, the results are based solely on the way in which learners rate themselves rather than through standards or behaviour, as some other personal style inventories do, and it only gives relative strengths within the individual learner, not in relation to others.

Having endured the scrutiny from more than 1500 studies, refereed articles, dissertations, and papers since 1971, Kolb's model is not without criticisms from fellow academics – and even a healthy number of critics of the critics – who claim variously that it pays insufficient attention to the process of reflection,[22] that the claims made for the four different learning styles are extravagant,[23] that the empirical support for the model is weak[24] and that it is not at all clear where such things as goals, purposes, intentions, choice and decision-making fit into the learning cycle.[25] Yet others maintain that Kolb's theory locates itself in the cognitive psychology tradition, and overlooks or mechanically explains and thus divorces people from the social, historical and cultural aspects of self, thinking and action,[26] that the idea of a manager reflecting like a scientist in isolation on events is like an 'intellectual Robinson Crusoe'[27] and that it is practical argumentation with oneself and in collaboration with others that actually forms the basis for learning.[28]

Nonetheless, in the words of many of his detractors and others,[29] Kolb's contributions cannot be underestimated. Whatever its limitations, by presenting a model of experience and learning in a scientific form, he has provided a thorough learning model, the theory of which, says Kolb, 'has held up well, but I think if anything it's only starting to be recognized empirically'.[30] As such, it has given industry and commerce a way of helping managers into a more professional place.

EBM's contribution

My optional approach, which is part of the prospective learning methodology, is not to supplant any of the accredited experiential learning approaches, whether they be Kolb's 'Observe-Assess-Design-Implement' cycle, Stephan Haeckel's 'Act-Sense-Interpret-Decide' cycle, Ralph Stacey's 'Choose-Act-Discover' cycle or Joseph Firestone's 'Decide-Act-Monitor-Evaluate' cycle. In fact, they are essentially all the same, depending on a well-trodden organically focused methodology structured around a reflection module with their own individual strengths and weaknesses. Rather than tinker with the underlying theory or practice, my own small contribution is, using Kolb's wellsprung approach, to reposition the methodology from 'learning' in general to decision-making in particular, to enhance the 'memory' component of the learning cycle and to ensure that lessons learned are transmitted across and down the managerial generations. The principle is that if companies and other organizations can augment their evidential base with better decision-relevant substance, the quality of the subsequent reflection and consequent learning will be improved, with beneficial implications for productivity and competitiveness. And if this erudition is then allowed to be inherited down the generations, industry and commerce will not have to keep on relearning its prior advances – with yet further impact on corporate profit and national wealth.

Kolb's Experiential Learning Theory (ELT)

Kolb's four-stage Experiential Learning Theory (ELT)[31] is that learning from experience is two-dimensional – individuals first grasp experience and then transform it. The former is done by feeling and doing, what he calls 'concrete experience', and by thinking and theorizing, what he calls 'abstract conceptualization'. The latter is done by watching and reflecting, so-called 'observation/reflection', and by doing or application, what he calls 'active experimentation', which allows the 'testing' of what is learned in new situations. Simply, to be effective experiential learners, individuals must first perceive information, reflect critically on it, compare how this fits into individual experiences and, finally, consider how this information offers new ways to act. It's a 'watch-mind-emotion-muscle' process.

The first stage, concrete experience, involves learners in a role-play, a live or video demonstration, a case study, or a testimonial. In the second, reflective observation, the learners are asked to review the experience from many perspectives. Questions are asked – for example, 'What happened?' or 'What was observed?'. The third stage is abstract conceptualization, where learners develop theories and look at patterns. Further questions are asked, such as 'How do you account for what you observed?', 'What does it mean for you?', 'How is it significant?', 'What conclusions can be drawn?' and 'What general principles can be derived?'. In the final active experimentation phase, learners explain what has been learned through the questions and suggest how the principles can be applied. The result is another concrete experience, but this time at a more complex level. The process is often represented as a cycle but Kolb's reading is that it should really be approached as a continuous spiral.

Although the process can be undertaken without help if learners are disciplined and imaginative enough, it is most effective with the help of a facilitator, whose role is principally supervisory within a functional responsibility of ensuring that learners develop their observational skills, their reflective skills, their conceptualization skills and their imagination. Above all, the facilitator needs to be analytic, objective and – probably most important of all – incisively provocative to encourage creative thinking.

Such it is with Experience-Based Management, with a few variations to shift its emphasis to decision-making.

EBM's learning stages: reflection

In its own six-stage schema, EBM arrives at Kolb's reflection stage with a lot more preparation to improve the memory component of the process (see Figure 6.1, p. 124). The 'Planning Stage', which I outlined in Chapter 7, will have pinpointed the main areas of organizational knowledge loss and designated a broad plan to preselect prime experiences from which the institution needs to learn. Stage 2, which I have covered in Chapters 8 and 9, will have implemented the 'Capture the evidence' plan to complement the data and information documented in the archive with a deliberate strategy to secure as much short-, medium- and long-term decision-relevant tacit knowledge as possible.

EBM'S Stage 3, 'Reflection', is almost identical to Kolb's two reflection and conceptualization stages, and involves recalling and interpreting the experiences and understanding the relationships of events using both individual memory and *all* the organization's repositories.

Preferably in a group situation consisting of all the decision-makers involved, the preselected learning opportunities identified in Stage 1 are examined as soon after the event as possible, with decision-makers stepping back from task involvement to review what actually happened. Involving learners in role-plays, live or video demonstrations is optional but my own experience is that theatrics or a TV presenter's skills are not very high on most managers' list of personal competencies.

Unceremonious and off-the-record discourse is, though, so the oral delivery of case studies or testimonies is often a more productive way of initiating the reflection and conceptualization phases. Depending on individual personalities and the group dynamics of project teams, there are several approaches that can be used.

One is for individuals to orally deliver a detailed chronological 'diary' of how their particular decision was made, explaining the justifications at each critical determination point. Depending on the complexity of the decision, individuals should be encouraged to deliver their testimonies of their decision-making process in as short a time as possible, perhaps even with a predesignated time limit, a discipline that should enhance memory processes, hone observational scrutiny, enrich both language and communication skills and reveal ingrained attitudes and beliefs. Importantly, their recall should be based on the evidence that can be recalled from their memory and validated in the archive and their oral debriefings, including those of their main operatives, the content of which provides the decision-maker with a coexisting shopfloor perspective.

Another is for individuals to allow themselves to be questioned by their decision-making associates about the chronology and justifications for their determinations.

Both methods provide an evidence-rich and rigorous method for individuals to orally muse their way through something as complex as modern-day decision-making. Even timelines on their own – exactly what managers did and when – can often be very revealing.

The Lessons Audit

Importantly, the depositions should refer to historical precedent with an emphasis on precedent *within* the organization; also to relevant theory and other decision-making approaches such as the decision tree. From that, learners are encouraged by the facilitator to make sense of the information and extract meaning for both themselves and their employer (and, if relevant, wider society), in particular identify patterns of behaviour and outcomes, even formulating their own theories. By reviewing the chosen experience from as many perspectives as possible, the learners are encouraged to put the experiences into some sort of overview in an organization-, job- and person-specific context. In the case of strategy-type issues, it would be important to also consult the repository of long-term OM, the organization's corporate history and even others' corporate histories.

To oblige the decision-making skew, my next stage involves learners jointly evaluating how their prior decisions could have been different in the *exact* historical circumstances of the time – specifically, how, using the benefit of hindsight, their changed decisions could have elicited a more productive outcome. This culminates in a jointly written list of 'lessons' specific to the chosen experience – a so-called Lessons Audit, the objective being to produce a list of dos, don'ts and other counsel for consideration next time an experience of a similar nature arises. The lessons are broken down into strategy-type conclusions and operational-type suppositions. With a suitable preface, Stage Five's 'The Lessons Audit' then becomes a definitive notice of new knowledge which the organization can pass on to selected others, both those elsewhere within the company and, when they arrive, new entrants, with the rider that this learning should provide the starting point for their own decision-making process. I like to describe this as 'leg-up', the means by which new knowledge can be shared across the organization and down the generations.

It is this formulation that provides one of several more knowledge 'platforms' that provide other opportunities for even better experiential learning.

Reprocessing

The second 'knowledge platform' is designed to emerge in the ensuing Stage 6 'Reprocessing'. In this stage, learners orally 'test' the lessons on a variety of different scenarios such as changed raw material circumstances, increased competition, lack of finance, specified outside regulation and so on – any circumstances that managers *think* may be the upcoming decision-making variables. For this, it is useful to draw on the predictions of industry economists and other analysts, whose opinions can be bought in but are often found in the news pages of responsible newspapers and journals. Learners effectively predict what is likely to happen in the future and then suggest what actions should be taken to refine the way both the prior determination and the *refined* determination – the one that was reprocessed in Stage 4's 'Lessons Audit' – might be taken. It is a decision-making rehearsal, from which managers develop the more rigorous ability to make determinations that are based on the tried-and-tested past and can be applied beneficially to the less unfamiliar future.

In this phase it is helpful to attach to the different scenarios a figurative word picture, the objective being to be as graphic as possible. For an investment advisory company, which changes its research and portfolio analysts at short notice, this might be like 'divorcing and remarrying within the month'. A sharp sales downturn could be like 'finding an unwelcome relative in the spare bedroom with a dozen suitcases and 12 mislaid keys'. To top managers, a succession of senior defections could be like 'finding oneself in a room full of familiar strangers', while a glitch in a new product development could be like 'a confectioner without any baking powder'. The purpose of this exercise is to attach an informal and personal interpretation to the different events that challenge the learner to be thoughtful and inventive. It also provides a way of disconnecting the episode from the customary use of dry facts and figures that characterize most self-assessments. By associating events more familiarly, the occurrences and their associated 'decisions' become more contextually memorable, a device similar to how some people recall the names of new acquaintances.

Another useful exercise at this stage is for managers to devise a decision-making schema to deliberately achieve a downturn similar to the performance that the organization wants to improve. For example, if a recent product launch came out overdue and over budget by a factor of, say, two, managers then proactively work out the decision necessary to achieve this lower outcome in the same new circumstances anticipated for the next product launch. The discipline of trying *not* to improve is frequently educational in its own right, providing as it does a direct comparison with the proposed approach to *correct* prior performance.

Evaluation

Stage 6, 'Evaluation', occurs when an event of a similar nature to the chosen experience in Stage 3, 'Reflection', arises. Learners then retrieve the devised lessons of Stage 4, 'The Lessons Audit' and, using the dummy-run knowledge acquired in Stage 5, reinterpret the knowledge to oblige their employer's new circumstances.

After a decision has been taken but before it is implemented, the decision-maker justifies the determination concisely *in writing* with an institution-specific precedent (if possible) and an accompanying rationalization under the basic headings 'The Decision', 'How' and 'Why'. Citing precedent will provide evidence that the decision has been made contextually while the complementary justification imparts the necessary attendant conceptualization, useful – with the earlier Stage 4 'Lessons Audit' – for further experiential learning down the line. It also averts later memory lapse and – if learning is actively championed by the employer – encourages managers to be less defensive than they might otherwise be – an important component of discovery and new knowledge.

Even then, this is not the end of the learning process. After the outcome becomes measurable, they again use the EBM learning spiral, akin to the DNA's double helix or a coiled steel spring, to assess whether revised practice can be turned into even better practice, in which case the Lessons Audit can be updated again.

In the multilinked chain of evolution, explicit knowledge has become tacit knowledge has become explicit knowledge. In essence, old knowledge has become new knowledge available to be reapplied, a process that supports the universal paradigm of progress being incremental and learning being continuous.

In addition to using prior experience as a tool to assess the many variants of decision-making before and after actual events, the logic of the EBM learning spiral is to make continual incremental improvements to real business situations. The more often reflection is undertaken, the more frequently the opportunity arises to modify and refine decision-making to better effect. On the basis that if one waits until after a task is completed, there is no opportunity to refine it until a similar task arises, there is also the option of starting the reflection stage *before* an experience is completed.

It may all sound like an elaborate process but, then, management was never intended to be uncomplicated or effortless. However, I maintain that it is better to get the front-end of decision-making right and make improvements than to spend as much, or even more, energy and money putting things right after the event.

It's a paradoxical thing, experiential learning. One would think that something as apparently simple as learning from experience would take a little less time to apply. But progressing from Piaget to Kolb has taken more than 80 years. Indeed, Kolb's own efforts have been in train for around a quarter of a century, and he has wearily stated that his experiential learning theory only started to be recognized empirically after more than ten years.

The interesting question is why the business educational establishment has taken so long to more fully capitalize on a prime educational tool and why so few organizations make use of it. In operational terms, relatively few resources are even targeted at its development, while organizations and managers are even now undecided about the value of hindsight. Given industry and commerce's importance and the fact that productivity growth is withering, it must surely rate as one of the twenty-first century's more weighty imperatives so that organizations of all sorts – businesses, government, non-government organizations, charities and so on – can be more proficiently managed.

Notes

1.   Aldous Huxley, *Texts and Pretexts: An Anthology of Commentaries*, London: Chatto & Windus, 1932.
2.   Fernando Olivera, 'Memory Systems in Organizations: An Empirical Investigation of Mechanisms for Knowledge Collection, Storage and Access', *Journal of Management Studies*, September 2000.
3.   Labour Force Survey, April 2005, using figures from the 2001 census.
4.   The Business School Admission website at: http://www.businessschooladmission.com/teaching_methods.asp, devoted to information needed to help students gain admission into top MBA programmes.
5.   Stephen Brookfield, *The Skilful Teacher*, San Francisco: Jossey-Bass, 1990.
6.   E.M. Forster, quoted in *The Observer*, London, 7 October 1951.
7.   Jean Piaget, *Play, Dreams and Imitation in Childhood*, New York: W.W. Norton, 1951.
8.   Maria Montessori, who died in 1952 aged 82, was primarily a physician – in fact, the first woman in Italy to qualify as such. As a result of her interest in the needs of 'uneducable' children, she initially developed a teaching programme that sought to teach skills by developing repeatable exercises. The success of her method then led her to question 'normal' education, for which she developed a methodology that emphasized self-education and self-realization through independent activity.

This connected with a further element reversing the traditional education system whereby active teachers instruct a passive class. In the Montessori system, the teacher-observer only intervenes when individual help is needed, the theory being that a child will learn naturally if put in an environment containing the proper materials such as 'learning games' (for example, toys, household utensils, plants and animals that are cared for by the children, and child-sized furniture). Physical exercise is also stressed in accordance with a belief that motor abilities should be developed along with sensory and intellectual capacities.

9.   John Dewey, *Democracy and Education: An Introduction to the Philosophy of Education,* New York: The Free Press, 1916.

10. Kurt Lewin, *Field Theory in Social Sciences,* New York: Harper & Row, 1951.

11. Kurt Lewin, 'Action Research and Minority Problems', *Journal of Social Issues,* vol. 2, 1946.

12. Born in New Jersey, Chris Argyris is a psychology, economics and organizational behaviour graduate of Clark, Kansas and Cornell universities and a faculty member of Yale and Harvard. His academic interests have ranged from the impact of formal organizational structures, control systems and the management on individuals, organizational change – in particular, the behaviour of senior executives in organizations – the role of the social scientist and, with Donald Schön, individual and organizational learning. They proposed what they called double-loop learning, a theory of personal change that involves learning to change underlying values and assumptions. It is a theory linked to their theory of action which says that changes in values, behaviour, leadership, and helping others, are all part of, and informed by, individuals' theories of action. An important aspect is the distinction between an individual's espoused theory and what they actually do. In reality, people always behave consistently with their theories-in-use even though they often do not act congruently with what they say. The four parts to the theory in action learning process include the discovery of espoused and theory-in-use, invention of new meanings, the production of new actions and the generalization of results. Argyris calls the gap between espoused theory and actual behaviour 'skilled incompetence'. The behaviours that support the cover-ups, or defensive routines, hinder the learning that is needed to bring about individual and organizational changes for improvement. So-called defensive reasoning seriously impairs the potential for growth and learning. His publications include: *Interpersonal Competence and Organizational Effectiveness,* Homewood, IL: Dorsey Press, 1962; *Knowledge for Action. A Guide to Overcoming Barriers to Organizational Change,* San Francisco: Jossey Bass, 1993: *Personality and Organization,* New York: Harper Collins, 1957; *Integrating the Individual and the Organization,* New York: Wiley, 1964; *Organization and Innovation,* New York: R.D. Irwin, 1965; *Intervention Theory and Method: A Behavioral Science View,* New York: Addison Wesley, 1970; *Increasing Leadership Effectiveness,* New York: Wiley-Interscience, 1976; *Inner Contradictions of Rigorous Research,* New York: Academic Press, 1980; *Reasoning, Learning, and Action: Individual and Organizational,* San Francisco: Jossey-Bass, 1982; *Strategy, Change and Defensive Routines,* Boston, MA: Pitman, 1985; *Action Science: Concepts, Methods, and Skills for Research and Intervention,* San Francisco: Jossey-Bass, 1985; *Overcoming Organizational Defenses. Facilitating Organizational Learning,* San Francisco: Allyn and Bacon, 1990; *Knowledge for Action. A Guide to Overcoming Barriers to Organizational Change,* San Francisco: Jossey Bass, 1993.

13. Boston-born Donald Schön was a Yale and Harvard graduate in philosophy. His academic focus has been how to help educators teach professionals to be effective, particularly in relation to the functions of the university and the ways in which educators prepare students for the professions. Like Dewey, Schön felt that people learn by doing with others. Schön taught philosophy at the University of California and the University of Kansas. From 1957 to 1963 he worked as a senior staff member in Arthur D. Little Inc., where he formed the New Product Group in the Research and Development Division. Under the Kennedy administration he was appointed director of the Institute for Applied Technology in the National Bureau of Standards, Department of Commerce, where he continued through 1966. He died in 1997.

14. R. Saljo, 'Learning in the Learner's Perspective: Some Common-sense Conceptions', Report no. 76, Institute of Education, University of Gothenburg, as summarized in P. Banyard and N. Hayes, *Psychology: Theory and Application,* London: Chapman & Hall, 1979.

15. Etienne Wenger's work into situated learning and the social construction of knowledge led to the conception of communities of practice. His publications include: *Communities of Practice: Learning, Meaning, and Identity,* Cambridge: Cambridge University Press, 1998; *Cultivating Communities of Practice,* Cambridge, MA: Harvard Business School Press, 2002.

16. Fritz Perls, who died in 1970 aged 77, was born in Berlin and educated in medicine and psychoanalysis. Escaping from Hitler's regime in 1933, he moved to South Africa and to the US,

where he met and collaborated with Paul Goodman on a basic text for the theory and new method of Gestalt therapy that contained so-called awareness exercises. In the 1960s Perls became more widely known through his work at California's Esalen Institute.

17. Professor George Elton Mayo, who died in 1949 aged 69, was the founder of the Human Relations Movement and of Industrial Sociology. His main claim to fame was the research he carried out at the Hawthorne Works of the Western Electric Company in Chicago, which made telephone equipment. Among the main conclusions were that job satisfaction increased through employee participation in decisions rather than through short-term incentives whilst work satisfaction depended to a large extent on the informal social relationships between workers and their bosses. The best vehicle for achieving this was informal groups (rather than formal work teams), as they provided their members with the basic needs for communication and cooperation. Yet management should be aware that, once forged, the group maintained a strong grip over workers' behaviour and productivity. Researchers concluded that changes in output could be attributed to changes not only in work conditions but also in work attitudes and social relations. See Elton Mayo, *The Social Problems of an Industrial Civilization*, New York: Ayer, 1945.

18. P.M. Senge, *The Fifth Discipline. The Art and Practice of the Learning Organization*, New York: Random House, 1990; *The Fifth Discipline Fieldbook: Strategies and Tools for Building a Learning Organization*, New York: Doubleday, 1994; *The Dance of Change: The Challenges to Sustaining Momentum in Learning Organizations*, New York: Doubleday, 1999; and *Schools That Learn: A Fifth Discipline Fieldbook for Educators*, New York: Doubleday, 2000.

19. Robert Flood and Norma Romm, *Diversity Management – Triple Loop Learning*, New York: Wiley, 1996. The authors introduce the twin notions of diversity management and triple-loop learning. A 'loop of learning' is depicted as a cyclic process built around a general question. Three such loops are identified: the How? loop is built around the question 'Are we doing things right?'; the What? loop is built around the question 'Are we doing the right things?'; and a Why? loop is built around the question 'Is rightness buttressed by mightiness and vice versa?'

20. Born in 1939, David Kolb was educated at Knox College and Harvard. Besides his work on experiential learning, he is also known for his contribution to thinking around organizational behaviour. With Roger Fry he created his famous model of learning out of four elements: concrete experience, observation and reflection, the formation of abstract concepts and testing in new situations. The authors argue that the learning cycle can begin at any one of the four points, and that it should really be approached as a continuous spiral. They have helped to challenge the models of learning that seek to reduce the potential to one dimension such as intelligence. Through his wife, Alice, Kolb is associated with Experience Based Learning Systems, Inc., a research and development company devoted to advancement of the theory, research and practice of experiential learning.

21. D.A. Kolb, *Experiential Learning: Experience as the Source of Learning and Development*, Englewood Cliffs, NJ: Prentice-Hall Inc.

22. D. Boud (ed.), *Reflection. Turning Experience into Learning*, London: Kogan Page, 1985.

23. P. Jarvis, *Adult Learning in the Social Context*, London: Croom Helm, 1987; and M. Tennant, *Psychology and Adult Learning*, London and New York: Routledge, 1997.

24. Ibid.

25. A. Rogers, *Teaching Adults* (2nd edn), Milton Keynes: Open University Press, 1996.

26. M. Reynolds, D. Holman, K. Pavlica and R. Thorpe, in *A Critique, Management Learning*, London: Sage, 1997.

27. Ibid.

28. Ibid.

29. S. Brookfield, *The Skilful Teacher*, op. cit.; P. Cross, *Adults as Learners*, San Francisco: Jossey-Bass, 1981; P. Jarvis, *Adult & Continuing Education* (2nd edn), London: Routledge, 1995; J. Kemp, G. Morrison and S. Ross, *Designing Effective Instruction*, NJ: Prentice-Hall, 1996. M. Knowles, *"The Adult Learner: A Neglected Species*, (4th edn), Houston, TX: Gulf Publishing, 1990; W.J. McKeachie, *Teaching Tips: Strategies, Research and Theory for College and University Teachers*, Lexington, MA: D.C. Heath and Company, 1994; J. Peters, P. Jarvis *et al.*, *Adult Education*, San Francisco: Jossey-Bass, 1991.

30. David Kolb, 'What Kolb Says', *National Teaching and Learning Forum*, vol. 1, no. 5, 1992.

31. David Kolb, *Experiential Learning: Experience as the Source of Learning and Development*, NJ: Prentice Hall.

The Future of the Past

One must always maintain one's connection to the past and yet ceaselessly pull away from it. To remain in touch with the past requires a love of memory. To remain in touch with the past requires a constant imaginative effort.

Gaston Bachelard, French scientist, philosopher, literary theorist[1]

For a world that has created so much wealth, there is a curious poverty in hindsight. With memory so fickle, little is recorded about how exactly it was done, even less is reflected upon, much is not learned, even more is not taught and the world is a poorer place for it.

One would imagine that if experience was considered valuable – as it is – its loss to the employer would not be treated in such a cavalier manner. Yet, although employers encourage the flexible labour market, they do very little to combat the resultant memory loss. Equally puzzling is the way in which both academics and managers disassociate institution-specific OM with the ability to make good and better decisions.

I can't remember the number of times I have had conversations with both populations on the subject I first called corporate and business history. Almost without exception, their reaction was either indifference or hostility, although when I substituted the words 'organizational memory' and/or 'experience', some acknowledgement of its importance might surface. But as soon as its relevance to decision-making and productivity is raised – particularly how instructors either don't teach it and/or how managers inexpertly apply it – the eyes glaze over. It's the Black Hole of administrative process.

Given the absence of apparent concern about the subject, the complacent – the majority, it seems – could well argue that industry and commerce is up and running in a way that has provided the greatest level of progress in the shortest amount of time ever. To change would require elemental adjustments in the behaviour of both academics and managers, not least the admission by both that their performance might be less than picture-perfect. Not the easiest of things to do, so why not just let the current system ride?

The problem with this suggested line of reasoning is the extent of resources inherent in current production which, in any lower-productivity undertaking, are much greater than they might otherwise be – in many cases, hugely excessive. Without the next level of productivity gains, costs will not take long to outpace the investment benefits.

I have already suggested that business education is partly responsible in that it devotes little specific attention to teaching managers *how* to make good and better decisions and that managers' ability to experientially learn from their employers' own experiences is now hugely affected by their self-encouraged hire'n'fire policy. To correct the iceberg-like productivity problem that they precipitate, ostrich-like business educators and institutions have to become more familiar with how to manage organizational memory to its *fullest* extent.

I have also suggested that the better decision-making that would emanate from more efficient experiential learning processes would make it easier and quicker to implement change, that fewer mistakes would be continually repeated, that wheels would not have to be constantly reinvented and productivity improve. As a consequence, prices and taxes would be lower, the quality of life higher and – to repeat Peter Drucker's[2] vision – there would be fewer social tensions and polarization would be less evident, as would radicalization and possibly even class war.

How one point can make a difference

Drucker's sociological consequences aside, bottom-line profits are normally easy to quantify, as are comparative prices and taxes but how can one evaluate the benefits in an actual operational context? Looking specifically at the manufacturing sector in the US, the UK, Germany and France, McKinsey Global Institute's (MGI) research[3] to which I've already referred in Chapter 4 (that which showed a strong correlation between management practices and national productivity rankings) also found that just a one-point improvement in performance across three management techniques – lean manufacturing, which minimizes waste, talent management, which retains good employees, and performance management, which rewards achieved goals – would generate a 5.1 per cent increase in return on capital employed (ROCE). Over a five-year period, MGI calculated that this improvement would equal the creation of $700 billion in value in all four countries. And this is just for manufacturing.

MGI assessed the use or non-use of each management technique and then compared each respondent's score over a recent five-year period with several key financial metrics, including ROCE relative to the sector research. On the basis used, the study computed that if the UK manufacturing sector were to increase its management performance score by the same one point, it could achieve an 80 per cent increase in its total factor productivity – and a level of productivity far above the US. It is a figure that flags up two glaring realities; how small is the actual improvement necessary for low-productivity companies to be able to compete with higher-productivity companies and, given the nature of the decision-making beast, how difficult that small margin is to realize.

Also instructive – and entirely pertinent – are MGI's observations about how organizations and governments have approached the productivity challenge. Its research has demonstrated repeatedly over the past decade that productivity at the sector level has been driven by the degree to which companies were exposed to competition. Hence, MGI suggests that governments should remove barriers to competition (such as excessive regulation). Which is exactly what many governments have been trying to do for years, usually unsuccessfully.

With US companies having the highest average management scores, it might seem safe to assume that plenty of competition in an economy would promote good management practice. Not so, says MGI. It could find no direct correlation between the level of competitive intensity and the adoption of good management practices. Although there were well and poorly managed companies in both competitive and less competitive environments, MGI did find, however, that good management practices had a more pronounced impact on the bottom line in a competitive environment. This imparts another subtle, but important, distinction in the conventional argument because the efforts by managers in less competitive environments actually had little impact on organizations. The highest productivity levels were, says MGI, likely to be achieved only when governments created the right competitive conditions *and* managers used the best management techniques. Their conclusion was that manufacturing companies could achieve the same productivity goals by better management – at little or no cost to governments or the sector.

In fact, MGI's reference to manufacturing, which is generally the more productive of today's business sectors, does not refer to the potential elsewhere in industry and commerce, notably in the larger service/knowledge areas, where – in Drucker's words[4] – capital and technology are not factors but tools of production. The difference is that a factor can replace labour, whereas a tool may or may not. What Drucker is saying is that managing machinery is not the same as managing people. Organizations may seem to be treating their employees as automatons, but people are not machines and their management requires a different approach.

Working smarter is the answer

Whether in manufacturing, or service/knowledge, MGI's study communicates another not insubstantial crumb of intelligence: that much of the effort to improve productivity is, in itself, inefficient. As reasoned, a more industrious way of improving productivity is to get managers at the sharp end of business and commerce to revive the century-and-a-quarter old counsel of Frederick Winslow Taylor and his modern-day inheritor Peter Drucker to 'work smarter', by making good and better decisions. Of course governments would continue to have to help within the macro-environment, but their efforts would not be the equivalent of having to battle against a very strong headwind.

More practically, better decision-making would help end the austere choice that managers regularly make between investment and, when poor value for money kicks in, disinvestment. When the latter happens, the piece of the production jigsaw that invariably suffers is labour, which, in its own cruel way, then further contributes to the wider dis-continuity treadmill and lost organizational knowledge, doing nothing to help organizations experientially learn. It's a roller-coaster problem that feeds off itself and inhibits managers from responding more imaginatively in their decision-making.

When lined up against its British neighbour, France is an excellent example of working smarter. Generally considered as overly bureaucratic (at least in the UK), its productivity is, in fact, 11 per cent higher than the similarly populated UK plc.[5] Perversely, France also has much higher unemployment. It spends heavily on public services and employs a quarter of all its workers in state companies. Its roads are immaculate, its trains run on time, it has one of the world's best public health services and has corporate winners in industries ranging from aerospace, automotive, pharmaceuticals and oil. For every 100 hours worked in the UK, the French labour just 70 hours.[6] With higher unemployment, fewer working mothers and early retirement, only 63 per cent of French adults of working age actually work, compared with 75 per cent in the UK. In terms of gross salary, average remuneration is 29 per cent lower than the average £25 170 earned in the UK, but the lower pay buys almost as much. Houses are cheaper, mortgages for first-time buyers receive tax relief, there are more generous child benefits and other allowances and French supermarkets deliver a trolley-load at a striking discount compared to their English counterparts. The French save on average one-sixth of their earnings. And inward investment accounts for a quarter of all new jobs in France.

In a special report[7] enquiring how, for example, car manufacturer Peugeot was able to barter a 35-hour week and still achieve plant output levels of 114 per cent of its theoretical capacity, *The Sunday Times* deemed the country's management education – in particular its emphasis on strategic decision-making – as the key. Echoing the UK's Work Foundation observation that Britain's main competitors all organize their workplaces more intelligently and creatively, it concluded that French managers are better planners, thanks to the way France prepares its future decision-makers. The country's brightest and most able are passed through the Grands Ecoles, postgraduate schools of which the civil-service college Ecole Nationale de l'Administration (ENA) is the most celebrated. The ENA teaches a way of thinking where higher management concentrates on strategic decision-making, an approach that now pervades French management culture. Alongside the Polytechnique, another elite college, their graduates provide France's senior politicians, policy advisers, almost the entire cadre of senior civil servants and half the directors of the country's 200 largest companies. In the words of Sir Francis Mackay, Britain's largest investor in France as chairman of contract caterers Compass Group and retailer Kingfisher: 'France is probably the most can-do country in Europe.'

I am not suggesting that France is somehow impervious to poor decision-making (its productivity is still 15 per cent behind the US,[8] so there is still much room for improvement) or that its route is necessarily the best. I suggest only that its emphasis on teaching good decision-making confirms the discipline's priority as a management skill and that it should be both better taught and better learned. What I have tried to argue is that better decision-making is part of improved experiential learning which, in turn, is part of a more professional approach to managing organizational memory under that larger corporate banner called knowledge management, itself the most important constituent in the even bigger umbrella called the information age that, more fittingly, should be called the knowledge age. I also suggest that existing processes to teach managers how to make good and better decisions are not particularly effective and that it is in the tried-and-tested knowledge of an organization's *own* experiences – those that walk out of the front door and are forgotten and/or distorted, even by people who stay within the organization – where institutions can find much added value.

Where is business going?

So, what is the future of the past in business? On experience to date, it has a decidedly unclear outlook given industry's and business teaching's widespread disregard for organizational memory's inbuilt worth.

That OM is acknowledged as a worthy subject by a few scholars is unassailable. Researchers have confirmed that new knowledge can be created by combining existing, dispersed knowledge.[9] Storing and using stored knowledge effectively can buffer the organization from the disruptive effects of staff turnover,[10] facilitate coordination,[11] contribute to the development of innovative products,[12] and may even serve to rebuild an organization.[13] Other academics have argued that: decisions are likely to be more effective when considered in terms of the organization's history than when made in a historical vacuum;[14] the benefits of collecting, storing and providing access to experiential knowledge are particularly relevant for multi-unit organizations where knowledge acquired at one site can be beneficial to other sites;[15] providing access to dispersed experiential knowledge can reduce the organizational costs of repeatedly developing solutions to common problems;

internal knowledge transfers can contribute to the development of organizational capabilities through the identification and replication of 'best practice';[16] and even that storing and using old knowledge are key components of organizational learning.[17] Yet, despite all this evidence that the past has a role in determining quality decision-making, mainstream business education still resists teaching future managers how best to do it.

These conclusions aside, the question of why management also widely disregards the fuller use of OM is equally bewildering but can probably be answered through the random example of an absorbing departmental seminar with the same title as this chapter held at Queen Mary College, University of London, in the summer of 2004 and at which several of Europe's top business historians used their medium to discuss how Ford could not have set up in Birmingham or Benetton in Leicester, how profit and wage rates have fared relative to each other in the US in the last part of the twentieth century and whether management consultants could be blamed for the Enron disaster. As with most business history seminars, just a handful of like-minded academics attended, even though the subject matter was relevant to other academics, government and industry.

For me, it was a classic representation of wider marketing failure, at least in the UK. As seen in their greater educational interest in corporate and business history, only the US and Japan have succeeded in some small measure in persuading their own constituencies that prior experience has a useful purpose. Business history academics like to think that the past has a future in education and training but they haven't yet found a persuasive way of selling the concept to other than their small captive audience. It is a failure that, sadly, demonstrates their own inability to appreciate one of the lessons from the subject they purport to teach – notably that almost all sales are demand-led.

Demand is the key

If business teaches us anything, it is that one first has to expose a demand for a product or service. This means that in business history's case it must provide the evidence to educationalists and industrialists that there is substantial value in applying past experience. Thereafter, the supply will follow – within the constraints, of course, of competition, affordability and content. In this statement, the operative words are 'applying past experience'. For knowledge practitioners in the business sector, whether academic or otherwise, this means that the way in which they research and document experience must be attuned to learning in oral debriefings, corporate histories and wider business history, the three most efficient, cost-effective and portable forms of knowledge capture. Currently, the first two products are mostly, although not entirely, undertaken by non-academics while the third is almost exclusively the preserve of scholars.

Oral debriefings are a relatively new product. Although some companies have experimented with the technique, few have used it for anything other than trying to discover why employees leave. In its traditional application it has been called the exit interview. The most accomplished practitioners are the US military, which has developed vast archives of oral testimony of wars since the Second World War specifically as an educational tool for successive generations, although there is little empirical evidence yet as to how effective the resultant learning has been. Equally, companies such as Ford, ARCO, Beckman Instruments, Bristol-Myers, Eli Lilley, Kaiser Aluminum and Chemical, Monsanto, Proctor & Gamble, Rohm and Haas and Standard Oil Company have also initiated oral history programmes but these have only been tentatively applied in decision-making. As illustrated in Chapter 8, the medium needs to be radically re-evaluated and re-designed as a learning tool.

The two other 'capture' mediums – corporate and business history – are still only minimally used and, as outlined in Chapter 9, they also need to be completely reassessed and reshaped as a learning tool. For the people who research and write them, the lesson is that just recording history for its own sake is not enough. They need to find a format that gives the discipline the success that historians in related disciplines have achieved. Specifically, they must begin to associate their genre with experiential learning, see themselves more as knowledge practitioners and conceive their marketplace beyond their traditional audience of academic colleagues and/or subject companies.

It is ironic that most of the development of these products was achieved by early practitioners such as American social commentator and writer Studs Terkel in oral debriefing, and Harvard's Professor Alfred Chandler and Oxford's Professor Charles Wilson in business and corporate history. it is a sobering fact not only that few researchers and authors have equalled or surpassed these modern-day pioneers but also that precedent has not appeared to be an influential factor in their work; otherwise, its application in education and industry would be significantly greater.

It is also true to say that the efforts of Terkel's, Chandler's and Wilson's successors have encountered enormous resistance from broader academia, whose view of client-sponsored corporate history, whether produced by academics or others, has been routinely contemptuous. This has been compounded by the attitude of subject companies which generally equate the genre with public relations rather than useful hindsight, a mindset that parades several other distinct managerial traits. One is that reflection triggers individual managers' insecurity, which in turn brings about defensive behaviour that sets off the associated reaction of denying any performance that is considered less than optimum. Another is the interrelated and powerful human trait called ego, which organizations often deem to be an essential requirement for their managers. Hence, any serious portrayal of their professional labours is instinctively resisted. Managers and the organizations that employ them need to see the medium less as a threat and more as an opportunity. In short, they have to demonstrate a corporate maturity that extends beyond defensive insecurity. Some managers and organizations have already demonstrated this, which suggests that the prospect is not unachievable.

Catch 22

And, finally, there is the actual experiential learning process itself. In this world, little is formalized in business instruction, the only regularized process being action learning, a methodology that has no recourse with the lost experience deriving from the flexible labour market or the other three innate chinks in the organization's learning chain, notably short and selective recall, and defensiveness. Clearly, nobody has been able to 'sell' the concept that localized experience is a powerful decision-making resource. Nor have organizations recognized it or demanded it. Other than a few specialists, practitioners have also not yet devised suitable approaches to either capturing or applying it. It's a chicken and egg thing, or, in modern literary terms, pure Catch 22. Without the one, the other is thwarted. In management-speak, this requires leadership by a champion or champions more effective and authoritative than those who have tried to date. The reality is that experiential learning, too, needs attention in conceptual terms; educators and managers have to first accept its validity as a teaching mechanism, and then decide on a procedural mechanism.

In the UK, this was actually attempted in the 1970s on the back of Mrs Thatcher's drive to promote popular capitalism. Thanks to the glassmakers Pilkington, a group of industrialists created the Business History Unit at the London School of Economics to champion the genre. There were strong hopes from Downing Street that it might make some contribution towards improving the quality of British management. More than two decades later, it is clear that the country's flagship business history institution has not lived up to the vision of its industrial founders. Original promises of permanent funding have never been realized, keeping its survival in constant doubt. Not only has it run a number of less-than-successful projects, its output as a research and teaching body also remains small alongside the other smaller business history centres around England and Wales. Applied teaching is also still a rare commodity in the UK, as it is in many other parts of the world.

My point is that when it comes to experiential learning, industry and related education have never got together in large enough numbers with mutual intent. This includes the discipine of knowledge management, which has, inexplicably, never ventured much beyond the random recording phase, expecting managers to magically learn from this evidence. Between them all, they have conspired to undervalue a genre that, if their attitude was more inspired, might have given the capture component of experiential learning a more constructive role.

This could still be achieved. If the theory of the demand-led marketplace is really a component of any successful product or service, industry could, if it mandated it, create the demand. By this I am suggesting that if someone has to lead the way, it should, once again, be industry, but this time with education *behind* it and the benefit of hindsight in front of it. After all, most teaching is predicated, supposedly, by perceived requirements, and education would have to be able to supply that demand.

In the wider world, the cry for experiential learning is constantly trumpeted, one of the more recent calls coming from a Pulitzer Prize winner[18] who, in the 1 January 2005 edition of *The New York Times*, proposed that today's society enjoyed a unique advantage. Unlike any previous society in history, ours, he wrote, has a detailed chronicle of human successes and failures at its disposal to warn of the consequences of their actions, thanks to historians, archaeologists, newspapers and television, 'Will we choose to use it?' For industry and commerce, the answer is rhetorical, at least for the moment. Its OM is scarcely recorded, let alone calculatingly used to help managers improve their decision-making skills. Experience-based management (EBM) is one approach that I'd like to think will provide the model and – using experiential learning's own precept – the basis for refinement and further development.

Restructuring learning within the corporate setting

For industry and commerce, the process of making the most of experiential learning may be more difficult to introduce than to structure. As with all important organizational functions, and especially one that encompasses an activity as fundamental as the control of an institution's intellectual capital, the utility first has to be acknowledged as important which, given the widespread unrecognized status of experiential learning to date, requires executive vision and a singular enthusiasm – not easy when managers typically do not see themselves as part of the problem.

This way of thinking was glaringly evident in a survey to launch the annual Investors in People (IiP) week in 2004 which concluded that senior managers, at least in the UK, saw productivity 'as someone else's problem'. Incredibly, an astonishing nine out of 10 managers acknowledged that 'workers' (it was unclear whether or not they included themselves in this category) needed to be employed more effectively and admitted that there was (still) no consensus on how this should happen.[19] Through organizations like the Confederation of British Industry, the Trades Union Congress, the British Chambers of Commerce and the new universities (the old poytechnics), IiP is one of dozens of poor-value schemes set up by government, industry and commerce over many years to help employers provide relevant training and development. Another example, dare I suggest it, of experiential non-learning?

This 'success rate' reinforces my view that any initiative as central to management, whether in the UK or elsewhere, has first to be managed top-down, preferably with board-nominated responsibility. Even better, it should be CEO-led. Anything else is likely to be seen as too threatening to top management. Whether by using a carrot or the stick, it is important thereafter to encourage a bottom-up approach for subordinates to seek, share and create knowledge. McKinsey calls this 'knowledge pull',[20] which is a grassroots desire on the part of individuals to tap into their company's intellectual resources. McKinsey acknowledges that creating databases or virtual team rooms isn't enough, since many employees resist using knowledge generated by other departments. Worse still, many people believe that the hoarding of knowledge is power, a philosophy that may help individuals but hurts companies.

The other critical element of any experiential learning programme is that it must endure, meaning that the current generation of decision-makers needs to ensure that the detail of their decision processes provides benefit for their successors and then *their* heirs. The process must span the generations; a missing link just weakens the chain. My own start–stop experience with organizations demonstrates that, in today's world of short job tenure, the 'not invented here' syndrome of many newly appointed CEOs can quickly sever the learning timeline. The commonplace managerial attitudes of 'One should never look back', 'We know better' or even 'We want to be able to make our own mistakes' also features large.

Whilst the inclusive process of 'capture it and learn from it' is plain enough, finding the correct organizational slot for the role is less clear, mainly because its interconnected components are kept separate and its output as a decision-making tool is as yet undefined by industry and commerce. Traditionally, the job of capturing an organization's explicit knowledge has been that of an archivist, whose role is mainly classification and filing of generated documentation, traditionally in physical form but, more recently, in electronic format. So, if tacit and other 'transient' knowledge, which requires more specialized collection skills, becomes part of the bill of fare, is it still an archive service?

The gathering of short- and medium-term memory has traditionally been assigned to someone in human resources. The high levels of job turnover suggest that it would be relatively easy for an organization to upgrade its role to broader OM collection not necessarily associated with employee departures. But does this enhanced product remain an HR role?

The task of recording the institution's long-term organizational memory – its corporate history – is usually given to a senior internal employee or outside historian. Finding a clear slot for this function is less clear given its perceived role as a celebratory vehicle once or twice every 100 years. Ideally, it is a product that should be updated every five years.

The other crucial arm of the process – teaching individuals how to use the collected evidence and apply prior experience – is generally perceived as a management development function, usually assigned to external business educators, sometimes a local business school.

Within any new institutional structure that might emerge, the organization clearly has to rationalize the various functions by deciding who might be best qualified to undertake the various 'capture' roles of organizational memory. Should these be individuals from inside the organization, who would need to be trained? Or should they be external individuals, who, given their more independent position, might be less familiar with organizational background but more objective and, given its importance, more relevant? Then, given that a large proportion of data/information management is now digitally based, how should the archivist/IT function be apportioned? After that, with OM secured, who is the best person to manage the key experiential learning element of improving decision-making? Human resources, the historian, the knowledge manager or specialized trainers?

Whoever is chosen, they must be attuned to the one single objective of being able to orchestrate better and continuous experiential learning among the organization's rolling employee base. To do this, they must be able to apply the past in ways that make it specifically relevant to their employers and their employers' future. Through lessons learned, erudition must be their harvest, the evidence of prior experience their vehicle and better decision-making their purpose.

So, where might a combination of all these various functions fit within the myriad functional corporate compartments?

Much, of course, depends on organizational structure, but my own view is that it is a more comfortable fit for the new discipline known as knowledge management (KM), that imprecisely defined activity that most organizations still think is more akin to information technology (IT) than experiential learning.

Most definitions of KM are unsatisfactory, and some are highly misleading, such as: 'The use of computer technology to organize, manage, and distribute electronically all types of information, customized to meet the needs of a wide variety of users'[21] and 'The process of capturing value, knowledge and understanding of corporate information, using IT systems, in order to maintain, re-use and re-deploy that knowledge'.[22] It is instructive that many of these characterizations neglect to emphasize the vital 'humanware' aspect of the discipline. By this I mean that it is of little use collecting, storing and distributing relevant data and information if individuals do not know how to apply the evidence. So, the conceptual appreciation and practice of KM needs to be redefined and upgraded. My personal preferred definition is closer to the Australian rendering of 'Organising, sharing and applying knowledge through the support of people and technology'[23] but with an added component: that KM is the processes by which organizations collect, disseminate and apply prior experience – both one's own and others' – with a view to leveraging old knowledge into new knowledge with the strict objective of improving productivity through better decision-making. I introduce 'productivity' because KM needs an identifiable focus – and particularly a seminal focus – otherwise managers tend to undervalue its importance.

This more pragmatic application of KM does not mean that archivists, information technologists, HR practitioners, corporate historians and business trainers are redundant. Quite the opposite. It means that there must be a new accommodation between all five disciplines so that each function is seen as having a common purpose. Top management needs to change its own mindset and those of corporate practitioners for a new organizational focus on the supervision of intellectual capital that extends beyond such things as technology and patent protection to wider organization-based experiential learning.

For many organizations, KM is already costing a fortune in hi-tech wizardry, much of which is wasted. To use an athletic analogy, they are running the equivalent of a marathon and dropping out before they breast the tape. To utilize their knowledge-spend more effectively, organizations have to go the extra mile, to learn to transform their old knowledge into new knowledge more efficiently. In short, they have to more fully manage their organizational memory.

Messages for the learning organization

Managers and their employers might be unfamiliar with formalized experiential learning but the related concept, the learning organization, is hardly an alien concept. Under the banner of the knowledge age, aficionados have been selling the model for more than a decade now. Experiential learning is – or should be – part of that movement.

It is instructive to weigh what some management gurus say about managers' role in the learning organization and their relationship with management information systems (MIS) and information technology (IT) – all disciplines that have a close association with experiential learning.

Peter Senge argues that the leader's role is that of a designer, teacher and steward who can build shared vision and challenge prevailing mental models. He or she is responsible for building organizations where people are continually expanding their capabilities to shape their future. Leaders, he says, are responsible for learning.[24]

G.P. Huber explicitly specifies the role of MIS in the learning organization as primarily serving organizational memory as well as three other processes – knowledge acquisition, information distribution and information interpretation. He notes that OM needs to be continuously updated and refreshed.[25]

Elsewhere, Chris Argyris points out[26] that most existing information systems focus on the convergence of interpretation and are not geared for multiple interpretations. He has argued that the 'massive technology of MIS, quality control systems, and audits of quality control systems is designed for single loop learning' and attributes overarching command-and-control structures for the 'gaps of knowledge' that top managers design to manage effectively. Single loop learning is designed to identify and correct errors so that the job gets done and the action remains within stated policy guidelines. 'Most organizations, often without realizing it, create systems of learning that suppress double loop inquiry and make it very difficult for even well designed information system to be effective'.[27]

In experienced-based management, I have adapted the prototypes created by the likes of Kurt Lewin and David Kolb in their non-business disciplines in a formalized, six-stage spiral sequence. Instead of using a scatter-gun approach to learning, I have included ways of preselecting the experiences from which to learn and which help overcome deficient memory in formats that are also user-friendly. Using the acquired evidence and a reflective schema, managers draw up a so-called Lessons Audit to their preselected scenarios. They practice decision-making by changing the circumstances and estimating how the decision might change. Then, when similar circumstances arise, managers return to the Lessons Audit and, in exactly the same way as in the previous phase, make new decisions based on their upgraded old knowledge. Once the outcome becomes measurable, they use the EBM spiral again to assess whether revised practice can be turned into even better practice. This stage supports the universal paradigm of progress being incremental and learning being continuous but, importantly, familiarizes managers with the mutable character of decision-making within a real-time (as apposed to theoretical) context. A managerial self-development tool geared primarily for employers, it has been designed as an instructional technique that can be taught both in business schools and for management development within organizations.

Decision-making made easier

In the Introduction to this book, I referred to the research study by Capgemini,[28] which found that senior managers were admitting that at least one in four of their decisions were wrong. They blamed this on having to make too many decisions, having to make them too quickly with too little information and without the time to consult with other people. On this last point internal consultation with between one and five people was rated by managers as the most significant factor in efficient and effective business decision-making.

Apart from increasing the number of managers, little can be done about the volume of decisions that managers claim they need to make. Decision-making is a necessary function of management although, depending on the quantity of defensive decisions – decisions taken because of poor determinations in the first place – an improvement in the overall quality of decision-making may cut down on managers' workload. Managers' second excuse – having to make decisions too quickly – is more easily solved. With the Capgemini study showing that a significant decision was being taken once a fortnight, the solution is to use the 'capture' tools inherent in EBM. These would help solve the problem of too little information of being reliant on colleagues whose memories may be short and selective and of not having access to those who have moved on to other employers. Once OM is captured, with EBM's in-built reflective methodology should make decision-making easier, quicker and more successful.

As I've pointed out, the way in which we function is mostly the result of premeditated decision-making. The better the latter, the better the former.

That the process of decision-making in business is not easy is not in question, whatever the learning process. As stated, prior evidential access on its own is not enough. Where real learning comes in is when the evidence is subjected to systematic and scrupulous reflection and then the institutional-specific lessons applied to changing circumstances.

Using another athletic metaphor, managers need to be both relay runners and pole vaulters. The organizations that employ them have to make sure that their baton is first passed and, then, rather than letting managers run *around* the hurdles, they need to ensure that part of their 'workout' regime is pole vaulting. For pole vaulting, read experiential learning, the discipline that allows individuals to do better than their predecessors.

Just like the BBC radio programme that introduced experiential learning to me all those years ago,[29] this sporty image – using individual world records and, collectively, the haul of gold medals that nations earn at Olympic Games – is apposite in another way. It provides a perfect depiction of how productivity and competition work in industry and commerce. Like best productivity, world records are the measure of finest performance at any particular time. Like most advances, they are incremental; they depend on an individual improving on prior performance – that is, experience – in a variety of ways, the most important being training, technology and attitude. The better individuals are at achieving top performance, the more gold medals they customarily earn at the Olympic Games. The more gold medals individuals receive, the more competitive are the nations they represent. Such is it in industry and commerce, with decision-making the chief conduit.

Indisputably, the productivity that the world has so far achieved has brought impressive benefits to many and has all been pulled off without much formal instruction in the art of decision-making. Like beating world records, continuing to move forward is becoming not only more difficult, but also very much more expensive, with the accruing benefits being disproportionately overtaken by costs, thanks to management dysfunction. The international competitive picture reveals huge variations in comparative outputs worldwide, so just imagine if the less productive organizations managed to equal the productivity of today's more productive organizations. And then picture what it would be like if those most productive organizations were to continue improving *their* outputs? This is the prospect, but decision-making has first to be elevated to a more professional level, as does the management of OM.

The history of management is the history of industrial change. However slowly, managers have been adapting to the shifting sands of innovation for more than 250 years. The latest seismic move has occurred is the way the developed world earns its living. Up to just a few decades ago, managers were managing a manufacturing and agricultural sector that employed the vast majority of workers. Today, they manage, or are trying to manage, a predominantly service sector employing up to around three-quarters of the labour force, where employees are now called knowledge workers. 'Trying to manage' is not an unmerited depiction of their efforts. The productivity of knowledge workers is not very high and the output in traditional sectors, although historically quite advanced, is now dragging its industrial feet.[30] Is service industry management really so different? And has old-style industry changed that much, sufficient to account for such halting productivity scores? The answer is yes, for reasons I have already discussed. The pervasive changes mean that both organizations and academia have to change their focus. Organizational memory was always an important component of this single most important managerial function but jobs discontinuity and knowledge loss was never the problem it is today.

'Education, education, education' may well be the war cry of progressive countries in the modern age but they overlook, or have forgotten, the crucial difference between skills and knowledge, and teaching and learning. In the world of productivity, skills without knowledge makes work a mechanical experience that restrains thinking, whilst teaching without learning just makes people more articulate. They say talk is cheap. It's not any more. It is time for educators, organizations and managers to let institutional DNA do its job.

Business and academia: intelligent cooperation

Experience teaches us that if you criticize a group of people, they will almost always back away from anything you might have to say. So why have I spent a book full of examples passing judgement against business academics and managers?

Well, experience also teaches that massaging an undeserving ego only reinforces the status quo and also that one must first get someone's attention for them to take any notice. I am hoping that both groups are also clever enough to spot an opportunity, in business academia's case a huge untapped resource of scholarship and in the case of organizations an improved bottom line.

With regard to business academics, they also work in an environment that hosts the necessary concentration of intellect to elevate teaching into learning. In addition, they serve a captive market, notably a huge body of rolling students who could start to make a significant difference within one generation. Moreover, someone has to integrate the academic and non-academic wings of this highly fragmented field, if only to provide the lead to encourage a better product and bring under one useful roof what work has been done. Better assimilation would also bring to each one the skills the other doesn't have. Even though non-academics may be more communicative, enterprising and/or proactive, academics would still have a better chance of giving experiential learning and decision-making the authority and credibility that it requires. In short, intelligent cooperation will be more effective than intractable separation.

If I am wrong then it has to be the non-academics who have to blaze the occupational trail. Either way, industry and commerce have to manage their organizational memory and want experiential learning as part of their instruction.

I have highlighted evidence showing that the current cycle of productivity growth is coming to an end and what will happen if nothing happens. Putting a philosophical spin on it, maybe it's the way that nations and societies rise and fall? Taking a look at just the last half-century, the UK's productivity growth has not been as good as Japan's and Germany's. Their eminence rose while the UK's fell. In the last ten years, Japan and German's productivity growth has tailed off, and the UK's current productivity growth is in fact slightly higher than these two powerhouses, opening up the speculative question whether (and how much) this edge may (or may not) be responsible for any change (real or apparent) in the three's comparative influence in the wider world.

Then there's the importance of experiential learning to the handful of BRICK countries whose opportunity to outdo the OECD has never been greater. All BRICK has to do is what the OECD is *not* doing. And what of the even wider question of the effectiveness of the Third World debt relief, further aid and the dismantling of trade barriers for *really* unproductive countries if those countries do not experientially learn? Singing for their supper in Hyde Park and elsewhere[31] would then have done little to get them out of the poorhouse. Applying hindsight for the benefit of decision-making is, I deduce, central to everyone's future. It always has been but, because of today's wider globalism, it is now even more so.

Two addendums

For two postscripts that harvest some contemporary experience-based lessons still to be learned in the First World and which contain a rare admission by one government of the less than adequate skills of its managers in just one public service sector, the news came in May 2004 that the European Parliament had outlawed 48 hour-plus working weeks. Opt-outs notwithstanding, the federal law-making body that represents the majority of the productivity-sliding OECD countries is, effectively, removing one of the few other ways in which they could help their electorates regain their lost edge. Had the current body of decision-makers been able to benefit from hindsight, they would have learned from the practice of the Soviet Union, whose law-makers similarly imposed fewer working hours on their employees when they opted to follow a policy of full employment. A decision not to reduce working hours in Europe would have been a good example of experiential learning's use of abstract conceptualization, in which the decision-makers would have been able to take the evidence of precedent, develop their own theories and conclusions and – hopefully – create new knowledge. No doubt the next generation of politicians will be able to draw a business lesson or two from their unsighted predecessors – if, that is, they're any better at the untutored skill of experiential learning.

And then, just months before this book went to print, Patricia Hewitt, the UK's Health Minister (nee Trade and Industry), publicly agreed with detractors[32] that billions of pounds *were* being wasted by National Health Service managers, who were asking for even more resources to implement government-initiated reforms.[33] With an awareness that much of the recent huge increase in NHS investment to almost £70 billion was showing no return in real output,[34] she admonished health managers for complaining about lack of funds, saying that there were major productivity gains to be had from the extra investment already in the system. In effect, she directed them to stop whingeing and start managing.

Hewitt's call to the organization employing the largest number of managers in the UK was mechanically repeated by the conference-holder's chief executive, Dame Gill Morgan, who, whilst confirming Peter Drucker's and this book's view that managers have to become more productive, added the routine chant 'but we also need the investment to continue'. It was a modified Oliver Twist request – 'Please, sir, I want some more'[35] – that Charles Dickens used to highlight the widespread hunger among Britain's urban poor and during the nineteenth century. Set in the modern day, Dame Gill Morgan's comment underlines another form of poverty – the plight of the unproductive organization and the hopelessness of the Hewitt/Morgan aspirations in the absence of any clear method of more effectively teaching managers *how* to make good and better decisions. Yet political history tells us that government decisions are prey to the same lack of experiential learning as managers; indeed, the poorer the primary decision-making by those designing strategy and making policy, the more difficult it becomes for those further down the managerial pecking order, as the example of the EU's 'stop working at 5 p.m.' diktat will no doubt substantiate.

In my Introduction I referred to the orthodox backstop exmployed by most economies trying to surf their way out of choppy waters: cut interest rates. My own fix is more enduring. Improve productivity, fast. However, to illustrate how slow 'fast' can actually be, I recall that the latest of numerous efforts to counteract the UK's productivity problem was in fact initiated in 1998 in the wake of New Labour's ascent to power.[36] Both the new prime minister and his chancellor acknowledged that there were too few first-class managers and too little productivity and pointed out that Britain could not be sustained with such low output levels. As a result, over the next 12 months, the government was going to examine the problem with others in industry and 'tear down every barrier to high productivity'. But despite their best efforts progress has been achingly slow, as evidenced by the latest Groningen dataset[37] (see Appendix 1), with the even later word from the Office for National Statistics that British workers are still almost a quarter less productive than their US peers and a tenth behind the average for the G7 group of the world's richest countries. High-unemployment France is still 11 per cent ahead. The good news is that the UK has become 3 per cent more productive than Germany at a time when the out-of-work total of the UK's largest export market was more than 11 per cent of the workforce.[38] In an attendant commentary, the Bank of England said – somewhat despairingly – that it was surprised that the large investment in information technology in the late 1990s (when the spend on computers rose to similar levels as that in the US) had not significantly improved British productivity.[39] In the business world, 'education, education, education'[40] and the other sticking plasters did not, unfortunately, include any great emphasis on proper experiential learning. Nor did industry and commerce make any allowance for the huge negative effect of the actively encouraged flexible labour market on the ability of organizations to benefit from their own experiences.

I also mixed quite a few other metaphors to point out that the shortsighted were not listening to the longsighted (and not only in the UK, as there are a score of even less productive OECD countries) with the result that institutions were becoming increasingly deaf. No disrespect intended to the visually impaired or hard of hearing, but there *is* a solution – a hearing aid in a form that takes knowledge management into its next evolutionary phase. For organizations that already do KM, just turn up the volume. It'll give you hindsight. It is time for education and business to do experiential learning properly.

In the classical myths, the acquisition of wisdom – embodied by the Greek goddess Athena – looms large. Athena was sprung from the forehead of Zeus, the supreme God. In today's world, wisdom needs a similar figurehead. Chief executives take note: some of you have already crossed the Maginot Line; many others are hovering just above. You don't have to be virginal, stately, armoured or breastplated to be Divine. To throw a thunderbolt or two, you just need to be a patron of better decision-making. At its heart is the application of that building block called experiential learning and its components known as organizational memory, reflection and new knowledge. Weightless they might be, valueless they are not.

Notes

1. Gaston Bachelard, *Fragments of a Poetics of Fire: A Retrospective Glance at the Lifework of a Master of Books*, trans. Kenneth Haltman, Dallas: Dallas Institute of Humanities and Culture Publications,1988.
2. P.F. Drucker, 'The New Productivity Challenge', *Harvard Business Review*, November–December 1991.
3. Stephen J. Dorgan and John Dowdy, 'How Good Management Raises Productivity', *The McKinsey Quarterly*, no. 4, 2002.
4. Drucker, 'The New Productivity Challenge', op. cit.
5. Groningen Growth and Development Centre and the Conference Board, *Total Economy Database*, August 2004 at: http://www.ggdc.net.
6. International Monetary Fund, 2002.
7. 'Why the French are on a Winner', *Sunday Times*, 5 December 2005.
8. Groningen Growth and Development Centre and the Conference Board, *Total Economy Database*, op. cit.
9. M. Schultz, 'The Uncertain Relevance of New Knowledge: Organizational Learning and Knowledge Flows in Multinational Corporations', paper presented at the Academy of Management, San Diego, 1998.
10. L. Arcote, S.L. Beckman and D. Epple, 'The Persistence and Transfer of Learning in Industrial Settings', *Management Science*, 1990.
11. J. Yates, *Control Through Communication*, Baltimore, MD: John Hopkins University Press, 1989.
12. A. Hargadon and R.I. Sutton, 'Technology Brokering and Innovation in a Product Development Firm'. *Administrative Science Quarterly*, December 1997; and C. Moorman and A.S. Miner. 'The Impact of Organizational Memory on New Product Performance and Creativity', *Journal of Marketing Research*, 1997.
13. M. Campbell-Kelly, 'Information Technology and Organizational Change in the British Census, 1801–1911', in J. Yates and J. Van Maanen (eds), *Information technology and Organizational Information: History, Rhetoric and Practice*, Thousand Oaks, CA: Sage, 2001.
14. J.P. Walsh and G.R. Ungson, 'Organizational Memory', *Academy of Management Review*, 1991.
15. P.S. Goodman and E.D. Darr, *Computer-aided Systems for Organizational Learning: Trends in Organizational Behaviour*, New York: John Wiley, 1996; and 'Computer-aided Systems and Communities: Mechanisms for Organizational Learning in Distributed Environments', *Management Information Systems Quarterly*, vol. 22, no. 4, 1998, pp. 417–40.
16. G. Szulanski, 'Exploring Internal Stickiness: Impediments to the Transfer of Best Practice within the Firm', *Strategic Management Journal*, winter special issue, 1996.

17. A. Casey, 'Collective Memory in Organizations', *Advances in Strategic Management*, 1997; R. Duncan and A. Weiss, 'Organizational Learning: Implications for Organizational Design', in B.M. Staw (ed.), *Research in Organizational Behavior*, Greenwich, CT: JAI Press, 1979; B. Levitt and J.G. March, 'Organizational Learning', *Annual Review of Sociology*, 1988; H.A. Simon, 'Bounded Rationality and Organizational Learning', *Organizational Science*, vol. 2, no. 1, 1991, pp. 125–34.

18. Jared Diamond, 'The Ends of the World as We Know Them', *New York Times*, 1 January 2005. Diamond won the 1998 Pulitzer Prize in general non-fiction for *Guns, Germs and Steel: The Fates of Human Societies*. He is the author of *Collapse: How Societies Choose or Fail to Succeed*, New York and London: Viking, 2004.

19. Ruth Spellman, chief executive of Investors in People, quoted in *The Times*, 15 November 2004, referring to survey by the Future Foundation to launch annual IIP Week.

20. Susanne Hauschild, Thomas Licht and Wolfram Stein, 'Creating a Knowledge Culture', *McKinsey Quarterly*, no. 1, 2001.

21. http://www.sirsi.com/glossary.html.

22. http://www.documentmanagement.org.uk/pages/glossary.htm.

23. http://www.finance.gov.au/pubs/AnnualReport99-00/gloss.htm.

24. Peter Senge, *The Fifth Discipline: the Art and Practice of the Learning Organization*, New York: Doubleday, 1990.

25. G.P. Huber, 'Organizational Learning: The Contributing Processes and the Literatures', *Organization Science*, February 1991.

26. Chris Argyris, 'Organizational Learning and Management Information Systems', *Accounting, Organizations, and Society*, vol. 2, no. 2, 1977, pp. 113–23.

27. Chris Argyris, 'Double-loop Learning in Organizations', *Harvard Business Review*, vol. 55, no. 5, 1977, pp. 115–25.

28. The Capgemini *Business Decisiveness Report*, August 2004 as reported in *The Times*, 16 August 2004.

29. See the Preface and Acknowledgements, p.xiii.

30. OECD, *Economic Outlook 2004*.

31. Refers to the series of pop concerts in July 2005 in the G8 countries and South Africa.

32. Patricia Hewitt, NHS Confederation annual conference, Birmingham, 17 June 2005.

33. Two-thirds of the NHS's chief executives thought that there was not enough money to fulfil targets, according to a poll of NHS chief executives, NHS Confederation annual conference, Birmingham, 17 June 2005.

34. Office for Statistical Analysis study in 2004 showing that, using 1995 output levels, the NHS could achieve the same results with £6 billion less investment. In July 2005 the Healthcare Commission reported that one in three hospital trusts in England were running deficits which contributed to the NHS overspending its budget by £500 million in 2004. This included 138 out of 590 trusts that failed to break even, 72 out of 303 primary care trusts (GP, dentist and mental health services) that failed to balance their books and 50 out of 173 acute hospital trusts which overspent.

35. Charles Dickens, *Oliver Twist*, 1837.

36. Labour Party Conference, Blackpool, 29 September 1998.

37. Groningen Growth and Development Centre and the Conference Board, *Total Economy Database*, op. cit.

38. Office for National Statistics, 12 September 2005. The full ONS figures showed that the UK's productivity growth actually collapsed to zero in the third quarter, with the performance for the full year to September 2005 registering a 0.4 per cent increase – a 15-year low – down from 0.6 per cent in the second quarter and 0.9 per cent in the first quarter. Even using the alternative 'output per hour' measure, productivity also failed to rise in the third quarter, with the full year performance dropping by 0.3 per cent compared with a year earlier. In an effort to downplay the figures, the Treasury released the information two days before the Christmas break and bizarrely insisted that the country was still 'making good progress in narrowing the productivity gap' with its main competitors.

39. 'British Workers Struggle in the Productivity Stakes', *The Daily Telegraph*, 13 September 2005.

40. 'Education, education, education' was one of the mantras on which New Labour was elected to government in 1997.

GDP Per Person Employed 1950–2003 (1999 EK $)

	1950	1960	1970	1980	1990	2000	2001	2002	2003
Australia	21 352	27 008	33 627	39 989	43 999	54 668	56 149	56 585	57 183
Austria	10 951	19 157	31 966	44 149	49 897	57 557	57 681	58 623	58 874
Belgium	17 874	22 702	35 027	48 086	56 798	66 718	66 364	66 940	67 935
Canada	25 077	32 368	40 485	44 820	49 498	57 733	58 165	58 774	58 505
Denmark	19 251	25 403	34 095	39 870	45 396	55 989	56 735	57 555	58 374
Finland	11 090	16 534	26 079	33 384	42 181	54 438	54 251	55 361	5 666
France	13 484	22 077	34 168	44 418	54 253	60 724	60 726	61 165	61 595
All Germany					47 121	57 420	57 732	58 195	58 782
West Germany	13 672	23 721	35 909	46 220	54 686				
Greece	7 340	12 071		33 518	35 472	42 126	44 151	45 506	46 441
Iceland			30 919	43 994	48 402	50 676	51 182	51 933	52 951
Ireland	10 914	14 947	22 564	32 821	46 455	64 509	66 660	69 965	70 064
Italy	12 901	18 581	34 304	45 534	53 676	61 465	61 387	60 783	60 355
Japan	5 416	10 250	23 959	34 019	44 600	49 955	50 438	50 910	52 384
Luxembourg	27 187	32 786	43 713	49 987	64 439	79 394	76 132	74 951	75 678
Netherlands	20 796	29 057	39 222	47 558	51 957	54 854	54 019	54 565	54 579
New Zealand		32 842	37 102	39 174	39 799	43 934	44 151	44 805	45 095
Norway	15 446	22 466	31 551	40 025	47 744	61 034	62 337	62 895	63 630
Portugal	6 209	10 032	18 336	24 863	28 723	35 199	35 325	35 366	35 237
Spain	6 806	10 383	21 940	37 314	46 969	51 458	51 027	51 067	50 937
Sweden	16 867	21 972	32 388	35 811	40 914	53 140	52 708	53 733	54 649
Switzerland	25 162	32 656	44 584	50 673	51 437	53 372	53 055	52 936	52 706
Turkey	2 923	5 205	8 202	11 150	16 000	20 485	19 753	21 494	23 338
UK	19 076	23 129	29 682	35 587	42 549	52 764	53 460	53 949	54 665
US	28 701	37 044	46 635	50 720	58 159	69 730	69 960	71 601	73 116

2 *The World Competitiveness Scoreboard 2004*

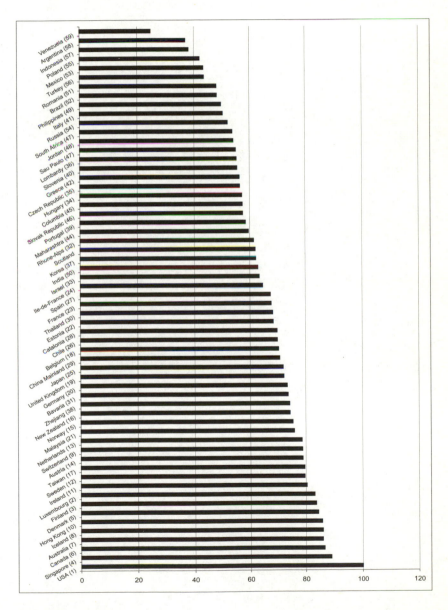

With kind permission of IMD International, Switzerland, *World Competitiveness Yearbook 2004*, www.imd.ch/wcc.

3 *OECD Productivity Scorecard 2003 (1999 EK $)*

1999 US$ GDP/capita

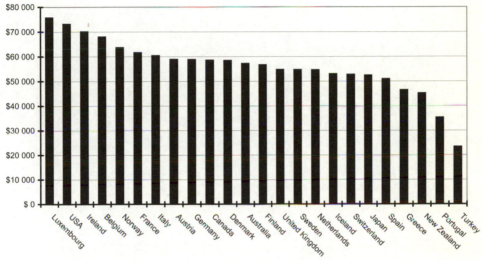

Source : Groningen Growth and Development Centre and The Conference Board, *Total Economy Database* , August 2004, http://www.ggdc.net.

4 *Productivity as a Percentage of US Productivity*

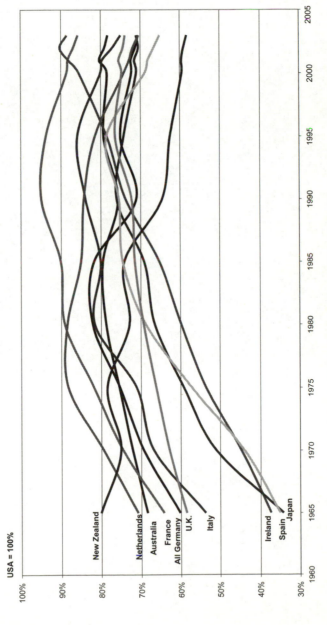

Productivity as %-age USA Productivity

USA = 100%

New Zealand
Netherlands
Australia
France
All Germany
U.K.
Italy
Ireland
Spain
Japan

100% 90% 80% 70% 60% 50% 40% 30%

1960 1965 1970 1975 1980 1985 1990 1995 2000 2005

Source: Groningen Growth and Development Centre and The Conference Board, *Total Economy Database*, August 2004, http://www.ggdc.net.

Index

acquisitions 54–5
action learning 65–6, 117, 190
action research 175
adaptive learning 46
Addis 157
AIDS 109
Apple Corporation 99
apprenticeships 65
Argyris, Chris 183, 194
Arthur D. Little consultancy 119

banking 103
Barnet Council (London) 95
Beagle 2 (UK space project) 19–20
Benetton 118
BHU (Business History Unit (London School
     of Economics)) 67
biographical debriefing 140
Blue Circle 158
Boeing 119
BP 118, 120
Bradford & Bingley 158
Branson, Sir Richard 156
Britannia Building Society 156
business education 5–6, 48, 53–73, 185
     business history 55–6
     corporate history 55–6
     creativity 56–7
     decision-making 47–8
     imagination 56–7
     management 196–7
     Owen Report 61
     shortcomings 58–9
     and success 57
     United Kingdom 61–70
business ethics 65
business history 45, 55–6, 65, 66–9 see also
     corporate history
     associations 164
     demand for 189–90
     film 169
     future of 188–9
     Internet 169
     Japan 82
     United States 82, 169
Business History Unit (London School of
     Economics) (BHU) 67

business research 64
Butterworth 165

Centre for Corporate Strategy and Change
     (University of Warwick) 138
Centre for History of Chemistry 137
CEOs (chief executive officers), succession
     23–4
Chaparral Steel 118–19
chief executive officers (CEOs), succession
     23–4
China, SARS virus 85
Citicorp 99
company directors 63
compensation culture 97
competitiveness scoreboard 203
copyright, oral debriefing 144–5, 146–7
Cordiant 84
corporate amnesia 16–17, 43 see also
     organizational memory (OM)
     Apple Corporation 99
     Citicorp 99
     Ford motor company 99
     IBM 99
     Israel 109–10
     New Zealand 105–6
     South Africa 107–9
     United Kingdom 101–4
     United States 98–100
corporate history 149–70 see also business
     history
     academia 164–5
     authors 166
     code of conduct 163–4
     demand for 189–90
     editorial objectivity 165–6
     educational use 167–70
     externally funded 149
     history of 161–2
     improvement 163–6
     independent 149–51
         with company cooperation 151–3
     limitations 162–3
     management of 165–7
     project managers 166–7
     sponsored 154–6
         disasters 156–9

successful 159–61
unauthorized 151
corporate poaching 23
corporate survival 172–3
costs
  of decision-making 96–8
  increases in 33
Courtaulds 167
Coutts 159–61
creativity 56–7
critical incident debriefing 141

data 90
Davenport-Hines, Dr Richard 157–8
deception, culture of 87
decision-making 20–22, 27–8, 171–3, 185–6,
    187–8, 195–6
  business education 47–8
  costs of 96–8
  specificity 91
  techniques 8–9
defamation, oral debriefing 146
defensive learning 116–17
defensive reasoning 84–7
  political 85–6
deflation 3
Dewey, John 175
Digital Equipment Corporation (DEC) 138–9
diversity management 184
double-loop learning 46, 176, 183
downsizing 79–80
  tax 79–80
Drucker, Peter 4, 76, 89, 91–2, 186–7

EBM see experience-based management
ECB (European Central Bank), interest rates
    3
Economic and Social Research Council
    (ESRC) 64, 67
economic history 53, 68–9
education, secondary 32, 49
ELT (experiential learning theory) 178–9
employee transit audits 129–30
employees
  tenure 39–42
  training 39
  turnover 39–42, 79–80, 81–3
  costs 42–4
  undervaluation of 18
Enron 64–5
enterprise ethic, United States 82
Ernst & Whinney 165
ESRC (Economic and Social Research
    Council) 64, 67
ethics 65
European Central Bank (ECB), interest rates
    3
European Union (EU) see also Eurozone

accounting irregularities 32
productivity 35
working hours 197–8
Eurozone, gross domestic product 2–3
exit debriefing 141
experience, experiential learning 176–8
experience-based management (EBM)
    12–13, 124, 178–82
  corporate histories 149–70
  employee transit audits 129–30
  evaluation 181–2
  evidence capture 142–4
  knowledge charts 128
  knowledge retrieval plans 130–31
  learning stages 179–82
  lessons audit 180
  oral debriefing 133–48
  planning 128–31
  project maps 128–9
  reflection 179–80
  reprocessing 180–81
experiential learning 5, 17–20, 45–6, 65–6,
    91–2, 98–113, 171, 173–8 see also
    experience-based management (EBM)
  capture 120–21, 122–3, 123–4
  case studies 118–20
  demand for 190–91
  design 123
  endurance of 192
  experience 176–8
  group dynamics 175
  history of 46–7
  improvement principle 118
  job rotation 121
  knowledge sharing 121–2
  Kolb approach 174
  learning histories 119–20
  learning style inventory 177
  management of 127–8
  memory systems 122–3
  mentoring 121–2
  origins 174–5
  postmortems 119
  selective learning 118–19
  social networks 121–2
  storage 120–21
  tacit input 119–20
  United States 98–100
experiential learning theory (ELT) 178–9

failure 95–113
  admission of 85
  rewarding 80–81, 93
fair trade 18–19, 28
flexible labour market 39–42, 79–80
  attitudes to 44
Ford motor company 119–20
  corporate amnesia 99

France, productivity 187–8
Franklin, Benjamin 50
freedom of information, oral debriefing 146
Fyffes 156–7

GDP *see* gross domestic product
General Motors 119
George Ballantine 157
Germany, productivity 35
Gestalt therapy 183
Glaxo 157–8
Groningen Total Economy Database 2, 4, 55
gross domestic product (GDP)
    Eurozone 2–3
    per person employed 201, 205

Haberdashers' Company 165
Heinz 151
Hewitt, Patricia 198
Hewlett-Packard 119
history of business 45
history of science 82
The History of Standard Oil Company 150
Hodge, Margaret 85–6
hospital hygiene 20
hostile defensiveness 86–7
HSBC, report on declining productivity 2–3
human resources 63

IBM, corporate amnesia 99
ICI (Imperial Chemical Industries) 68–9, 80
IiP (Investors in People) 192
imagination 56–7
immigration, United States 82
IMPM (International Masters in Practising Management) 61
incidental learning 115–16
information 90
information systems (IS) 33
    management 34
Institute of Chartered Secretaries & Administrators 159
Institute of Directors, training courses 63
International Masters in Practising Management (IMPM) 61
International Telephone and Telegraph Corporation (ITT) 152
Investors in People (IIP) 192
involuntary learning 115–18
Iran, earthquake reconstruction 86
IS (information systems) 33
    management 34
Islington Council (London), exploitation of children in care 85
Israel
    construction industry 110
    corporate amnesia 109–11

marketing 109–10
productivity 110
ITT (International Telephone and Telegraph Corporation) 152

Japan
    business history 82
    productivity 35, 81–3
job churn 79–80, 81–3
job rotation 121

KM (knowledge management) 26, 87–90, 193–4
knowledge 90–91 *see also* corporate amnesia; organizational memory (OM)
    acquisition 7
    attitudes to 44–5
    cost of loss 42–4
    ownership of 6, 15–16
    sharing 121–2
    tacit 16–17, 45
knowledge charts 128
knowledge management (KM) 26, 87–90, 193–4
Knowledge Preservation Project 16–17
knowledge pull 192
knowledge retrieval plans 130–31
Kolb, David 173, 177–8, 184
    experiential learning theory (ELT) 178–9
Kraft 116

labour productivity 75
learning
    action 65–6
    adaptive 46
    defensive 117
    double-loop 46, 176, 183
    experiential *see* experiential learning
    incidental 116
    involuntary 115–18
    multiple-loop 177
    organizational 24–5, 27, 46–7, 185
    planned 116
    proactive 116
    prospective 117–18
    restructuring of 191–5
    selective 118–19
    single-loop 46, 176
    transformational 177
    triple-loop 177
    types of 7–8
    unconscious 115
learning histories 119–20
learning organizations 87–90, 194–5
learning style inventory 177
Lewin, Kurt 175
Libya, compensation for terrorist attacks 85

liquidity trap 3
London School of Economics, Business
    History Unit (BHU) 67
Lonrho 151, 157
Los Alamos 16–17

management
    advances 33–4
    beliefs 34–5
    business education 196–7
    in complex organizations 172–3
    increase in 172
    ineffectiveness 32–3
    information systems (IS) 34
    reflectiveness 45–6, 64–5
    by rote 96
    service sector 196
    untrained 25–6
    wasted productivity 22, 28
management consultants 22
management practices, productivity 186–7
management research 64
management skills 20–22, 172
    United Kingdom 101
management training 25–6
Mayo, George Elton 183–4
MBAs 59–61
    United Kingdom 61–4
McKinsey Global Institute (MGI) 186–7
medical negligence 31, 49
memory systems 122–3
mentoring 121–2
mergers 54–5
MGI (McKinsey Global Institute) 186–7
Microsoft 119
Mintzberg, H., and Lampel, J. 60–61
money laundering 32
Montessori, Maria 182–3
Morgan, Dame Gill 198
MRSA (methicillin-resistant staphylococcus
    aureus) 20
multifactor productivity 75–6
multiple-loop learning 177

N. M. Rothschild & Sons 141
National Aeronautical and Space
    Administration (Nasa) 16
National Audit Office (UK) 97
National Health Service (NHS) 24–5, 34, 87,
    104
    investment 36
    productivity 198, 200
Network Rail 81
New Zealand
    corporate amnesia 105–6
    management culture 105
    overseas acquisitions 106
    performance-based incentives 105

productivity 104–5
public sector 107
Sheep Council 105–7
NHS see National Health Service
Nomura 151–2

Office for National Statistics (ONS),
    productivity 98
OM see organizational memory
oral debriefing 133–48
    biographical 140
    confidentiality 145–6
    copyright 144–5, 146–7
    critical incident 141
    defamation 146
    demand for 189–90
    editing 144
    evidence capture 142–4
    exit 141
    false memory 142
    freedom of information 146
    history of 135
    in industry 136–9
    interviewers 142
    introduction letter 142–3
    participation 139–40
    payment 147
    process 143–4
    questions 143–4
    release forms 144–5
    research 143
    subject 140
    by telephone 147–8
    transcripts 144
    types of 140–41
    US military 135–6
    video recording 141
organizational learning 24–5, 27, 46–7, 185
organizational memory (OM) 5–6, 10–12,
    83–7 see also corporate amnesia
    capture 192–3
    corporate histories 149–70
    defensive reasoning 84
    oral debriefing 133–48
    responsibility for 192–3
    selective recall 83–4
    short recall 83–4
Owen Report (on business education) 61

Perls, Fritz 183
Phoenix Assurance 158
Piaget, Jean 174
Pilkington, Sir Alistair 66, 67
Pilkington Brothers 66–7
planned learning 116
poaching, corporate 23
police, productivity 25, 29, 31
Powergen 95

PPP (purchasing power parity) 4
proactive learning 116
productivity 1–5, 75–94, 196, 197
    calculation 75–6
    comparative 76–7
    culture of deception 87
    declining 77–8
    European Union (EU) 35
    France 187–8
    Germany 35
    historical 76–7
    improvements, history 78–9
    Israel 109
    Japan 35, 81–3
    labour 75
    low, costs 44
    management practices 186–7
    McKinsey Global Institute (MGI) 186–7
    measurement 86–7
    multifactor 75–6
    National Health Service (NHS) 24–5, 198,
        200
    New Zealand 104–5
    Office for National Statistics (ONS) 98
    as a percentage of US productivity 207
    police 25, 29, 31
    potential 77–8
    South Africa 107
    targets 87
    total-factor 75–6
    United Kingdom 35–9, 100–2, 198–9
    United States 81–3
    wasted 22
project maps 128–9
prospective learning 117–18
purchasing power parity (PPP) 4

RAE (Research Assessment Exercise) 64, 69
railways, United Kingdom 36
RAMBA (real-alternative MBA) 61
raw materials, overexploitation of 18
Reader, Bill 68–9
real-alternative MBA (RAMBA) 61
reflectiveness 45–6, 64–5
reframing learning see double-loop learning
Research Assessment Exercise (RAE) 64, 69
rewarding failure 80–81, 93
N. M. Rothschild & Sons 141
Royal Insurance 158

SARS virus, China 85
Schön, Donald 183
science, history of 82
secondary education 32, 49
selective learning 118–19
selective memory recall 83–4
Semco 115
short memory recall 83–4

single-loop learning 46, 176, 194
skilled incompetence 183
social networks 121–2
Social Science Research Council (SSRC) see
        Economic and Social Research Council
        (ESRC)
South Africa
    AIDS 109
    civil service 108
    corporate amnesia 107–9
    productivity 107
    stock losses 109
    Unilever 108–9
South African Development Community 109
Standard Oil Company 150
start-ups 54–5
Staveley Industries 156
subject debriefing 140
succession, chief executive officers (CEOs)
        23–4
Sullivan & Cromwell 152–3

tacit knowledge 16–17, 45, 90–91
Taxpayers' Alliance (TPA) 97
Taylor, Frederick Winslow 78
Teacher's Whiskey 157
time and motion studies 78
total-factor productivity 75–6
Toyota 165
training 39
transformational learning 177
triple-loop learning 177, 184

unconscious learning 115
unemployment, youth 31–2, 49
Unilever 156, 161–2
United Kingdom
    agricultural sector 103–4, 115
    business education 61–70
    company directors 63
    complaints, failure to make 37
    corporate amnesia 101–4
    finance sector 103
    foreign languages 37
        education 50
    foreign ownership of business 62, 72
    government, management consultants 22
        costs 28
    human resources 63
    local government 102–3
    management skills 101
    MBAs 61–4
    prices 37, 50
    productivity 35–9, 100–2, 198–9
        measurement 86–7
    public sector projects 102, 103
    railways 36, 103
    wealth creation 37–8

United States
  business history 82, 169
  corporate amnesia 98–100
  enterprise ethic 82
  experiential learning 98–100
  immigration 82
  military, oral debriefing 135–6
  productivity 81–3

video recording, oral debriefing 141

'working smarter' 187–8
World Bank Group Historical Office 137
Wright brothers 15–16

youth unemployment 31–2, 49

About the Author

Arnold Kransdorff is the originator of the concept known as corporate amnesia: what happens when businesses and other kinds of cooperative organization literally lose their memory. He is an expert in knowledge management, the leading UK authority on the consequences of the flexible labour market and a fervent proponent of experiential learning, for which organizational memory (OM) is the indispensable evidential base for good decision-making. The author's characterization of OM is the institution's DNA, the organization-specific know-how accrued from experience that characterizes its ability to perform.

This is his second book on this important aspect of intellectual capital, which most organizations carelessly discard in the wake of the actively encouraged flexible labour market. With a wide historical knowledge of industry and a deep understanding of the strategic and tactical issues facing international business, he is an enthusiastic proponent of the principles of the learning organization. His work is widely published in academic journals, trade journals and the national press. A guest lecturer at many UK and overseas business schools, he is a former award-winning financial analyst and industrial commentator for the *London Financial Times* and the recipient of an Award of Excellence from *Anbar Management Intelligence*, the world's leading guide in management journal literature. He has assisted in the RSA's Inquiry on 'Tomorrow's Company', the ESRC-commissioned study on 'Management Research', the CBI's deliberations on 'Flexible Labour Markets' and the Washington, DC-based Corporate Leadership Council's study on 'New Tools for Managing Workforce Stability'.

His UK-based company, Pencorp, is a leading corporate history publisher and management consultancy specializing in helping organizations better cope with imposed change and the stop-start consequences of a mobile workforce, for which they have pioneered the use of Oral Debriefing techniques in management development, succession planning and post-implementation reviews. The author can be contacted on ak@corporate-amnesia.com or through the websites www.corporate-amnesia.com and www.pencorp.co.uk.